Praise for the Kiss, Bow, or Shake Hands *series*

"In this global economy, ANYONE who leaves the U.S. is a fool if they don't read up on their destination's customs. *Kiss, Bow, or Shake Hands* is THE definitive authority on how to conduct yourself around the world. You can easily offend your prospects and there is no faster way to kill the most lucrative business deal. *Kiss, Bow, or Shake Hands* has been immeasurably helpful over the years."

—Louis Altman, President, New Hampshire International
Trade Association (NHITA), and President, GlobaFone

"*Kiss, Bow, or Shake Hands* has been an invaluable resource for international businesspeople for years. Don't leave home without it."

—Joe Douress, Vice President,
LexisNexis Martindale-Hubbell

"*Kiss, Bow, or Shake Hands* is a great resource of cultural and business-related information. The material is concise and easy to read. The cultural information is unique, educational, and fun! It's a book that can be enjoyed by a great number of people, from a student, to a leisure traveler, to the most sophisticated business person."

—Joanna Savvides, President,
World Trade Center of Greater Philadelphia

"In my work, I train employees of multinational corporations on how to manage the intercultural aspects of an international assignment. *Kiss, Bow, or Shake Hands* is a tremendous resource for the growing number of individuals in today's global workforce who find themselves working across international borders and on assignment outside their home country."

—Carolyn Ryffel, Senior Manager of Intercultural Services,
Cartus, Chicago, IL

"To help achieve success in communicating globally about our business, there are critical tools never far from my reach: my laptop or BlackBerry, my phone, and Terri Morrison's *Kiss, Bow, or Shake Hands*."

—Sherry Nebel, Vice President–Communications,
Connexion by Boeing

KISS, BOW, OR SHAKE HANDS: LATIN AMERICA

How to Do Business in
18 Latin American Countries

- CULTURAL OVERVIEWS
- TIPS FOR DOING BUSINESS • KNOW BEFORE YOU GO
- NEGOTIATING STRATEGIES
- PROTOCOL

TERRI MORRISON AND WAYNE A. CONAWAY

BUSINESS

AVON, MASSACHUSETTS

To Nica, Brendan, and Alex
Forever Wise, Forever True, Forever Loved
y a Antonio
Mi Vida
—TERRI MORRISON

To my Parents
I hope I was a good long-term investment.
—WAYNE A. CONAWAY

And to the late George A. Borden, Ph.D.,
a gifted friend.

This book includes material previously published in *Kiss, Bow, or Shake Hands* by
Terri Morrison, © 2006, F+W Publications, Inc.

Published by Adams Media, an F+W Publications Company
57 Littlefield Street
Avon, MA 02322
www.adamsmedia.com

ISBN 10: 1-59869-217-8
ISBN 13: 978-1-59869-217-4

Printed in the United States of America.

J I H G F E D C B A

Library of Congress Cataloging-in-Publication Data
is available from publisher.

This publication is designed to provide accurate and authoritative information with
regard to the subject matter covered. It is sold with the understanding that the publisher is not engaged in rendering legal, accounting, or other professional advice. If
legal advice or other expert assistance is required, the services of a competent professional person should be sought.
 —From a *Declaration of Principles* jointly adopted by a Committee of the
American Bar Association and a Committee of Publishers and Associations

Many of the designations used by manufacturers and sellers to distinguish their
product are claimed as trademarks. Where those designations appear in this book
and Adams Media was aware of a trademark claim, the designations have been
printed with initial capital letters.

Maps © Map Resouces.

This book is available at quantity discounts for bulk purchases.
For information, please call 1-800-289-0963.

Contents

Preface

IN THE DOZEN YEARS since the original edition of *Kiss, Bow, or Shake Hands* was originally published, the world has changed in remarkable ways. Several countries have dissolved (such as the Soviet Union), others have been absorbed (East Germany), and some have emerged (Azerbaijan). Trade barriers have been lifted (such as for South Africa and Vietnam) and economies have radically shifted (Ireland and India).

The interesting thing is that over twelve years—throughout all of the massive political and economic changes—the cultures, values, and belief systems of major ethnic groups have remained constant.

For example, many Latin American executives have adapted to international business practices, yet they appreciate knowledge of their styles and cultural values. Just understanding Hispanic name order and titles will give you an advantage other executives who do no research.

As Goethe said, "There is nothing more terrible than ignorance in action" (*Es ist nichts schrecklicher als eine tätige Unwissenheit*).

During my life, I have seen World War, reconstruction, terrorism, and tremendous advances in technology. On this increasingly interconnected planet, businesses need to acknowledge that people are not alike all over the world—the more you respect local attitudes toward families, work, and religion, the more successful you will be in those locales. Priorities in Lima are not equivalent to those in Los Angeles.

It is a pleasure to introduce you to this important book. Review it before you embark on your international trips. Gain the information you need on business practices, cognitive styles, negotiation techniques, and social customs. Give the right gift; make the right gesture. Read *Kiss, Bow, or Shake Hands: Latin America*.

—HANS H.B. KOEHLER,
the former Director of the Wharton Export Network

"Audi alteram partem."
—HEAR THE OTHER SIDE.

Introduction

WHAT WILL YOU NEED TO KNOW in 2010 or 2020 to work in Latin America? As Hans Koehler pointed out in his Preface, we live in changing times. As of this writing, Chile's first female President is implementing policies to reduce poverty and promote equality, while Bolivia and Venezuela have embraced more extreme "populist, anti-yanqui" movements. Politics and economies change. But many of the cultural tenets presented in *Kiss, Bow, or Shake Hands* took hundreds or thousands of years to develop. These stable precepts help us understand why people behave differently around the world, and they will help you to avoid committing global marketing faux pas like these:

The Ford Motor Company was unsuccessful at marketing the Ford Pinto in Brazil. Ford had not realized that "Pinto" is a slang term in Portuguese for "small penis." Few Brazilian men were willing to be associated with a Pinto. (Ford managed to save its investment by changing the name of the car to Corcel, Portuguese for "horse.")

McDonald's Corporation settled a group of lawsuits for $10 million in 2002. Why were they sued? Because of their French fries and hash browns. After 1990, McDonald's stated that only pure vegetable oil was used to cook their fries, implying that they were prepared in a "vegetarian" manner. However, the oil contained the essence of beef flavor, which is an anathema to Hindus and vegetarians worldwide. Most of the money from the lawsuit was donated to Hindu and other vegetarian causes.

As these examples show, an unintentional misstep can threaten or destroy your costly international marketing efforts. It also reflects the benefit of learning the language of your target countries, and corroborating translations locally.

Kiss, Bow, or Shake Hands: Latin America is organized in a clear, consistent manner to help you easily find the data you need to avoid many of the errors others have made before you.

The work to develop this volume resulted in not only this book, but much additional information that is available on our Web site *www.kissboworshakehands.com*. The Web site also contains information on official world holidays, recommendations for learning foreign languages, gift-giving suggestions, legal data, and hundreds of articles like "Subtle Gestures," and "Lie To Me." *Kiss, Bow* is now part of a larger electronic database—*Kiss, Bow, or Shake Hands: Expanded Edition*. You are also welcome to contact us at 610-725-1040 or e-mail *TerriMorrison@getcustoms.com* with your questions or comments.

Each chapter in this new edition focuses on a single country, and all are organized into sections, such as in the following example for Brazil:

What's Your Cultural IQ?
Three quick questions to gauge your knowledge

Tips on Doing Business in Brazil
Five business-related highlights

Country Background
Demographics, History, Type of Government, Language, and The Brazilian View (perspectives from the country's viewpoint)

Know Before You Go
Natural and human hazards

Cultural Orientation
A cultural anthropologist's view. This section is described in detail in the introductory chapter.

Business Practices
Including sections on Punctuality, Appointments, and Local Time; Negotiating; and Business Entertaining

Protocol
With discussions of Greetings, Titles/Forms of Address, Gestures, Gifts, and Dress

And many Cultural Notes on a variety of subjects are scattered throughout the chapters.

(For more details on Titles/Forms of Address, Mailing Addresses, etc., we also recommend an excellent book called *Merriam-Webster's Guide to International Business Communications*, by Toby D. Atkinson.)

Please remember that you will work with individuals, and there are always exceptions to every rule. For example, *Kiss, Bow, or Shake Hands: Latin America* suggests that many Hispanics have a strong sense of personal honor, have an exceedingly strong network of family and friends, and are sensitive to being reprimanded in public. (This is reflected in the proverb *"Quién a uno castiga, a ciento hostiga."* "He that chastens one, harasses one hundred.") Somewhere there is probably a reserved, quiet, and emotionless Latin manager, without any family or friends, who never takes umbrage at a punishing tone in public. Just because we haven't met him (or her) doesn't mean that no such person exists.

The process of communication is fluid, not static. The success of your intercultural interactions depends upon you, and the quality of your information. *Kiss, Bow, or Shake Hands: Latin America* provides you with the best and most current data possible on what foreign business and social practices to expect in your efforts at globalization.

"The most universal quality is diversity."
—MICHEL DE MONTAIGNE, 1580

Cultural Orientation

FOR EACH OF THE COUNTRIES in *Kiss, Bow, or Shake Hands: Latin America* there is a Cultural Orientation section. The study of cultural orientation gives us a model for understanding and predicting the results of intercultural encounters. It is, however, a model—a theory. New discoveries continue to be made about why we act the way we do.

Furthermore, communication always takes place between individuals, not cultures. Few individuals are perfect representations of their culture. Citizens of the United States of America are generally known for addressing one another by first names, a habit that most of the world does not follow. However, there are many U.S. citizens who are more comfortable with formality, and prefer to use last names and titles. This does not make them any less like U.S. citizens. It just makes them individuals.

Many global executives adopt the manners of their targeted countries, so why do U.S. executives need to study foreign ways? There are a variety of reasons.

First of all, many foreign businesspeople often cannot or will not imitate U.S. mannerisms. Can you afford to leave them out of your business plans?

Second, you might wish to sell to the general public in a foreign market. The average foreign consumer is certainly not going to have the same habits or tastes as consumers in the United States of America.

Third, although your business counterpart in Brazil may act or speak like an American or Canadian or Australian at times, he isn't. He probably is not even thinking in English; he is thinking in Portuguese. Knowing how Brazilian people tend to arrive at decisions gives you an edge. And don't we all need every business advantage we can get?

The following page begins a breakdown of the information in the cultural orientation section.

Cognitive Styles: How We Organize and Process Information

The word "cognitive" refers to thought, so "cognitive styles" refers to thought patterns. We take in data every conscious moment. Some of it is just noise, and we ignore it. Some of it is of no interest, and we forget it as soon as we see/hear/feel/smell/taste it. Some data, however, we choose to accept.

Open-minded or Closed-minded?

Studies of cognitive styles suggest that people fall into *open-minded* and *closed-minded* categories. The open-minded person seeks out more information before making a decision. The closed-minded person has tunnel vision—he or she sees only a narrow range of data and ignores the rest.

Something that might surprise you is that most experts in cultural orientation consider the citizens of the USA and Canada to be closed-minded.

Open-minded people are more apt to see the relativity of issues. They admit that they don't have all the answers, and that they need to learn before they can come to a proper conclusion. Frankly, there are not many cultures like that. Most cultures produce closed-minded citizens.

Here's an example: Most theocratic (governed by religious leaders) cultures are closed-minded. That's one of the characteristics of such a culture: God tells you what is important. Anything outside of those parameters can be ignored. From a business point of view, that can be a weakness. For example, Islam prohibits charging interest on a loan. There can be no argument and no appeal: Charging interest is wrong. Obviously, running a modern banking system without charging interest is challenging.

So why are Canada and the USA closed-minded?

Assume that someone from an Islamic country tells a North American that the United States of America is evil and should become a theocracy. The North American is likely to scoff. The United States a theocracy? Nonsense! Why, the separation of church and state is one of the most sacred precepts established by the founding fathers of the United States of America.

That North American is being closed-minded. He or she is refusing to even consider the Muslim's reasoning. A truly open-minded person would consider the proposition. He or she might reject the possibility after due thought, but not without a complete evaluation.

In fact, a person who wants to study cultural orientation should consider such questions. Granted, most businesspeople would probably decide that the United States of America should not become a theocracy. But considering the topic can lead to some useful insights. Perhaps most important is the concept that much of the world does not share the United States' predilection for the separation of church and state. This separation is a specifically Western notion, which evolved out of the hundreds of years of European religious wars that followed the Protestant Reformation.

In point of fact, most cultures tend to produce closed-minded citizens as long as things are working fairly well. It often takes a major disaster to make people open-minded. For example, the citizens of many former Communist nations are now becoming open-minded. Their old Communist ideology has fallen apart, and they realize they need new answers.

Associative or Abstractive Thinking?

Another aspect of cognitive styles is how people process information. We divide such processing into *associative* and *abstractive* characteristics.

A person who thinks associatively is filtering new data through the screen of personal experience. New data (we'll call it X) can only be understood in relation to similar past experiences (Is this new X more like A, or maybe B?). What if X is not like anything ever encountered before? The associative thinker is still going to pigeonhole that new data in with something else (X is just another B). On the other hand, the abstractive thinker can deal with something genuinely new. When the abstractive person encounters new data, he or she doesn't have to lump it in with past experiences (It's not A, it's not B or C—it's new! It's X!). The abstractive person is more able to extrapolate data and consider hypothetical situations ("I've never experienced X, but I've read about how such things might occur").

Obviously, no country has more than its share of smart (or dull) people. However, some cultures have come to value abstractive thinking, whereas others encourage associative patterns. Much of this has to do with the educational system. A system that teaches by rote tends to produce associative thinkers. An educational system that teaches problem-solving develops abstractive thinking. The scientific method is very much a product of abstractive thinking. Both northern Europe and North America produce a lot of abstractive thinkers.

Particular or Universal Thinking?

One final category has to do with how thinking and behavior are focused. People are divided into *particular* versus *universal* thinkers. The particularistic person feels that a personal relationship is more important than obeying rules or laws. On the other hand, the universalistic person tends to obey regulations and laws; relationships are less important than an individual's duty to the company, society, and authority in general.

Not surprisingly, the previous categories tend to go together in certain patterns. Abstractive thinkers often display universalistic behavior: It requires abstractive thought to see beyond one's personal relationships and consider "the good of society" (which is a very abstract concept).

Negotiation Strategies: What We Accept as Evidence

In general, let us assume that everyone acts on the basis of his or her own best interests. The question becomes: How do I decide if this is a good deal or not? Or, in a broader sense, what is the truth?

Different cultures arrive at truth in different ways. These ways can be distilled into *faith*, *facts*, and *feelings*.

The person who acts on the basis of faith is using a belief system, which can be a religious or political ideology. For example, many small nations believe in self-sufficiency. They may reject a deal that is overwhelmingly advantageous simply because they want their own people to do it. It doesn't matter that you can provide a better-quality product at a much lower price; they believe it is better that their fellow citizens produce the product, even if they produce an inferior product at a higher cost. Presenting facts to such a person is a waste of time. His or her faith operates independently from facts.

Clearly, people who believe in facts want to see evidence to support your position. They can be the most predictable to work with. If you offer the low bid, you get the job.

People who believe in feelings are the most common throughout the world. These are the people who "go with their gut instincts." They need to like you in order to do business with you. It can take a long time to build up a relationship with them. However, once that relationship is established, it is very strong. They aren't going to run to the first company that undercuts your offer.

Value Systems: The Basis for Behavior

Each culture has a system for dividing right from wrong, or good from evil. After a general statement concerning the values of the culture, this section identifies the culture's three value systems (Locus of Decision-Making, Sources of Anxiety Reduction, and Issues of Equality/Inequality). These following three sections identify the Value Systems in the predominant culture of each country.

Locus of Decision-Making

This section explores how much a culture prizes individualism as opposed to collectivism. Some countries, such as the USA, are very individualistic, while others, such as China, are very collectivistic. A person in the United States may consider only himself or herself when making a decision, while a person in China must abide by the consensus of the collective group.

Such pure individualism and collectivism is rare. In most countries people consider more than just themselves, but are not bound by the desires of the group.

It is possible to consider the loci of decision-making as a series of concentric circles. In the center, in the smallest circle, is the individual. The next circle, slightly larger, is usually the family. Many cultures expect each individual to consider "What is best for my family?" prior to making any decisions. The next circle represents a larger group. It could be an ethnic group, a religion, or even the individual's country. Some cultures expect individuals to consider the best interests of the entire, expansive group.

Of course, when a person is acting as representative for a company, the best interests of the company may be paramount.

Sources of Anxiety Reduction

Every human being on this planet is subject to stress. How do we handle it? How do we reduce anxiety?

We can identify four basic sources of security and stability that people turn to: interpersonal relationships, religion, technology, and the law. Frequently, a combination of sources is used.

A person who must decide on an important business deal is under stress. If this person is your client, it may help you to know where he or she will turn for help and advice. This is especially true when the person turns to interpersonal relationships. If an executive is going to ask his or her spouse for advice, you had better make sure that you have made a good impression on that spouse.

Issues of Equality/Inequality

An important characteristic of all cultures is the division of power. Who controls the government, and who controls the business resources?

"All men are created equal" is a sacred tenet of the United States of America. Despite this, prejudice against many groups still exists in the United States.

All cultures have disadvantaged groups. This section identifies some sectors that have unequal status. These can be defined by economic status as well as by race or gender. Only the most industrialized nations tend to have a large, stable middle class. Many countries have a small, rich elite and a huge, poverty-stricken underclass.

Issues of male-female equality are also analyzed in this section. It is useful for a female business executive to know how women are regarded in a foreign country.

Never forget that this model represents cultural patterns that may or may not apply to each individual you contact and get to know. Utilize this information as a guideline and remain open to the new experiences we all encounter abroad.

"*Vérité en-deca des Pyrénées, erreur au-dela.*"
—BLAISE PASCAL, 1623–1662

"There are truths on this side of the Pyrenees
which are falsehoods on the other."
—TRANSLATION: GEERT HOFSTEDE

MAP OF LATIN AMERICA

ATLANTIC OCEAN

Honduras
PAGE 122

Nicaragua
PAGE 146

Mexico
PAGE 133

Belize
PAGE 14

Cuba

Haiti

Dominican Republic

Guatemala
PAGE 111

Panama
PAGE 159

Caribbean Sea

El Salvador
PAGE 100

Costa Rica
PAGE 77

Venezuela
PAGE 204

Guyana

Suriname

French Guiana

Ecuador
PAGE 89

Colombia
PAGE 64

PACIFIC OCEAN

Brazil
PAGE 39

Peru
PAGE 181

Bolivia
PAGE 26

Paraguay
PAGE 170

Chile
PAGE 51

Argentina
PAGE 1

Uruguay
PAGE 193

The Malvinas

Argentina

Argentine Republic
Local short form: Argentina
Local long form: República Argentina

Cultural Note

When Spain ruled Argentina, immigration was restricted to Spaniards. However, after Argentina gained independence in 1816, immigration from all over Europe was encouraged. The new Argentinians were not only Spanish but Italian, English, Irish, German, Polish, Jewish, and Ukrainian. By the 1990s, the majority of new immigrants were from the Pacific Rim.

▶ WHAT'S YOUR CULTURAL IQ?

1. Argentina has produced some extraordinary authors. Match the writer with his work:

   a. Jorge Luis Borges   1. *Kiss of the Spider Woman*
   b. Manuel Puig   2. *Prisoner Without a Name,*
   c. Jacobo Timerman   *Cell Without a Number*
                                  3. *Labyrinths*

   ANSWER: a. 3; b. 1; c. 2. Jorge Luis Borges wrote a multitude of highly acclaimed poems and short stories, and was a strong influence on the development of magic realism. Manuel Puig authored novels about popular culture in Argentina, including *Betrayed by Rita Hayworth* and *Kiss of the Spider Woman*. He lived most of his life in Brazil. Journalist Jacobo Timerman's works included *Prisoner Without a Name, Cell Without a Number*.

2. When he became an ally of Fidel Castro in 1953, Argentine-born revolutionary Ernesto Guevara Serna became known as "Che" Guevara. Why?

   a. He sneezed a lot.
   b. Latin Americans often call Argentines "che."

c. He stammered.

d. C-H-E is an acronym of the Cuban revolution.

ANSWER: b. Argentines use the interjection "che" so often that has become a nickname for all Argentines.

3. The tango is both the national dance and a national obsession in Argentina. TRUE OR FALSE: In 1954, a tango artist named Astor Piazzolla so outraged some Argentine tango fans that he received death threats.

ANSWER: TRUE. For years, Astor Piazzolla had been one of Argentina's top tango musicians, leading tango bands with his bandoneon (a type of accordion). In 1954, Piazzolla performed a radically different "new tango," which broke decades of tango conventions. This brought him many fans—and vociferous protests from traditionalists.

▶ TIPS ON DOING BUSINESS IN ARGENTINA

- Compared with other South Americans, Argentines have a reputation for seriousness and melancholy. To call someone or something "not serious" is one of the most damning accusations an Argentine can make. A formal, sober manner is appropriate.
- On the other hand, when somber Argentines become amused, you know that they have become comfortable with you. Argentine banter is full of putdowns, from comments about your wardrobe to your weight. Don't be offended.
- Executives may work irregular and extended hours, sometimes lasting until 10:00 P.M. An 8:00 P.M. business appointment is not unusual.
- In most cases, a good personal relationship with your prospects is a prerequisite for conducting business. (The Internet is changing some aspects of this.) Meetings begin and end with small talk, so always allocate extra time at the end of a meeting for polite conversation.
- Appropriate, refined attire is very important—particularly in the capital, Buenos Aires. Businesspeople should bring a conservative wardrobe in order to be taken seriously.

▶ COUNTRY BACKGROUND

Demographics

About 85 percent of Argentines are of European descent, primarily Spanish or Italian. Indians, mestizos (people of mixed Indian and Spanish ancestry), and blacks together make up only 15 percent of Argentina's 40 million people (2006 estimate). There are also significant numbers of French, English, and German immigrants. Buenos Aires boasts the largest number of Jews in Latin America; they are commonly referred to as *los rusos* (the Russians) because most of the early Jewish settlers emigrated from Czarist Russia.

History

The original Amerindian inhabitants of Argentina were nomadic hunters and gatherers more warlike than agricultural. They killed the first Spanish explorers to arrive in 1516, and even forced the abandonment of the first Buenos Aires settlement some twenty years later. Their ultimate fate was similar to that of their North American brethren: they were defeated and hunted down.

Buenos Aires gained importance late during the Spanish reign, when it was designated as the capital of the new viceroyalty of Río de la Plata in 1776. This Spanish viceroyalty lasted for scarcely four decades.

Napoleon's conquest of Spain prompted the Argentines to declare temporary self-rule in 1810. This led to a full declaration of independence in 1816, under the grandiose title of the United Provinces of Río de la Plata.

Fighting quickly broke out, as many provinces refused to be ruled by Buenos Aires. The territory of Río de la Plata divided into modern Argentina, Bolivia, Paraguay, Uruguay, and southern Chile. Even the old, established cities of northern Argentina resisted domination by the upstart port of Buenos Aires. Not until 1880 was Argentina fully united.

Military coups preceded and followed Juan Perón's dictatorship between 1946 and 1955. After Perón's banishment to Spain, Argentina had another thirty years of military rule (there were some short episodes of civilian leadership during those decades). In 1973 he returned briefly to office, and when he died, power was transferred to his wife, Isabel Perón.

In 1976, threatened by terrorism and hyperinflation, most Argentines were relieved when the military seized power. But stability was restored at the cost of human rights. The plight of the *desaparacidos* (the "disappeared") began to be covered in the media when the mothers of thousands of missing Argentine citizens started keeping a public vigil for family members who had become victims of the military. The "Dirty War" lasted until 1983, and up to 30,000 Argentines disappeared—kidnapped, tortured, and illegally executed.

After a few years, brutality, corruption, and bad monetary policy made the junta unpopular. The junta decided to distract the populace by invading the British-held Malvinas (or Falkland) Islands in 1982. To the junta's surprise, the United Kingdom fought to hold the territory. Argentina lost the Falkland War, and the humbled junta ceded power to an elected government in 1983.

The economy of Argentina suffered through a loan default in 2001, which was the largest in history to that point. Riots and resignations followed. After a series of five presidents in two weeks, Eduardo Duhalde became president and made some significant economic decisions in order to be eligible for aid again from the International Monetary Fund. In May of 2003 Nestor Kirchner was elected president, and he became noteworthy for his decision to persecute those responsible for the human rights abuses between 1976 and 1983.

Type of Government

La República Argentina is a federal republic. Argentina has twenty-three provinces; its capital is Buenos Aires. The president is both the chief of state and head of government. The cabinet is appointed by the president. The legislative branch is a bicameral National Congress. It consists of the Senate and the Chamber of Deputies. In the judicial branch, nine Supreme Court judges are appointed by the president with the Senate's approval. Current information on the government of Argentina can be found with the Embassy of Argentina, at *www .embassyofargentina.us*.

Cultural Note
Juan Domingo Perón founded a political dynasty. But despite her fame, Eva (Evita) Perón, his second wife, was never president—she died while her husband was in office. Perón's third wife, Isabel, succeeded to the presidency after he died in office in 1974. And Carlos Saul Menem, president from 1989 to 1999, was a member of the Justicialista Party—the modern-day Peronist Party.

Language

Spanish is the official language, although many people speak English, and an estimated 1,500,000 people speak Italian. German and French are also commonly spoken. The heavy influence of Italian on Argentine Spanish makes it unique on the continent. Ethnologue, a catalogue of world languages, references twenty-six languages in Argentina—one of which is extinct. For further data on the various languages of Argentina, visit *www.ethnologue.com*. The site provides well-researched databases and maps of information on the languages of the world.

The Argentine View

Church and state are officially separate, but about 90 percent of the population consider themselves Roman Catholic. Protestants, Muslims, and Jews account for the remainder.

There are many reasons suggested for the somber outlook of many Argentines. None of them can be proven. This, however, is a fact: Buenos Aires has a large percentage of people who have sought psychiatric help. The city also has more mental health practitioners than any other city in Latin America.

Like the French, Argentines tend to consider themselves more cultured than people from most countries. This can hamper their business dealings with people from nations Argentines have been known to look down upon.

For a country with many European attitudes, the Argentines still may exhibit a substantial amount of machismo. Antiglobalization sentiment has increased in Argentina since the nation's 2001 economic crisis.

☑ Know Before You Go

Most of Argentina is relatively safe from natural disasters. The exceptions are the San Miguel de Tucumán and Mendoza areas in the Andes, which are subject to earthquakes.

Violent windstorms (called *pamperos*) can strike the Pampas and northeast; heavy flooding may also occur.

The greatest risk to travelers is from street crime, which has often been an issue in Argentine politics. Such crime is not usually violent, but often manifests as scams and car theft. Corrupt officials, especially rural policemen, have been known to extort fines from travelers. This seemed to be on the increase since the economic dislocations of 2001.

In 2005, Argentina ranked 97th out of 158 countries (they tied with Algeria, Mada-gascar, Malawi, Mozambique, Serbia and Montenegro) in Transparency International's Corruption Perception Index. (See *www.transparency.org* for further information.)

While they rarely affect foreigners, there are still active territorial disputes in Argentina. These include the UK-administered Falkland Islands (Islas Malvinas), the South Georgia Islands, and the South Sandwich Islands. In 1995 Argentina ceded the right to settle the dispute by force. The Beagle Channel Islands dispute was resolved through papal mediation in 1984, but armed incidents have persisted since the 1992 discovery of oil in the region. Argentina's territorial claim in Antarctica partially overlaps British and Chilean claims.

The convergence of the Argentina-Brazil-Paraguay borders is a locus of money laun-dering and smuggling. Travelers to this region may find themselves interrogated upon their return to their home country.

⊙ CULTURAL ORIENTATION

Cognitive Styles: How Argentines Organize and Process Information

Strong European influences make Argentines less open to discussion of new ideas than the citizens of most other Latin American countries. Those with higher educations are more apt to be abstractive in their thinking, although associative, experiential thinking is the rule of thumb. Strong personal relationships make Argentines more concerned about the consequences of an action than about the action itself.

Negotiation Strategies: What Argentines Accept as Evidence

There is a decided conflict among the forces of feeling, faith, and facts. Argentines look at problems from a subjective perspective, but these feelings are usually influenced by faith in some ideology (primarily the Catholic Church, a political party, or ethnocentrism). Facts are always acceptable as long as they do not contradict either feeling or faith.

Argentines have been evaluated to have a higher-than-average ranking in uncertainty avoidance. This may make Argentines averse to risk and somewhat unwilling to accept change.

Value Systems: The Basis for Behavior

Humanitarian values are strong, but consumerism is resulting in a more materialistic society. The following three sections identify the Value Systems in the predominant culture—their methods of dividing right from wrong, good from evil, and so forth.

Locus of Decision-Making

A single, high-ranking individual usually makes business decisions, but decisions are also made with the best interest of a larger group in mind. The most honored group is the extended family, from which one gains his or her self-identity. Kinships and friendships play significant roles in decision-making. Some cultural anthropologists believe that Argentines are less collectivist than their Latin American neighbors, and chart a high individuality index.

Sources of Anxiety Reduction

Although the older generations are still attached to the Church and the extended family for their security, the younger generation is putting more faith in the social structure. This sometimes leads to unrealistic allegiance to a strong political figure or ideology.

Issues of Equality/Inequality

Those who are in power consider themselves entitled to the privileges that come with the office. Argentines have been measured to have a higher-than-average masculinity index. Although machismo is still very strong, it is being challenged on all fronts. There are now more women than men in school, and women are taking a leading role in both politics and business.

▶ BUSINESS PRACTICES

Punctuality, Appointments, and Local Time

- Visitors are expected to be punctual. However, do not be surprised if your Argentine counterpart is late. In general, the more important the person, the more likely it is that he or she will keep you waiting.
- Guidelines for punctuality are different for social occasions. Even North Americans are expected to be thirty minutes late (or more) for dinner or parties; to show up on time would be impolite. But be on time for lunch and for events with a scheduled starting time, such as the theater.
- When it is important to know if your Argentine counterpart expects promptness, you can ask, *"¿En punto?"* (on the dot?).
- Remember that many South Americans and Europeans write the day first, then the month, then the year (e.g., December 3, 2010, is written 3.12.10 or 3/12/10). This is the case in Argentina.
- Your first appointments in Argentina should be with potential representatives (sometimes called *enchufados*)—individuals who have high-level contacts in your industry segment. The person you ultimately select opens the doors and can greatly facilitate the process of doing business in Argentina. Get a list of potential *enchufados* or local representatives through your embassy or your company's legal or accounting firm.
- Be certain you hire the correct Argentine personnel; it can be very difficult to change or fire your local representative.
- Argentine executives may put in a very long day, often lasting until 10:00 P.M. The ability to keep irregular business hours is the prerogative of an important executive.
- The country of Argentina is three hours behind Greenwich Mean Time (G.M.T. − 3), making it two hours ahead of U.S. Eastern Standard Time (E.S.T. + 2).

Negotiating

- Visitors are often surprised that, despite its European manners, the pace of business negotiations is much slower than in Europe.

Do not be surprised if it takes you several trips to accomplish your goal. One reason business moves slowly is that Argentina is a bureaucratic and litigious country. Even after the top decision-maker has agreed to something, many others must concur.

- Argentine negotiators have a reputation for toughness, yielding very little. Part of their immobility is due to the fact that they are generally averse to risk.

- Personal relationships are far more important than corporate ones. Each time your company changes its representative, you will virtually be starting from scratch. New alliances must be built up before business can proceed.

- Whenever you want to deal with the Argentine government, it is vital to have an Argentine contact to act as an intermediary. Without one, you probably won't even get an appointment.

- Don't assume that each portion of a contract is finalized once agreement on that section has been reached. Until the entire contract is signed, each part is subject to renegotiation.

- Expect the final contract to be long and detailed.

Business Entertaining

- Business meals are popular and are usually held in restaurants; offers to dine in Argentine homes are relatively infrequent.

- To summon a waiter, raise your hand with your index finger extended or call out *mozo* (waiter) or *moza* (waitress). Don't adopt the local habit of making a kissing noise to attract a waiter; although common, it is considered impolite.

- Business lunches are less common outside of Buenos Aires; it is still common for people to go home to eat lunch.

- Argentines do not usually discuss business over meals; meals are considered social occasions.

- Since dinner does not begin until 10:00 P.M. (or later on weekends), Argentines have tea or coffee and pastries between 4:00 and 6:00 P.M. If you are in a meeting during that time, you will be offered something. Accept something to drink, even if you don't want it.

- When dining, keep your hands on the table, not in your lap.

- There are several complexities involved with pouring wine, which a foreigner can unknowingly violate. For example, pouring with the left hand may be an insult.
- Taxes on imported liquors are enormous. When you are invited out, your host will be paying, so don't order imported liquors unless your host does so first. Try a local drink instead; most types of liquor are produced in local versions.
- To indicate that you are finished eating and have had enough, cross your knife and fork (with the prongs down) on your dinner plate.
- Argentina produces some of the best beef in the world; expect to see a lot of it at meals. Parrillada, a mixed grill of beef, beef, and more beef is very popular. Every variety of cut is included, from the udders on up. Many Argentines eat meat twice a day.

Cultural Note

Try to avoid offering any political opinions. Be especially cautious about praising Argentina's neighbors (notably Chile). Argentina has fought wars with all of them.

Most Argentines are anxious to put the Falkland Islands War behind them, so avoid bringing up the subject. However, if it is discussed, remember to refer to the islands by their Argentine name, the Malvinas Islands.

The Argentine style of banter may seem odd, as it may include mildly derogatory comments about your wardrobe or your weight. Don't take it seriously; indeed, it is a sign that your Argentine colleague is getting comfortable around you.

Argentines are great sports fans. Talking about sports is always a good way to open a conversation. Soccer (called *fútbol*) is the most popular sport. U.S.–style football is *fútbol americano*.

Many older Argentines love opera, so it may be a good topic to discuss. Restaurants and sightseeing are also fine topics.

⊚ PROTOCOL

Greetings

- Close male friends shake hands or embrace upon meeting; men kiss close female friends. Close female friends usually kiss each other. The full embrace *(abrazo)* may entail a hug, a handshake, and several thumps on the shoulder, often ending with another handshake.

- Except when greeting close friends, it is traditional to shake hands briefly and nod to both men and women.

Titles/Forms of Address

- Travelers should be attentive to Argentina's unique naming conventions; they are different from many other Spanish-speaking cultures.
- Rather than include the surnames of both parents in their full names, Argentines generally use just one surname (or family name). For example, a business card might say: "Señor Alberto Paz," or "Señor Alberto Paz Esteban." In both cases, Paz, or Paz Esteban would be his father's name. His mother's surname will probably not appear.
- The word *de* may be used in surnames, particularly by women who want to add their husbands' family names to their own.
- While Argentines may have double first names on their business cards (like María Teresa or José Antonio), they might not use both those names in person—or in print. If you have not been told which first name they use, you should address them by their surnames.
- Appendix A contains further data on Titles and Forms of Address.

Gestures

- The Argentine people converse at a closer distance than North Americans or northern Europeans are used to—often with a hand on the other person's lapel or shoulder. Restrain yourself from backing away; an Argentine will probably step forward to close the distance.
- Maintaining eye contact is very important—something that North Americans may find difficult while speaking to a person at such close quarters.
- A pat on the shoulder is a sign of friendship.
- The gesture that some North Americans use to mean "so-so" (twisting the flat, open hand from side to side) is common in Argentina. The meaning is the same.

- A sweeping gesture beginning under the chin and continuing up over the top of the head is used to mean "I don't know" or "I don't care."
- With thumb and middle finger touching (as if holding a pinch of salt), one taps them with the index finger to indicate "hurry up" or "a lot."
- Avoid placing your hands on your hips while speaking.
- Make sure to cover your mouth when either yawning or coughing.
- Sit only on chairs, not on a ledge, box, or table.
- Don't rest your feet on anything other than a footstool or rail; it is very impolite to place them upon a table.
- Eating in the street or on public transportation is considered impolite.

Gifts

- High taxes on imported liquor makes this a highly appreciated gift. Scotch and French champagne are popular. Don't bring wine; the Southern Cone produces an abundance of quality wines.
- As in any country, gifts should be beautifully designed and of superior workmanship. If the item is produced by your corporation, the corporate name or logo should appear discreetly, not be emblazoned over the whole surface.
- Avoid giving knives; they symbolize the severing of a friendship.
- Electronic gadgets like iPods are popular.
- Argentina is a major cattle producer, and thus a major leather producer. Avoid bringing leather gifts.
- If you are invited to an Argentine home, bring a gift of flowers, imported chocolates, or whiskey. Bird of paradise flowers are appreciated.

Dress

- Dress is very important for making a good impression in Argentina. Your entire wardrobe will be scrutinized.
- While Argentines are more in touch with European clothing styles than many Latin Americans, they tend toward the modest and the subdued. The provocative clothing popular in Brazil, for example, is rarely seen in Argentina.

- Business dress in Argentina is fairly conservative: dark suits and ties for men; white blouses and dark suits or skirts for women.
- Men may wear the same dark suit for evening wear. Women should wear a dress or skirt.
- Both men and women wear pants as casualwear. If you are meeting business associates (outdoor barbecues, called *asado*, are popular), avoid jeans and wear a jacket or blazer. Women should not wear shorts, except when invited to a swimming pool.
- Indian clothing is for Indians; don't adopt any native costumes, no matter how attractive. The same goes for gaucho outfits.
- Bring lightweight clothing for the summer, and topcoats and sweaters for the winter (especially since central heating is not universal). Don't forget that the seasons in South America are the reverse of those in the Northern Hemisphere.
- Don't wear anything outside that can be damaged by water during Carnival. Drenching pedestrians is a favorite Carnival pastime of the young.

Cultural Note

A common Argentine saying is that Argentina has always been "blessed by resources but cursed by politics." Despite its turbulent political history, Argentina has remained one of Latin America's most prosperous nations.

Today the Republic of Argentina is once again a democracy. Its military junta stepped down after the country's loss to Great Britain in the 1982 Falkland Islands War. As of 2004, the military has remained in the background, even during the mass protests caused by the economic meltdown of 2001.

Belize

Former: British Honduras

Cultural Note

Although the history of Belize is heavily laced with pirates, it nevertheless is one of the most peaceful countries in Central America. Unlike its neighbors, Belize has not suffered even a single coup, major uprising, or guerrilla war.

For the first decade after independence, Belize depended upon British troops stationed there to protect its sovereignty against territorial aggression from Guatemala. However, after Guatemala finally recognized Belize's independence in 1991, the British troops were withdrawn and Belize created its own army of some 1,000 men.

▶ WHAT'S YOUR CULTURAL IQ?

1. TRUE or FALSE: The first Europeans to claim Belize were from the United Kingdom.

   ANSWER: FALSE. Actually, the Spanish claimed Belize first, but they never bothered settling it. It was an Englander, Peter Wallace, who established the first European settlement in Belize in 1638. Spaniards expelled the British settlers three times (in 1754, 1759, and 1765), but the British always returned after the Spanish forces left.

2. Many of the first European settlers came to Belize to pursue careers as what?
   a. Farmers
   b. Missionaries
   c. Pirates
   d. Puritans and other religious exiles

   ANSWER: c. Belize, the one area of Central America free of Spanish settlements, had long been a haven for the pirates and privateers who preyed on Spanish ships. Piracy declined in the seventeenth century (in part because the British revoked the charters of its privateers), leading some pirates to settle down.

3. Belizeans are proud of their varied and spectacular wildlife. TRUE or FALSE? The mountain cow is the national animal of Belize.
ANSWER: TRUE. The mountain cow—better known as the tapir—is the national animal of Belize. Tapirs are protected, and are the largest land mammal in the tropics, weighing up to 600 pounds. Belize's national bird is the spectacular keel-billed toucan.

▶ TIPS ON DOING BUSINESS IN BELIZE

- Belize is Central America's youngest independent nation; it was the colony of British Honduras until 1981. There are two political parties: the People's United Party (PUP) and the United Democratic Party (UDP). Whichever party is out of power often tries to inflame public opinion by denouncing the local plans of non-Belizeans. Curiously, once that party achieves power, they tend to be relatively cooperative with outside businesspeople and investors.

- Relations between Belize and its neighbors are now cordial, although Guatemala claimed parts of Belizean territory until 1992.

- Although Belize's official language is English, visitors may be surprised that the Creole dialect of English spoken by most Belizeans is unintelligible to many foreign speakers of English. However, Belizean businesspeople can converse in conventional English.

- Business in Belize is concentrated in the areas of tourism, agriculture, and forestry. However, Belize has recently become a banking haven.

- As of this writing, foreigners could buy Belizean citizenship for about U.S. $50,000. Citizenship can be acquired without even visiting the country! (The Belizean Political Reform Commission recommended in 2000 that section 26(1)c of the constitution—which allowed so-called "economic citizenships"—be deleted. But no action has been taken.)

Cultural Note

Belizeans are as relaxed about street addresses as they are about most other things. Many houses and buildings do not have street numbers, nor do all streets have names. To find a particular address, get directions from a well-known landmark.

▶ COUNTRY BACKGROUND

Demographics

Belize is the second smallest nation in Central America. It is slightly larger than El Salvador. With only 290,000 people (2006 estimate), it is also the least-populated country in Central America.

The bulk of Belize's population is of mixed ancestry. Spanish-Indian Mestizos make up 49 percent of Belizeans. Blacks and black-white mulattos (collectively known as Creoles in Belize) account for 25 percent, and Amerindian (primarily Mayan) for 11 percent.

The Garifunas are also known as Garinagus or Black Caribs. While their genetic heritage comes mostly from Africa, their culture and language is primarily Amerindian. Some friction exists between the Garifunas and the more populous Creoles.

History

In 1638, the British pirate Peter Wallace established the first European settlement in Belize, near the mouth of the Belize River. Then another British pirate, Bartholomew Sharp, began regular timber exports from Belize in 1660. He shipped valuable logwood, which provided dyes for textiles. His success brought other British loggers to Belize, who collectively became known as the Baymen.

The first African slaves were brought to Belize for the timber-cutting industry between 1700 and 1710. This combination of African and European ethnicity was the origin of Belize's Creole population.

The Spanish drove out the Baymen in 1754, 1759, and 1779. Each time, the Spanish did not stay, and the Baymen soon returned. The beginnings of local government emerged in 1765, when the Baymen established Burnaby's Code. With the discovery of synthetic dyes, mahogany replaced logwood as Belize's most important export.

The 1783 Treaty of Paris confirmed Britain's right to conduct logging in Belize, but prohibited the establishment of agriculture. From then on, Belize would not be able to produce enough food to feed itself, and became dependent upon outside imports.

Slavery was outlawed in 1838, but the black population of Belize was still subject to restrictions, such as a prohibition against ex-slaves from receiving Crown land grants.

A few white families became wealthy and owned most of Belize's land. In 1853 the country established a local legislative assembly, dominated by the landowners.

In 1862, while the United States of America was embroiled in the Civil War (and unable to enforce the Monroe Doctrine), Belize formally became the British colony of British Honduras, ruled by a lieutenant governor who was subordinate to the governor of Jamaica. The post of British Honduras' highest official, the lieutenant governor, was raised to governor in 1884. This meant Belize was no longer subordinate to the governor of Jamaica.

Creole soldiers, recently returned from service overseas in World War I, rioted in 1919. Many date the start of the Belizean independence movement to this incident, known as the Ex-Servicemen's Riot.

Due to the vulnerability of Belize City to hurricanes, the capital was moved fifty miles inland to the new city of Belmopan in 1973.

British Honduras became the independent nation of Belize in 1981.

Cultural Note
The people of Belize have a distinct style of popular music and dance called *punta*. Of West African origin, Punta dance is unique in that the feet remain stationary. Instead, the rest of the body—especially the hips—moves. It is especially popular among the Garifuna.

Type of Government
Since independence from the United Kingdom in 1981, Belize has been a constitutional monarchy. In the executive branch there is a prime minister and a Cabinet, and there are two legislative houses: the Senate and the House of Representatives.

The monarch of the United Kingdom (currently Queen Elizabeth II) is the chief of state, represented by a governor-general (who is a native of Belize). The prime minister is head of the government.

For current government data, check with the Embassy of Belize at *www.embassyofbelize.org*. An interesting, excellent source for additional information is *www.belize.gov.bz*.

Language

The official language of Belize is English. However, the dialect of English spoken by much of the Creole population is unintelligible to most foreigners. While the speech patterns sound familiar, the overall speech is not generally understood by outside English speakers.

There are nine languages currently spoken in Belize. If English and Creole English are categorized as separate languages, the majority language of Belize is actually Spanish. Also spoken is Plautdietsch, a dialect of German spoken by the 6,000 Mennonite farmers in Belize. Most of the other languages are indigenous Amerindian tongues.

For further data on the various languages of Belize, see *www .ethnologue.com*.

The Belizean View

There is no official religion in Belize, and the constitution guarantees freedom of religion. However, the country has a national prayer, which includes Christian references.

Roman Catholics make up almost exactly 50 percent of the population. Some 27 percent of the remainder are Protestants, divided among Pentecostalists, Anglicans, Seventh-Day Adventists, Mennonites, Methodists, and Jehovah's Witnesses. About 14 percent of Belizeans follow non-Christian religions, and over 9 percent are not members of any organized religion. Ever since the Anglican Church established the first Belizean school in 1816, most primary schools in Belize have been run and staffed by churches. Traditionally, most schools were supported by Roman Catholics (who ran over half the schools in Belize), the Anglicans and the Methodists. In recent years, evangelical churches (such as the Assemblies of God) have opened schools. Primary education is free in Belize.

Isolated behind its barrier reef, Belize has been (and continues to be) ignored for the most part by outside forces. Race relations among the wide variety of ethnic groups are relatively good. The Creoles have formed the backbone of Belizean urban society for decades.

Belize is an anomaly in Central America—a new nation with an English-speaking heritage surrounded by Spanish-speaking countries. Belizeans cannot agree on whether they live in a Central American country or a Caribbean country. Certainly, the Caribbean influence (and through that, their heritage from the United Kingdom) is predominant among the business class and along the coast. But in the interior, where the majority of inhabitants are Spanish speakers who have immigrated from Mexico or Guatemala, the heritage is very much Latin American.

Belize has no oil, coal, or hydroelectric resources. The cost of electricity is high, as is the cost of air conditioning. Most Belizeans do without air conditioning.

The people of Belize have come to view their wildlife protectively. Posters showing local animals with the slogan "This Is Their Land Too" abound. Land is constantly being set aside as nature reserves, and many species are protected.

In Belize, the influence of the United States of America has long eclipsed the influence of the United Kingdom. Since World War II, it is estimated that one in every five Belizeans emigrated to the USA, legally or otherwise.

Cultural Note

Both the terms "Fever Coast" and "Mosquito Coast" refer to part of the Central American coastline on the Caribbean. The term Fever Coast is generally used for the coasts of Belize, Guatemala, and Honduras. The Mosquito Coast is technically a larger area: from Belize all the way down to Panama. Either way, Belize marks the northern end.

☑ Know Before You Go

The greatest hazard to visitors comes from vehicles. Traffic accidents are the leading cause of accidental death in Belize. Most such accidents occur in Belize City; victims include bicyclists and pedestrians.

Street crime is also a concern—again, primarily in Belize City.

Malaria is present throughout Belize, and is a leading cause of hospital admissions.

Road conditions vary in rural areas. Many are unpaved and become muddy during rainstorms. If you drive, be careful not to hit any of Belize's wildlife—especially the tapirs.

Of course, keep alert for weather emergencies while in Belize. Hurricanes and other tropical storms have caused widespread dislocations and destruction.

Marijuana is widely available in Belize. While Belizeans are rarely prosecuted for using marijuana, foreigners may be. In tourist areas, the greatest hazard often comes from rowdy foreigners under the influence of alcohol or drugs.

When you leave Belize, expect a thorough search of your luggage. Belizeans are very protective of their wildlife, and they are determined that none of their endangered exotic birds be smuggled out (either live or in the form of eggs).

▶ CULTURAL ORIENTATION

This information reflects the cultural orientation of the majority of English-speaking businesspeople in Belize. It is not applicable to Belize's other ethnic groups, including the Spanish speakers concentrated in the interior and border areas.

Cognitive Styles: How Belizeans Organize and Process Information

In Belize there is a basic tendency to accept information on any topic for discussion. Their beliefs are arrived at through association and experiential thinking. They look at each particular situation rather than using universal rules or laws to guide their behavior.

Further research needs to be done among the Belizeans.

Negotiation Strategies: What Belizeans Accept as Evidence

An individual's feelings about a topic or situation are the primary source of the truth. Faith in an ideology of class structure may influence that perception as well. Typically, an argument based entirely on quantifiable data is not convincing to the majority of Belizeans.

Value Systems: The Basis for Behavior

Class distinctions are more fluid in Belize than in its neighboring countries. The following three sections identify the Value Systems in the predominant culture—their methods of dividing right from wrong, good from evil, and so forth.

Locus of Decision-Making

Individuals in Belize are responsible for making their own decisions. The majority culture falls somewhere in the middle between individualism and collectivism. The effect of business decisions on one's family must be considered, but ultimately the decision belongs to one individual (almost inevitably a man).

Sources of Anxiety Reduction

Belizeans tend to be a remarkably relaxed people. They do not feel the need for strict laws and regulations to give order to their lives. This puts them in contrast with most of their Latin American neighbors. Belizeans are often unconcerned about ambiguity; for example, village government currently works without strict delineation of powers and responsibilities by the central government. Belizeans also tend to be willing to take risks, in business and in other aspects of their lives.

Issues of Equality/Inequality

Historically, Belize was a slave society, with a few white landowners bringing slaves from Africa to work in agriculture—from logging to sugar production. While some very wealthy families remain, there is a smaller differential between rich and poor in Belize than in many Latin American nations. Despite relative poverty among many Belizeans, race relations are fairly quiet. However, in regard to gender, Belize is a very masculine society. As the Political Reform Commission noted, women are rare in government. Except for women who have inherited businesses, Belizean women are infrequently seen in executive roles.

▶ BUSINESS PRACTICES

Punctuality, Appointments, and Local Time

- Business hours are generally 9:00 A.M. to noon, and 1:00 P.M. to 5:00 P.M., Monday through Friday. Government offices and many shops are open approximately the same hours.

- As a foreigner, you are expected to be punctual to all business appointments. Professionals in Belize's small business community tend to be on time.
- Outside the business community, Belizeans tend to have a casual relationship with time.
- Belizeans, like many Europeans and South Americans, write the day first, then the month, then the year (e.g., December 3, 2010, is written 3/12/10 or 3.12.10).
- Before you arrive, make appointments at least a week in advance.
- Keep an eye on the weather forecast. Hurricanes and tropical storms can disrupt your entire business schedule.
- Some businesses keep Saturday morning hours—but, to compensate, they usually close early on Wednesday.
- Official holidays are listed at *www.kissboworshakehands.com*.
- Belize is five hours behind Greenwich Mean Time (G.M.T. – 5), which is the same as U.S. Eastern Standard Time.

Negotiating

- It will be difficult to conduct business without hiring a local contact, preferably a native of Belize. (Remember, anyone can buy Belizean citizenship; that does not make him or her an expert on Belizean business.)
- Just as many Belizeans vote for political leaders on the basis of their personality rather than their platforms, business decisions are often dependent upon the personality of the individual. A Belizean must like you in order to do business with you.
- Business is done from the top down in Belize. A company's top executives make the decisions.
- English (not Creole English) is used in business transactions. All materials should be translated into English. Spelling follows the British pattern.
- Your business cards should be printed in your native language on one side, and the translation in English on the other. These should be presented with the English side facing your Belizean colleague.

- Expect delays. Deadlines and completion dates, even when put in writing, are flexible.
- Avoid discussing local politics, religion, or race. Good topics are sports, the natural beauty of Belize, and places you have visited in the UK or in Latin America.
- It is a good idea to be informed about local culture and history, or at least to show curiosity about Belize.

Business Entertaining
- Breakfast is known as "tea" in Belize. It is a light meal eaten around 6:30 or 7:00 A.M.
- Lunch is known as "dinner" in Belize. It is the main meal of the day, and the usual choice for a business meal. It is usually served between noon and 1:00 P.M.
- Confusingly, the evening meal is also called "dinner" in Belize. Another term for eating the evening meal is "drinking tea." Obviously, if you are confused by an invitation to dine, ask what time you should arrive. This meal begins anytime from 6:00 to 8:00 P.M. It is a lighter meal than the noon dinner.
- Traditionally, the meal ends with the main course. There is no dessert, coffee, or after-dinner drink.
- Belizean tradition holds that you accept any food or drink offered to you, and that you eat everything on your plate. Claiming that your doctor prohibits you from eating certain foods is the only acceptable excuse for declining, and you should inform your host of this issue before you arrive.
- Belizeans tend to have large families and small dining tables, so families often eat in shifts. The men are always served first. As an honored guest in a private home, a foreign businesswoman might be allowed to eat with the men.
- In a restaurant, Belizean men may refuse to let a woman pay (unless everyone has agreed in advance to pay for their own food). If a businesswoman wants to pay, she should make arrangements in advance with the waiter or the restaurant.

▶ PROTOCOL

Greetings

- The standard greeting between men is the handshake. Men will shake hands with women, but women rarely shake hands with other women.
- Older women often hug visitors, usually with just one arm.
- The handshake is also used when departing.

Titles/Forms of Address

- Among English-speaking Belizeans, address people by their surnames, prefixed with "Mister," "Mrs.," or "Miss." ("Ms." is not in common use in Belize.)
- The only titles in common use are "Doctor" for anyone with a Ph.D., and "Professor" for college teachers.
- Among Spanish-speaking Belizeans, use the traditional Spanish forms of address that are listed in Appendix A.

Gestures

- Because so many Belizeans have lived in the United States of America, North American gestures are understood and used in Belize.

Gifts

- Gift giving is not traditionally part of doing business in Belize.
- When invited into a home for a meal, bring wine, liquor, or a dessert.
- Further guidelines on gift giving are available at *www.kissbow orshakehands.com.*

Dress

- In theory, businessmen should wear a dark suit and tie for business meetings. Women should wear a dress. If you are in a conservative business such as banking, this is appropriate garb.
- The same outfits are appropriate for the most formal of social occasions in Belize.

- When not at business-related events, jeans or other casualwear are standard. However, women should not wear revealing or tight clothes on the street.
- In practice, because of the heat, attire tends to be much more casual. Even the prime minister rarely dons a jacket or tie.

Cultural Note

When Belize achieved independence in 1981, the design of its flag was somewhat controversial because of its strong similarity to the dominant political group—the People's United Party (PUP). Public opinion was divided on the flag, because it was supposed to be a symbol of unification. Therefore, some additions were made in deference to the opposition—the United Democratic Party. Two horizontal red stripes were added at the top and bottom.

Bolivia

Republic of Bolivia
Local long form: Republica de Bolivia

Cultural Note

Bolivia has one of the largest natural gas reserves in South America. It exports some of the gas (e.g., one contract runs through 2019 with Brazil), but the government plans to increase exports. However, the path is precarious. In October of 2003, President Gonzalo Sánchez de Lozada dared to suggest that Bolivia start exporting their natural gas through Chile, and massive protests were staged. The furor ultimately led to his resignation.

⯈ WHAT'S YOUR CULTURAL IQ?.

1. Why were Bolivians irate about selling natural gas through Chile?
   a. Bolivians want to keep the gas to themselves.
   b. Bolivia lost a war with Chile in 1883, and still resents it.
   c. Peru offered Bolivia more money than Chile, and the Bolivian populace found out.

   ANSWER: b. Bolivia has never forgiven Chile for annexing Bolivia's entire coastline back in 1883. This may sound like ancient history, but those (like former president Gonzalo Sánchez de Lozada) who forget the Bolivian-Chilean animosity do so at their own risk. Bolivian presidents still commemorate an annual "Day of the Sea" with a vow to regain their seacoast, and landlocked Bolivia still maintains a navy that patrols Lake Titicaca.

2. What is the capital of Bolivia?
   a. La Paz
   b. Sucre
   c. Santa Cruz
   d. a and b
   e. b and c

ANSWER: d. Unique among the Americas, Bolivia has two capital cities. La Paz is the permanent capital, but Sucre is the summer capital. Santa Cruz is the most populous city.

3. TRUE or FALSE? Today Bolivia's Potosí Mine produces tin, but hundreds of years ago it yielded so much silver that the expression "as rich as Potosí" became a popular expression throughout Europe and the Americas.
ANSWER: TRUE. Unfortunately, the silver in Potosí was exhausted decades ago.

▶ TIPS ON DOING BUSINESS IN BOLIVIA

- The Spanish dialect spoken in Bolivia is very conservative. Unlike the Spanish used in most of Latin America, Bolivians retain the second-person plural *(vosotros)* form of verbs.
- Although Bolivia is traditionally a male-dominated country, Bolivian women are increasingly common in the workplace. Foreign businesswomen are no longer viewed as a novelty.
- Business is conducted at a leisurely pace. The best way to break into the market is with a local representative who knows how deals are done. Because business is conducted on a personal level, agreements are made between people, not companies. You will need the right person to introduce you. Be certain to contract with the correct individual—once you sign an agreement, you may not be able to change your representative.
- In 2005 Bolivia elected its first indigenous President, Evo Morales. President Morales supported left-wing policies and politicians in Latin America. Avoid political discussions with your Bolivian associates, but if they do arise, be extremely sensitive to their viewpoints.
- In the 1990s, Bolivia tried to develop its vast natural resources instead of relying so heavily on foreign aid. It privatized various state-owned companies—the airline, telephone, oil, and power companies. It also became an associate member of Mercosur (the Southern Cone Common Market) in the 1990s and signed a free trade agreement with Mexico. If the government can stabilize, there is great potential for growth.

⊚ COUNTRY BACKGROUND

Demographics

Almost half of Bolivia's 9 million population (2006 estimate) is involved in agriculture. Mining now occupies only some 3 percent of the workforce. A full two-thirds of the population lives outside urban areas. Full-blood Indians (Quechua and Aymara) account for over half of the Bolivian populace. About 30 percent are mestizo (mixed Indian and European heritage), and 15 percent are of European descent.

History

Once part of the powerful Inca empire, Bolivia was conquered by the Spanish in 1538. Naming the area Upper Peru, the Spanish found that Bolivia possessed the mineral wealth they so avidly sought. The huge silver mines at Potosí, discovered in 1545, were the richest in the world. Until the silver was depleted, Potosí was one of the biggest and wealthiest cities in North or South America.

In 1809 Bolivia rebelled against Spanish rule, a revolt that inspired independence movements throughout the entire Southern Cone. But unlike the other countries, Bolivia was known to contain great mineral wealth. The Spanish fought for sixteen years to keep Bolivia a colony. Bolivia finally gained its independence in 1825. The country was named after its liberator, Simón Bolívar.

At the time of its independence, Bolivia was much larger; it even had a seacoast and a port on the Pacific. Unfortunately, a quarter of this land was lost in several wars with neighboring nations. The War of the Pacific (1879-1883) resulted in the loss of Bolivia's seaport of Antofagasta to Chile. Bolivians have never reconciled themselves to this loss, and to this day they maintain a small navy—just in case they ever get the coast back. The loss of its only access to the Pacific has been blamed for many of Bolivia's problems, as the country even lacks large navigable rivers to connect it with the outside world.

Bolivia's territory was further reduced in the Chaco War of 1932 to 1935. For a century, neither Bolivia nor Paraguay felt the need to delineate their borders in the desertlike Chaco region. But in the

1920s, oil was discovered there, and the two countries fought for control of the Chaco. Both countries agreed to a truce in 1935, but Bolivia lost most of the Chaco in the subsequent peace negotiations. The loss of the Chaco also cut off Bolivia from the Paraguay River, its only remaining outlet to the sea.

Despite its mineral wealth, Bolivia has the lowest per capita income of any country in South America. There is a large underground economy, due largely to coca production. The United States of America has backed coca eradication programs, which generate large anti-American sentiment among poor Bolivians. Recently, Bolivia has begun exporting natural gas to Brazil and other countries.

The past few decades have been turbulent for Bolivia. The violent narco-regime of General Luis García Meza ended in a coup in 1981. Unable to maintain a stable government, the military recalled the Congress, and a civil government was installed in 1982. Since that time the military has eschewed direct political involvement. Bolivia's economy subsequently suffered hyperinflation, which by 1985 had reached 24,000 percent a year. Great sacrifices were made to stabilize the economy. Changes in the political landscape in 2006 under President Evo Morales may include relaxation on restrictions for growing coca leaves, and increased controls over the natural gas industry.

Type of Government

The Republic of Bolivia is a multiparty republic with two legislative houses, the Chamber of Senators and the Chamber of Deputies. The president is both the chief of state and the head of the government.

Bolivian heads of state do not necessarily complete their entire term of office. President Hugo Bánzer Suárez resigned for health reasons in August 2001. In October of 2003, massive protests brought down the government of his successor, President Gonzalo Sánchez de Lozada. Ostensibly, these protests were over the government's plan to export natural gas via a pipeline through Chile (and from there by ship to the USA). However, many of the protest leaders were traditional coca-growers, who were opposed to the government's U.S.-backed coca eradication policy. This resulted in the 2005 election of Chile's first indigenous President, Evo Morales.

For current government data, check with the Embassy of Bolivia at *www.bolivia-usa.org*.

Language

Bolivia has three official languages: Spanish, Aymara, and Quechua. While all businesspeople speak Spanish, many of the Indians speak their native Aymara or Quechua. These are not the only Amerindian languages; linguists have identified forty-four distinct languages in Bolivia, six of which are now extinct. Spanish is the language of the business community and is linguistically conservative.

For data on the various languages of Bolivia, see Ethnologue at *www.ethnologue.com*.

The Bolivian View

Although Protestantism has been making some gains, 93 percent of Bolivians are Roman Catholics. Catholicism is the official religion, but freedom of worship is guaranteed by law. Protestants and Jews each number 2 percent of the population. Seventh Day Adventists and Mennonites are among Bolivia's fastest-growing Protestant religions.

Bolivia is a nation with many factions. Groups are divided by ethnicity, wealth, and language. Amerindians are subdivided by tribe. Unions remain powerful; protests by unions have brought down more than one Bolivian government.

The family remains the single most powerful social unit. Nepotism is considered proper at all levels of society.

There is hostile sentiment toward those countries that took Bolivian land over the past two centuries: Brazil, Paraguay, and especially Chile. Anti-Americanism and antiglobalization protests break out periodically.

Cultural Note

Bolivia has not been known for political stability. Since independence in 1825, it has had sixteen constitutions and almost 250 governments. Its presidents have ranged from a woman (Lidia Gueiler Tejada, elected in 1980 and ousted by a coup the same year) to a brutal lunatic (Mariano Melgarejo) who, during the 1870 Franco-Prussian War, decided to march the Bolivian army eastward to aid France. (He turned back when it began to rain).

☑ Know Before You Go

Foreign visitors to the country of Bolivia are at risk of altitude sickness. Altitude sickness presents a problem in areas over 6,000 feet above sea level. There is no effective predictor of who will succumb and who won't. People of different ages, sexes, and health are struck down.

The best way to avoid altitude sickness is to acclimate yourself. Once you get to 6,000 feet, you should spend at least two nights at that altitude, repeating this acclimation period at each increase of 3,000 feet. La Paz is the highest capital city in the world—at 13,000 feet.

Earthquakes occur with some frequency, and automobile accidents are a major hazard.

Bolivians are generally heavy smokers. Individuals who are sensitive to cigarette smoke may encounter difficulties.

Between March and April, flooding occurs in the northeast.

⊙ CULTURAL ORIENTATION

Cognitive Styles: How Bolivians Organize and Process Information

The basic tendency of the Bolivians is to be open to discussion of new ideas, but this is tempered by a strong ethnocentrism in each of the several ethnic groups. Those with higher educations have learned to think abstractively, but associative, experiential thinking is the rule. Very strong kinship ties make Bolivians more concerned about the consequences of an action than about the action itself.

Negotiation Strategies: What Bolivians Accept as Evidence

There is much conflict between the forces of feeling, faith, and facts. Basically, Bolivians look at problems from a subjective perspective. The word of a friend or family member (feelings) has the highest validity, but a strong faith in an ideology (e.g., the Catholic Church, a political party, or ethnocentrism) may override an individual's feelings. Facts are always acceptable as long as they do not contradict the other two forces.

Note that it is difficult for Bolivians to disagree with someone they like. Their true opinion might not be evident.

Value Systems: The Basis for Behavior

The four ethnic groups—Quechua, Aymara, mestizos, and whites—have very different value systems. The following three sections identify the Value Systems in the economically and politically dominant white culture—their methods of dividing right from wrong, good from evil, and so forth.

Locus of Decision-Making

Decisions are usually made by an individual, but always with the best interests of a larger group in mind. Self-identity is based on the social system and the history of the extended family. Consensus forms the basis of community decision-making, with kinships and friendships playing major roles.

Sources of Anxiety Reduction

The Church has a great moral influence and gives a sense of stability to life. The nuclear family is extremely stable. Kin and family are the core of social structure, and great stress is placed on the bonds of responsibility among kin. There is a laid-back view of life that always allows time to talk with a friend. Deadlines are not a high priority.

Issues of Equality/Inequality

Ethnicity is the focus of much of national life and the white elite holds a strong bias against others. There are extreme contrasts between rich and poor. Machismo is very strong; women are still considered subordinate.

◉ BUSINESS PRACTICES

Punctuality, Appointments, and Local Time

- Business hours are generally 9:00 A.M. to 12 noon and 2:00 to 6:00 P.M., Monday through Friday. Some business people keep office hours on Saturday mornings as well.
- Punctuality is not a high priority in Bolivia. However, foreigners from North America, Europe, and Asia are indeed expected to be punctual.

- Bolivian business meetings rarely start on time. Expect your Bolivian counterparts to be late; do not get indignant. Some foreign-educated businesspeople or younger executives will be prompt.
- Be aware that social occasions have different rules. Even North Americans are expected to be fifteen to thirty minutes late for dinner or parties; to show up on time would be impolite. But be on time for lunch and for events with a scheduled starting time, such as the theater.
- When it is important to know if your Bolivian counterpart expects promptness, you can ask, "*¿En punto?*" (on the dot?).
- In Bolivia, as in most of Latin America, the date is written with the day first, then the month, then the year (e.g., October 2, 2011, is written 2/10/11). The U.S. pattern of month-day-year is uncommon in Bolivia.
- Mornings are best for appointments.
- Try to make appointments at least a week in advance.
- Allow yourself to get acclimated to the high altitude by arriving in Bolivia a day early.
- The best months of the year to conduct business in Bolivia are April and May, and September and October. Little business is accomplished in the two weeks before and after Christmas and Easter, during Carnival week (the week before Ash Wednesday) or during Independence Week (the first week in August). January through March is typically vacation time in Bolivia. For further holiday data in Bolivia, visit *www.kissboworshakehands.com*.
- Bolivia is four hours behind Greenwich Mean Time (G.M.T. – 4), making it one hour ahead of U.S. Eastern Standard Time (E.S.T. + 1).

Negotiating

- The pace of business negotiations in Latin America is usually much slower than it is in western Europe or North America. This is especially true in Bolivia, where trying to rush a deal by applying pressure will probably fail.
- Do not be surprised if it takes you several trips to Bolivia to accomplish your goal. Bolivians respond best to low-key, slow-paced negotiations.

- Vivid presentations that incorporate simulations or models will be well received.
- Personal relationships are far more important than corporate ones in Bolivia. With traditional Bolivians, every time your company changes its representative, you will probably be starting from scratch. Historically, a new relationship must be built up before business can proceed. Younger or foreign-educated Bolivians may put more emphasis on their relationship with your company, not its individual representatives.
- Don't assume that each portion of a contract is settled once an agreement on that portion has been reached. Until the entire contract is signed, each portion is subject to renegotiation.
- Bolivians will doubt your importance unless you stay at the most prestigious international hotels.
- Bolivians converse at a closer distance than do North Americans and northern Europeans. If you instinctively back away, a Bolivian will probably move forward to close up space. This physical closeness makes maintaining eye contact difficult for some foreigners.
- While many of the executives you meet will speak English, check beforehand as to whether or not you will need an interpreter.
- All printed material you hand out should be translated into Spanish. This goes for everything from business cards to reports to brochures.
- Sometimes Bolivians have trouble with foreign names, so be ready to hand out your business card when you are introduced.
- Bolivians are great sports fans. Talking about sports is always a good way to open a conversation. Soccer, which is called *fútbol* (U.S.-style football is *fútbol americano*), is the most popular sport.
- Families and food are good topics of conversation as well. Bolivians also appreciate visitors who know something about their country.

Business Entertaining
- Business meals are popular in Bolivia. They are usually held in restaurants; offers to dine in a Bolivian home are relatively infrequent.

- While one can discuss business over lunch, dinner is considered a social occasion. Do not bring up business over dinner unless your Bolivian counterpart does so first.
- Lunch is usually the largest meal of the day. Dinner may start anytime from 7:30 to 9:30 P.M. A formal dinner usually begins at 9:00 P.M.
- Most Bolivians are proud of their cuisine and usually prefer entertaining in restaurants that serve native dishes. However, other types of cuisine sometimes become trendy.
- Be warned that Bolivian food may contain very hot peppers.
- When dining, keep your hands on the table, not in your lap.
- Never eat with your fingers; there are utensils for everything. Even fruits such as bananas are eaten with a fruit knife and fork.
- Avoid pouring wine, if possible. There are several complex taboos about wine pouring (e.g., pouring with the left hand is an insult.)
- When eating at a Bolivian home, understand that everyone—including the guest—is expected to eat everything on his or her plate. Your hosts will encourage you to eat, and it is traditional for you to decline the first time your hostess asks if you want more. Wait until they insist, or you may be deluged with food. A compliment is taken as a request for more food, so hold your compliments until after the meal.
- Stay at the table until everyone is finished eating. It is polite to leave a home about thirty minutes after dinner is concluded.
- At a gathering such as a party, you may have to introduce yourself. Only at a formal party (or one hosted by a older person) can you expect that someone else will introduce you.
- Eating in the street is considered improper by older Bolivians.
- Avoid whispering; it is impolite to anyone out of earshot and arouses suspicion. Wait until you can talk to the person in private.

⊙ PROTOCOL

Greetings
- Except when greeting close friends, it is traditional to shake hands firmly with both men and women.

- Close male friends shake hands or embrace upon meeting; men kiss close female friends. Close female friends usually kiss each other. The full embrace *(abrazo)* may entail a hug, a handshake, and several thumps on the shoulder, ending with another handshake.
- Close friends of either sex may walk arm in arm. Women often hold hands.
- Good friends will greet each other at each encounter, even if they have greeted each other already that day.

Titles/Forms of Address

- While the Indian languages of Aymara and Quechua are (along with Spanish) official languages in Bolivia, all the businesspeople you meet will be fluent in Spanish, so Spanish titles may be used.
- Most people you meet should be addressed with a title and their surname. Only children, family members, and close friends address each other by their first names.
- Persons who do not have professional titles should be addressed as "Mr.," "Mrs.," or "Miss," plus their surname. In Spanish, these are:

  Mr. = *Señor*

  Mrs. = *Señora*

  Miss = *Señorita*

- When a person has a title, it is important to address him or her with that title followed by the surname. A PhD or a physician is called "Doctor." Teachers prefer the title *Profesor*, engineers go by *Ingeniero*, architects are *Arquitecto*, and lawyers are *Abogado*.

Gestures

- A pat on the shoulder is a sign of friendship.
- The gesture that some North Americans use to mean "so-so" (twisting the flat, open hand from side to side) indicates "no" in Bolivia. Bus and taxi drivers use this gesture to indicate that their vehicles are full. Street vendors use it to indicate that they have no more of something.
- Another gesture for "no" is a wave of the index finger.
- Beckon using a scooping motion with the palm down. Children can be summoned in this way, but adults may find it demeaning.

- Make sure to cover your mouth when yawning or coughing.
- Sit only on chairs, not on a ledge, box, or table. Manners dictate an erect sitting posture; don't slump.

Cultural Note

Indian clothing is for Indians; don't adopt any native costumes, no matter how attractive.

Wearing the bowler hat that Indian women wear will make you a laughingstock.

Don't wear anything outside that can be damaged by water during Carnival. Drenching pedestrians is a favorite Carnival pastime of the young.

Dress

- Business dress in Bolivia is conservative: dark suits and ties for men; light-colored blouses and dark suits or skirts for women. Men should follow their Bolivian colleagues' lead with regard to wearing ties and removing jackets in the summer.
- The formality of dress varies in different cities. La Paz will be very formal, (of course, the altitude of La Paz often makes it very chilly). In Cochabamba suits are normal business garments; and in freewheeling, tropical Santa Cruz, businessmen wear light-weight suits or go without a jacket.
- Dress to handle the weather in Bolivia. The lowlands are subject to great heat and humidity in summers. Most local people wear cotton in such weather. Don't forget that the seasons in the Southern Hemisphere are the reverse of those in the Northern Hemisphere.
- Sweaters are recommended during the winter or at night in high-altitude cities.
- Whatever the season, be prepared for sudden changes in weather and temperature.
- Men may wear the same dark suit for formal occasions (such as the theater, a formal dinner party, and so forth), but women are expected to wear different evening attire. The invitation will specify that the affair is formal. Tuxedos are rarely worn.
- Both men and women wear pants as casualwear. If you are meeting business associates, avoid jeans and wear a jacket or blazer. Women should not wear shorts.

Cultural Note

Gifts identified with the United States of America (such as T-shirts and caps) were popular in the past. However, the United States is no longer universally popular in Bolivia, because the U.S. policy of coca eradication has put thousands of coca farmers out of work. As Quechuan activist Leonida Zurita-Vargas pointed out, "because of the American drug problem, we can no longer grow coca, which was part of our life and our culture long before the United States was a country. . . . We (the Quechua) are used to chewing coca leaves every day, much as Americans drink coffee. We sustained ourselves by growing coca for products like shampoo, medicinal teas and toothpaste. We did not turn coca into cocaine; the chemicals needed for that are made in countries like the United States." The international community may have to deal with the coca growers. The former head of the coca-growers' federation, Evo Morales, was elected President in 2005.

Gifts

- Bolivians are favorably impressed by gifts. The intention is more important than the gift itself.
- As in any country, a gift should be of high quality. If the item is produced by your corporation, the corporate name or logo should appear discreetly, not be emblazoned over the whole surface.
- Bolivia's vast underground economy provides electronic items (both genuine and counterfeit) at a discount. Be careful to give only high-quality, cutting-edge gifts, with a means to support the product (e.g., iPods with gift certificates, etc.).
- Avoid giving knives; they symbolize the severing of a friendship.
- Popular gifts are fine leather briefcases, well-made chess and backgammon sets, and imported linen items. Kitchen gadgets can be popular.
- When invited to a Bolivian home, bring a gift of flowers, chocolates, wine, or whiskey. Avoid purple flowers, which are used at funerals, or yellow flowers, which signify enmity.

Brazil

Federative Republic of Brazil
Local short form: Brasil
Local long form: Republica Federativa do Brasil

Cultural Note

Despite its economic problems, Brazil is often regarded as a potentially rich country with strong industrial sectors, huge possibilities for agricultural production, and massive natural resources. An example of its potential for efficient utilization of resources is its processing of sugar cane into ethyl alcohol for fueling 1.5 million Brazilian cars. Its natural resources include gold, nickel, tin, oil, and timber taken from its tropical rain forest in the Amazon River basin—a practice which is now internationally regarded as controversial.

▶ WHAT IS YOUR CULTURAL IQ?

1. In Brazil, a *jeito* is:
   a. The national dish
   b. An Afro-Brazilian religion
   c. A way to sidestep a rule
   ANSWER: c. When an obstacle presents itself, Brazilians prefer to go around the rules. Such a maneuver is called a *jeito* or (if the maneuver is small) *jeitinho*. In business, it often consists of calling in a favor to have someone bend a regulation.

2. Many ethnic groups have come to Brazil in search of opportunity. For example, there are more Japanese in Brazil than in any other country except Japan. TRUE or FALSE: Japanese is the second most commonly spoken language in Brazil.
   ANSWER: FALSE. Germans got to Brazil earlier than the Japanese and established entire German-speaking enclaves, making German second to Portuguese as Brazil's leading language.

3. Brazil has had several capitals since the first one was established in 1549. Which of the following cities was created specifically to be the capital of Brazil?
   a. Salvador da Bahia
   b. Rio de Janeiro
   c. Brasília
   ANSWER: c) Brasília was built on undeveloped land in the interior to be the national capital of Brazil. By moving the capital inland, it spurred migration away from the crowded coastal areas. Salvador da Bahia was the nation's capital from 1549 to 1763; Rio de Janeiro was the capital from 1763 to 1960.

▶ TIPS ON DOING BUSINESS IN BRAZIL

- Brazilians do not consider themselves to be Hispanics, and they resent being spoken to in Spanish. Be sure your documentation—including business cards—is printed in both Portuguese and English.
- Brazil is Latin America's largest and most populous country. Be certain to understand the cultural background of your Brazilian client—it is a hugely diverse nation, and an individual's ethnicity, language, and belief systems can range from Portuguese to Japanese or Egyptian to German.
- Although it is common for Brazilians to deride their government and civil service, foreigners should not join in the criticisms. Most Brazilians are highly patriotic.
- Brazilians once had a monopoly on the production of natural rubber; however, they lost their monopoly when British adventurers stole rubber tree seeds and successfully grew rubber in East Asia. Ever since then, Brazilians have been sensitive to real or perceived theft of their natural resources. Today there is new emphasis placed on Brazil's proprietorship of the biodiversity of the Amazon.
- Brazilians are proud of their cultural achievement in the arts. Many Brazilian writers and musicians are known throughout the world, and visitors should have some familiarity with them.

▶ COUNTRY BACKGROUND

Demographics

Brazil's cultural heritage is rich and varied. The total population is approximately 188 million (2006 estimate). Of these, over half (54 percent) identified themselves as white—direct descendants of Europeans. Another 40 percent are of mixed heritage (mulatto or mestizo). The small remainder includes Brazilians of African, Asian or other descent. Persons solely of Amerindian descent account for just 0.1 percent of Brazil's population.

Brazil's population is concentrated on its two hundred miles of Atlantic coast. Over 90 percent of the people live on 10 percent of the land, and more than 15 million live in municipal São Paulo and Rio de Janeiro.

History

Unlike the Mayans or Incas, the Amerindians of Brazil have left few artifacts behind for archaeologists to study. Many tribes disappeared after contact with Europeans, through death or intermarriage with the colonists. Most of the tribes that remain today have adapted to interactions with modern civilization, although a few groups may remain hidden in the Amazon.

To contest occupation by other European powers, King João III of Portugal sent out the first colonizing expedition in 1531. Martim Afonso de Sousa established the settlement of São Vicente. This settlement would eventually become a profitable sugar-producing center, after African slaves were imported to work the plantations.

After nearly two centuries of searching, Portuguese explorers finally found gold in Brazil in the 1690s. Thousands of people poured into the goldfields of Minas Gerais. In the next hundred years, 400,000 Portuguese emigrants would come to Brazil, most of them lured by gold. Two million Africans were also enslaved and imported during the same period.

In 1807, Napoleon occupied Portugal, and members of the Portuguese royal family fled to Brazil. Rio de Janeiro was the seat of the entire

Portuguese empire from 1808 to 1821, but the Portuguese emperor became increasingly unpopular. After the emperor returned to Lisbon in 1822, Brazil declared independence. September 7 is Brazil's national holiday, which marks their independence from Portugal.

The new Brazilian empire experienced instability until its second emperor, Dom Pedro II, came of age. Ruling from 1840 to 1889, Dom Pedro II proved to be a dedicated, enlightened, and modest ruler. Industrialization came to Brazil, and coffee replaced sugar as the nation's most important export. Dom Pedro II was also the final emperor; the military overthrew him and proclaimed Brazil a republic in 1889.

Brazil's ill-defined borders were largely established in the nineteenth century. On its southern border, Brazil annexed what is now Uruguay in 1821. From 1825 to 1828, Brazil fought a war with Argentina for control of Uruguay, but neither side managed to win a decisive victory. After British intervention, Uruguay became an independent buffer state, largely separating Brazil and Argentina. Brazil and Argentina would fight another war from 1851 to 1852; this time Brazil was victorious.

On its southwestern border, Brazil fought in the 1864–1870 War of the Triple Alliance. This war pitted Brazil, Argentina, and Uruguay against Paraguay. It ended with Paraguay's defeat, allowing Brazil to annex some Paraguayan territory. In 1903, Brazil also took land from Bolivia.

Brazil's expansion to the north was stopped by the colonies of the United Kingdom, the Netherlands, and France (which today are Guyana, Surinam, and French Guiana).

By 1890, Brazil's sugar and coffee exports were eclipsed by rubber. The market for automobile tires exploded, requiring massive amounts of rubber. Brazil was then the world's sole producer of natural rubber, and the country once again experienced a sudden boom. But Brazil's monopoly on natural rubber was broken when plantations in Southeast Asia (using stolen Brazilian rubber tree seeds) began rubber production in 1910.

Brazil celebrated its modernity by inaugurating the new city of Brasília as the capital in 1960. Fueled by government spending, inflation soared. After several unpopular presidents in a row, the military seized power in 1964. Many Brazilians supported the coup at first, despite rights abuses. Faced with increased protests from the Brazilian people, the military allowed a presidential election to take place in 1985. Brazil has had free elections since then.

Type of Government

Brazil is a multiparty federal republic. The president is both the chief of state and the head of the government. There are two legislative houses: a Senate and a Chamber of Deputies. The ministers in the Supreme Federal Tribunal are appointed for life by the president and confirmed by the Senate.

For current government data, check with the Embassy of Brazil at *www.brasilemb.org.*

Language

Portuguese is the official language. Some segments of the population speak German, Spanish, Italian, French, English, or various Amerindian languages.

A total of 234 languages have been cataloged in Brazil by *www. ethnologue.com*. Of these, 192 of these are living languages, and 42 are now extinct.

The Brazilian View

There is no official religion in Brazil, but nearly 80 percent of the population identify themselves as Catholic. (Note that this includes syncretic Afro-Catholic groups with spiritualist beliefs; they are sometimes called Spiritist Catholics.) Protestantism is currently growing in Brazil, now accounting for over 23 percent of the population. The bulk of Brazilian Protestants belong to Pentecostal groups. There are also small numbers of Buddhists, Jews, and Muslims in Brazil. Indeed, virtually every religion on Earth is represented in Brazil.

The African heritage of many Brazilians may account for the large numbers of syncretic Afro-Catholic groups, which puts African gods into the realm of Catholic saints.

It has been speculated that Brazil's diverse, sprawling cultures respond best to strong, authoritarian leadership. This may be reinforced by the historic recollection of the rule of Emperor Dom Pedro II (1840–1889) as a golden age. Certainly, the Brazilian people have often accepted military dictatorships in times of crisis. Whether this has changed remains to be seen.

☑ Know Before You Go

Crime rates continued to spiral in cities like Rio de Janeiro—travelers should utilize precautions when working late or traveling alone in various urban areas. Even police can be a potential hazard for uninformed visitors. Real and suspected criminals have been tortured and killed, primarily from the large number of homeless, and from those who live in the slums *(favelas)* in the big cities. Prisons are hugely overcrowded, and riots over poor conditions break out on a regular basis.

There is still a prolific illegal wildlife trade in the Amazon Basin, and deforestation is a major problem. Air and water pollution are serious issues in Rio de Janeiro, Sao Paulo, and several other large cities.

The Amazon Basin holds potential hazards for travelers, from mosquito-borne diseases to poisonous insects. Consult with your physician for current inoculations and medical precautions before you travel to rural areas. Also, visit the Center for Disease Control Web site for information on outbreaks of virulent infections at *www.cdc.gov*.

The northeastern part of Brazil suffers from recurring droughts, while floods and frost occur in the south.

◉ CULTURAL ORIENTATION

Cognitive Styles: How Brazilians Organize and Process Information

Brazilians are open to discussions of most subjects, but home and family are private topics, and generally not talked about with incidental acquaintances. Brazilians tend to be more analytical and abstractive than other Latin Americans. They look at the particulars of each situation rather than looking to universal rules or laws.

Negotiation Strategies: What Brazilians Accept as Evidence

Brazilians tend to approach problems indirectly, allowing their feelings to dictate the solution. Facts are admissible as evidence, but they may change with the needs of the negotiator, and they seldom overrule subjective feelings.

Value System: The Basis for Behavior

There are large groups of Germans (who kept their own language) and Japanese (who learned Portuguese) that have their own value systems, which differ somewhat from other Brazilians. The following three sections identify the Value Systems in the predominant culture—their methods of dividing right from wrong, good from evil, and so forth.

Locus of Decision-Making

The individual is responsible for his or her decisions, but in Brazil family loyalty is the individual's highest duty. Nepotism is the influential family member's first obligation. The family is more important in Brazil than in any other Latin American country. It has been the single most important institution in the formation of Brazilian society.

Sources of Anxiety Reduction

The most significant kin group is the *parentela*—the relatives one recognizes from both families—which may include hundreds of individuals, all related to an illustrious ancestor. This creates a social structure that gives the individual a great sense of stability. The Catholic Church is an essential part of the culture and social life. Although many Brazilians are only nominal Catholics, the Church gives structure to their lives.

Issues of Equality/Inequality

The concepts of class and status are strong and may determine what job a person will have. Class is described in economic terms. There is a strong color bias. There are extreme contrasts between rich and poor, but the concept that powerful people are entitled to special privileges of office is being questioned. The macho male image prevails, and Brazilian men generally continue to expect women to be subordinate.

⊙ BUSINESS PRACTICES

Punctuality, Appointments, and Local Time
- Business hours are generally advertised as 8:30 A.M. to 5:30 P.M., but decision makers usually begin work later in the morning and stay later in the evening.
- The lack of punctuality is a fact of life in Brazil. Become accustomed to waiting for your Brazilian counterpart.
- Avoid any business transactions around Carnival, which is celebrated for up to a week before Lent begins on Ash Wednesday. The most spectacular festivities culminate on Fat Tuesday.
- Make appointments at least one week in advance. Never try to make impromptu calls at business or government offices.
- Try to make your appointments between 10:00 A.M. and noon, so that your business runs into lunch. It is important to host a good meal with a Brazilian prospect; it is a key part of building a relationship.
- Be prepared to commit long-term resources (both in time and money) toward establishing strong relationships in Brazil. Without such commitments, there is no point in attempting to do business there at all.
- Brazilians conduct business through personal connections and expect long-term relationships. Before you invest in a trip, hire an appropriate Brazilian contact in your industry to help you meet the right people. Your Brazilian contact (called a *despechante* in Portuguese) will be invaluable.
- A list of Brazil's official holidays is available at *www.kissbowor shakehands.com*.
- Most of Brazil is three hours behind Greenwich Mean Time (G.M.T. – 3), or two hours ahead of U.S. Eastern Standard Time (E.S.T. + 2). Western Brazil is four hours behind G.M.T., or one hour ahead of U.S. Eastern Standard Time.

Negotiating
- Be patient. It will usually require several trips to get through a bargaining process.

- During negotiations, be prepared to discuss all aspects of the contract simultaneously rather than sequentially.
- Seemingly, extraneous data may be reviewed and re-reviewed. Try to be as flexible as possible without making definite commitments.
- Sometimes Brazilians find aggressive business attitudes offensive—do not expect to get right to the point. Avoid confrontations, and hide any frustrations.
- If you change your negotiating team, you may undermine the entire contract. Brazilians value the person they do business with more than the firm name.
- Make sure you have a local accountant and *notario* (similar to a lawyer) or lawyer for contract issues. Brazilians may resent an outside legal presence.
- It is normal for a conversation to be highly animated, with many interruptions, many statements of "no" being interjected, and a great deal of physical contact.
- Brazilians are enthusiastic soccer (called *fútbol*) fans. Soccer is always a lively topic for conversation.
- Avoid deep discussions of politics and any topics relating to Argentina (Brazil's traditional rival).
- Brazilians use periods to punctuate thousands (e.g., 5.550 = 5,550).
- Be aware that Brazilians consider themselves Americans also. Do not use the phrase "in America" when referring to the United States of America.

Business Entertaining
- Ask your prospect's secretary to recommend a prestigious restaurant.
- Do not expect to discuss business during a meal. You should participate in the conversation, but not try to direct it too much. Wait until coffee is served to broach a work-related topic.
- Stay at a first-class hotel, and entertain there if the hotel has an excellent restaurant.
- If you are invited to a party, it will probably be given at a private club rather than at a home. Arrive at least fifteen minutes late.

- A snack consisting of cookies, cake, and beverages is usually served at 4:00 or 5:00 P.M.
- Brazilian dinners take place anytime from 7:00 to 10:00 P.M. Dinner parties can easily continue until 2:00 A.M., but it is not unheard of for dinner parties to break up as late as 7:00 A.M. the next morning!

▶ PROTOCOL

Greetings
- Greetings can be effusive, with extended handshakes common during the first encounter, progressing to embraces once a friendship has been established. Women often kiss each other on alternating cheeks. Depending upon your location in Brazil, they may kiss you twice if you are married, three times if single. The third kiss is supposed to indicate "good luck" for finding a spouse.
- It is polite to shake hands with everyone present in a group, both upon arrival and upon departure.

Titles/Forms of Address
- When applicable, titles such as "Doctor," "Professor," and so forth, are used to address business acquaintances. Or the term *Senhor* (Mr.) or *Senhora* (Mrs.) is used to precede the surname. Be aware that people may sometimes introduce themselves using their titles and their first names (e.g., Doctor John).
- Unlike the practice in Spanish-speaking countries, the order of names in Portuguese is first name, middle name, and, usually, two last names. The first surname is from the person's mother, and the second from the father. If an executive hands you a card with the name Joaquin Gilberto Silva Mantega, you would address him as Senhor Mantega. For further information on the properties and forms of address for Brazil, please consult Appendix A.

Gestures
- Brazilians communicate in extremely close proximity. They may keep in physical contact by touching arms, hands, or shoulders

during the entire conversation. They are friendly and outgoing, and physical interaction is simply an extension of the Brazilian persona—do not back away.

- The sign for "okay" in North America (a circle of first finger and thumb) is totally unacceptable in Brazil. It is considered vulgar.
- To signal "come here," extend your palm face down and wave your fingers toward your body.
- Snapping your fingers while whipping your hand up and down adds emphasis to a statement, or can indicate "long ago."
- To invoke good luck, place your thumb between your index and middle fingers while making a fist. This is also known as the "fig."
- Flicking the fingertips underneath the chin indicates that you do not know the answer to a question.
- Further information on gestures can be found at *www.kissbowor shakehands.com.*

Gifts

- Avoid giving anything black or purple, since these are colors of mourning.
- Avoid giving knives, which symbolize cutting off a relationship, or handkerchiefs, which connote grief.
- Giving a gift is not required at the first meeting. Instead, buy lunch or dinner, and consider the individual's tastes for future gift giving.
- Wait until after the formal meeting is over to present a gift. A relaxed social situation is the best time.
- Small electronic gadgets are appreciated—for example, calculators, iPods or CD players, digital cameras, and so forth. CDs or DVDs of popular movies and entertainers can be expensive in Brazil and make good gifts.
- Name-brand pens are appropriate.
- When invited to a home (an important occurrence), bring candy, champagne, or Scotch. Also bring something for the children— T-shirts or caps from prestigious universities or sports teams in your country, etc.
- Suggestions for further culturally appropriate gifts can be found at *www.kissboworshakehands.com.*

Dress

- Brazil is a tropical country, so expect the weather to be hot. Clothing made of natural fibers will be cooler and more comfortable. (The seasons in Brazil are the opposite of those in the Northern Hemisphere—July is midwinter, and January is summertime.)
- The colors of the Brazilian flag are green and yellow, so foreigners should avoid wearing this combination in any fashion.
- Conservative attire for women is very important in business. Any misstep in clothing or behavior will reflect upon your firm, and may even determine whether or not anyone will do business with you. Also make sure your nails are manicured.
- Only young people wear jeans (always clean and pressed). Men should wear slacks and long-sleeved shirts for casual attire.

Cultural Note

Brazil has a naturally advantageous location on the equator for a space program. Rockets can launch and enter orbit using less propellant, and carrying bigger payloads from the Alcantara rocket base. However, Brazil encountered setbacks with their program, like the explosion on the ground at the Alcantara base which killed twenty-one people in August of 2003. Subsequently, their first successful launch occurred in October of 2004. Other countries have expressed interest in sending their rockets into orbit from Brazil's tropical site.

Chile

Republic of Chile
Local short form: Chile
Local long form: Republica de Chile

Cultural Note

Chileans have a renowned reputation for achievement in many cultural fields. Literature, social science, and fine arts are considered prestigious areas of study. Since the 1920s, Chile has challenged Argentina's place as South America's biggest producer of books in the Spanish language.

A Chilean also created Latin America's answer to Mickey Mouse: Condorito, a cartoon condor dressed in a red beret, red shirt, and black soccer *(fútbol)* shorts. Created by the late cartoonist René Ríos Boettiger, Condorito is one of the most beloved cartoon characters in the world. Syndicated in every Spanish-speaking country, Condorito has been used to sell everything from food to Microsoft Windows.

▶ WHAT IS YOUR CULTURAL IQ?

1. TRUE or FALSE: The date of September 11th is remembered with sadness by many Chileans.
   ANSWER: TRUE, but not because of the terrorist attacks in the USA on September 11, 2001. The Chileans remember September 11, 1973, when the Marxist government of Salvador Allende was overthrown in a military coup backed by the CIA. The subsequent seventeen years of military rule were accompanied by repression, torture, and executions (although they also ushered in economic prosperity).

2. Which of the following is *not* true about Chile?
   a. If placed in Europe, Chile would stretch from the north of Scotland to the island of Gibraltar in the Mediterranean.
   b. Chile is almost as long as California.

   c. To fit the entire country on a television screen, Chile's weather maps have to divide the county into three parts.

   d. If placed horizontally, Chile would stretch across the Pacific Ocean at its widest point.

ANSWER: d. Chile is long, but not *that* long.

3. Which of the following famous Chilean authors have won the Nobel Prize for literature?

   a) Isabel Allende

   b) Gabriela Mistral

   c) Pablo Neruda

   d) None of the above

ANSWER: b and c. Of the three, only Isabel Allende has never received a Nobel Prize.

▶ COUNTRY BACKGROUND

Demographics

Because of the geography of the area, Chile has experienced a large degree of isolation and, as a result, is more ethnically homogeneous than most of South America. Of the 16 million people who live in Chile (2006 estimate), some 95 percent are mestizo (of mixed European and Indian blood), 3 percent are Indian (mostly Araucanian), and less than 2 percent are solely of European descent.

History

The first European settlers in Chile were Spanish explorers in search of gold and silver, who arrived after the defeat of the Inca empire in 1533. What they found instead was a fertile valley. Chile soon became part of the Spanish empire, governed from Peru.

Bernardo O'Higgins, Chile's renowned patriot, led a struggle for independence against the Spanish from 1810 to 1818. Helped by an army trained by Argentine patriot José de San Martín, Chilean independence was formally declared on February 12, 1818.

During the nineteenth century, Chile expanded its territories. A treaty with Argentina gave Chile control of the Strait of Magellan (although most of Patagonia went to Argentina). Chile twice fought

Peru and Bolivia for control of the Pacific coast. In 1883, Chile won the War of the Pacific, expanding the country's territory northward to an area rich in natural resources. Relations with Bolivia remain difficult to this day, as the now-landlocked Bolivia has never reconciled itself to the loss of its entire Pacific seaboard.

In 1964, Eduardo Frei, a Christian Democrat, was elected to the presidency. His program was marked by the slogan "Revolution in Liberty" and consisted of far-reaching social programs. But the Socialists and Communists felt that these reforms were insufficient, while conservatives saw them as excessive. In the next election, in 1970, Dr. Salvador Allende won with 36 percent of the votes over two other candidates, becoming the first freely elected Marxist leader in this hemisphere. But Allende did not have majority support in the Chilean Congress, and discontent grew as a result of shortages of food and consumer goods. Furthermore, in the USA, the Nixon administration decided that the presence of a new Marxist regime in the Americas was unacceptable.

On September 11, 1973, a bloody, CIA-backed military coup overthrew Allende, abolished the Congress, and banned political parties. A four-man military junta instituted a repressive regime. The leading general, Augusto Pinochet Ugarte, ruled as president and commander of the army.

In 1980, a new constitution was approved in a national plebiscite. Under it, General Pinochet was elected to an eight-year term, with the military junta acting as the legislature. At the end of that term, Pinochet allowed another plebiscite to decide if he should continue for another eight years. When he lost the plebiscite, he called for free elections in December 1989. As a result of that election, President Patricio Aylwin Azócar took office in March 1990 as the first elected president since 1970. Since then, political power has passed peacefully from one elected government to the next. In 2006, Chile swore in a new President, Michelle Bachelet, who was an unprecedented leader for a traditionally conservative, generally Catholic country. Prior to serving as President she was Secretary of Defense and supervised some of the same military personnel who had overseen her own imprisonment, torture, and her father's murder. One Chilean reporter explained her election thus: When we go into the booth, we vote with our souls, not our wallets.

Cultural Note

Many North American gestures have completely different meanings in other countries. In Chile, slapping your right fist into your left open palm is obscene, and displaying an open palm with the fingers splayed means "stupid."

Type of Government

The Republic of Chile is a multiparty republic with two legislative houses, the Senate and the Chamber of Deputies. The president is the chief of state as well as the head of the government.

Suffrage is universal and compulsory at age eighteen.

The current government is considered stable; however, it must still address continued problems from poverty. For current government data, check with the Embassy of Chile at *www.chile-usa.org*.

Language

The official language of Chile is Spanish, although English is spoken by well-educated businesspeople and in tourist centers. Chileans speak a very conservative form of Spanish. In most of Latin America, the second-person plural of verbs is ignored (the third-person plural is used instead). Chileans, however, continue to use the traditional second-person plural form of the verb.

Cultural Note

Although Spanish is the official language in both Chile and Argentina, the two countries often use different words for the same thing. For example:

Chilean cowboys are called *huasos*. Argentine cowboys are called *gauchos*.

Chile's slums are called *callampas*. Argentina's urban slums are called *villas miserias*.

Chile's national dance is the *cueca*. Argentina's national dance is the tango.

(Both are displays of dominance and submission in the form of a dance.)

The Web site *www.ethnologue.com* lists a total of eleven languages, two of which are extinct and several of which are endangered. Aside from Spanish, all the other languages are Amerindian—except for the Polynesian language Rapa Nui, spoken by the 2,500 natives of Easter Island (a Chilean possession).

The Chilean View

There is no official religion in Chile, but over 78 percent of the population identify themselves as Roman Catholics. As in most European countries, relatively few people attend church every Sunday. Protestants account for over 13 percent. There is also a small Jewish population. A sizable number of people consider themselves nonreligious or atheist.

Chile is prone to natural disasters (earthquakes, volcanoes, etc.), and some sociologists believe that this is the source of the traditional Chilean pessimism and fatalistic attitude.

In the past, ostentation was rarely seen in public. However, Chile's recent economic success has made public displays of wealth more common—if not acceptable to traditionalists.

Cultural Note

Family respect and loyalty are primary concerns in Chile, even taking precedence over business responsibilities. Extended families are often found living close together and tend to be very dependent upon one another. Machismo remains part of Chilean culture, but women have obviously made great strides in politics and business.

☑ Know Before You Go

Nature has bestowed many things upon Chile, including many dangers. Earthquakes and volcanoes are an ever-present hazard, as are tsunamis (tidal waves) caused by offshore earthquakes.

Some cities in Chile are elevated enough to cause altitude sickness in visitors. Altitude sickness can strike anyone, even if you have never experienced it before. There is no sure prevention except gradual acclimation to high elevation: once you get to 6,000 feet above sea level, spend at least two nights there. Repeat this acclimation period at each increase of 3,000 feet. Alcohol consumption tends to make the symptoms worse. Sunburn is also a danger at high altitudes, because there is less atmosphere to protect you from the sun.

There is a new hazard in the southernmost part of Chile: the Antarctic ozone hole in the atmosphere. As in high altitudes, sunburn can occur quickly. Sunblock and/or protective clothing (including sunglasses) are the best preventatives.

Many Chileans are heavy smokers. It can be difficult to find smoke-free establishments. International hotel chains tend to be the best at enforcing no-smoking rules.

Although Chile has its share of natural hazards, the country lacks the dangers associated with other Latin American countries. The roads—especially the main highways—are good, and Chileans are relatively safe, polite drivers. Armed robbery and kidnapping are rare. Corruption (aside from tax evasion) is uncommon. Even the Chilean traffic police (the Carabineros) tend to be honest; they make take an attempt to bribe them as an insult.

▶ CULTURAL ORIENTATION

Cognitive Styles: How Chileans Organize and Process Information

In Chile, information is readily accepted for the purpose of discussion. Negotiations may be extensive, with little movement from the initial position. Chileans educated abroad or in foreign business methods may process information conceptually and analytically, but most are associative in their thinking. Typically, Chileans see each problem as having a particular solution rather than looking to a universal rule or law.

Negotiation Strategies: What Chileans Accept as Evidence

In traditional negotiations, Chileans consider feelings more important than facts. The truth is considered to be subjective and personal. In addition, faith in a strong Catholic or Protestant ideology may form the basis for truth.

Value Systems: The Basis for Behavior

This is not a culture of conquerors but of cosmopolitans who assimilated all European cultures into their social strata through marriage. The following three sections identify the Value Systems in the predominant culture—their methods of dividing right from wrong, good from evil, and so forth.

Locus of Decision-Making

Chile has a collectivist culture in which the extended family is a dominating factor in the individual's decision-making process. The prospect that a bad decision could bring dishonor on one's group or family is always a factor in decision-making. Expertise is considered less important than membership in the appropriate group. Thus, kinship and friendship play a major role in a person's business associations. It is essential for a foreigner to become friends with Chileans with whom one wants to do business.

Sources of Anxiety Reduction

Chileans evidently have a high index of uncertainty avoidance. As a result, Chileans use laws and morality to give structure to their worldview. (This can be seen in how Chileans wait in orderly lines, as opposed to how some other Latin Americans crowd and push instead of queue.)

Social stratification has traditionally been strong in Chile. Marriage into the right family was considered essential, as family ties are a major determinant of success. Chileans used to accept their social class as destiny. However, the economic boom of the 1990s has made class structure less of a determinant. Although relatively few Chileans have gotten rich, the new entrepreneurs are not all from Chile's upper class.

Issues of Equality/Inequality

On a philosophical level, Chileans consider each individual to have equal rights, and no law needs to be passed to ensure this equality. On a practical level, black and Amerindian Chileans remain discriminated against. There is a small, traditional, class-conscious elite, a bigger middle class than in most other Latin American countries, and a large impoverished underclass.

The Chilean masculinity index has been charted as lower than average for Latin America, resulting in more equality for Chilean women, as evidenced by the election of their first female president in 2006.

▶ BUSINESS PRACTICES

Punctuality, Appointments, and Local Time

- Business hours are 9:00 A.M. to 5:00 P.M., Monday through Friday. A two-hour lunch is taken at 12:00.
- Be punctual at meetings. Punctuality is appreciated and expected from North Americans. Do not be offended, however, if your counterpart is thirty minutes late. On the other hand, everyone (even foreigners) is expected to arrive at social functions late. Be at least fifteen minutes late to a dinner and thirty minutes late to a party.
- Remember that many Europeans and South Americans write the day first, then the month, then the year (e.g., December 3, 2010, is written 3.12.10 or 3/12/10). This is the case in Chile.
- The best times to make appointments are from 10:00 A.M. to 12:00 and 2:30 to 5:00 P.M. Following up a late-morning appointment with a business lunch is also popular.
- Make appointments at least one week in advance of your arrival, and reconfirm them when you get there.
- A popular time for vacations is January and February (summer holidays). This is not the time to try to do business in Chile.
- Chile is four hours behind Greenwich Mean Time (G.M.T. − 4). This makes it one hour ahead of U.S. Eastern Standard Time (E.S.T. + 1). Chile goes on daylight saving time from mid-October through mid-March.

Cultural Note

The decision-making process is centralized, residing mostly with the upper-level *presidente* or *gerente general*. Next in importance comes the *gerente*, followed by mid- and low-level managers; all provide support to the upper levels. But all levels usually have input, so business transactions may take place at a slower pace than in North America or Europe. Be patient and expect delays. Several trips may be necessary to conclude a business transaction.

Negotiating

- Personal relationships are paramount in business relations in Chile. The initial visit should be by an upper-level executive, accompanied by midlevel executives. These midlevel executives are the ones who will make subsequent visits to conduct more detailed business negotiations. At a first meeting, spend most of the time establishing a rapport, then gradually steer the conversation toward introducing your firm.

- Attitudes toward trading with North America are positive, despite how Chile's admittance to the North American Free Trade Area has been delayed for years.

- Conservative values in politics, economics, and social attitudes prevail. Honesty and integrity are valued. A sense of humor is appreciated, but serious, businesslike behavior is expected.

- There is a strong sense of personal honor on the part of Chilean businesspeople. A single accusation of wrongdoing can follow a Chilean for his or her entire life. Consequently, avoid criticizing a person in public or doing anything that would cause him or her embarrassment.

- Chileans are straightforward and take negotiating quite seriously. A hard-sell approach, however, will not work. Have your bottom line and other terms clearly drawn out. Also outline a strong financial package with options such as nontraditional financing terms.

- Many women are professionally advanced in Chile, and a woman will have better success here than in most other Latin American countries.

- Show commitment to the business relationship through a willingness to provide continued service to your client, despite the long distances involved. Remember that Chileans strive to overcome the isolation imposed on them by geography.

- Making a good impression includes staying at one of the finer international hotels while in Chile.

- Chileans generally converse in closer proximity than North Americans or northern Europeans. Do not pull away from a person who is speaking quite close to you, even if you are uncomfortable. This may be interpreted as a personal affront.

- Try to cover any tattoos you may have while in Chile. To older Chileans, only criminals wear tattoos, although this attitude is changing among the young.

- Have business cards printed with English on one side and Spanish on the other. Present cards to everyone in a meeting except secretaries.
- Third parties are very important for making contacts in Chile. Banks and consulting firms can make introductions.
- The business atmosphere is more formal than in other South American countries. Proper etiquette and dress are expected.
- Chileans avoid behavior that may appear aggressive. Kindness and respect for others are valued.
- Learn a little about Chile's history, culture, economy, exports, and so forth, and be prepared to discuss them. Appreciation of Chile's history will impress and please your contacts.

Cultural Note

Chileans do not bargain in either stores or street markets. Note that it is illegal to sell something and fail to give a receipt. When a receipt is not issued, this often means that the merchant is not declaring the sale on tax reports. Both the buyer and the seller can be fined for this infraction; it is the buyer's responsibility to ask for the receipt.

▶ BUSINESS ENTERTAINING

- Breakfast is usually eaten between 7:00 and 9:00 A.M. Breakfast tends to be very light. A substantial number of Chileans eat breakfast in bed (which is possible because even middle-class families can afford a maid and/or cook).
- Lunch, the largest meal of the day, begins anytime from noon to 1:30. Lunch is often a multicourse meal lasting as long as two hours. (The higher-ranking the businessperson, the longer he or she can take for lunch.)
- Between 5:00 and 6:00 P.M., Chileans eat a snack called *once*. This consists of tea or coffee and light food, such as cookies or cheese. Some Chileans also drink alcohol at this time, which is where the "once" got its name. The traditional Chilean spirit is called *aguardiente*. *Once* is the Spanish word for "eleven," and there are eleven letters in the word aguardiente.

- Dinner is served between 8:00 and 9:00 P.M. Alcohol, in the form of a mixed drink, often starts the dinner. Wine or beer is served during the meal. Dinner ends with coffee, tea or yerba mate—and more alcohol. (Yerba mate is a caffeinated herb served in a gourd. It is more common in the Chilean south. See the entry under Paraguay on how to drink yerba mate.) Men often drink spirits after dinner and expect foreign businessmen to do the same; businesswomen are exempt from this ritual.

- Chileans are very hospitable and often invite foreigners into their home. If you are invited for drinks in the evening, you will probably be asked to stay for dinner as well.

- It is not customary to send a thank-you gift or note following an invitation to a Chilean home, but flowers or candy sent to the hostess in advance are appreciated. If you wish to convey your thanks, do so by telephone rather than by mail.

- Entertaining is often done in large hotels and restaurants. Make arrangements concerning the bill with the maitre d' in advance to avoid competition for paying. If you are a guest, reciprocate the hospitality at a later date.

- Proper table manners are very important in Chile. In general, follow European standards. Make an attempt to try everything that is served to you.

- Superstitious Chileans consider it bad luck to pass a salt shaker directly to another person. Instead, put the salt down on the table within reach of the person.

- There are several traditions concerning the pouring of wine in Chile. If you pour wine in the wrong way, you risk insulting your Chilean hosts. This includes pouring with your left hand, or pouring so that the wine splashes against the opposite side of the glass.

- Good topics of conversation include family, Chilean history, cuisine, wines, and sights that they might recommend—including Easter Island, a Chilean possession. Many Chileans are very interested in world travel, so mention other places you have visited. Skiing and fishing are very popular in Chile. Topics to avoid include local politics, human rights violations, and religion. Do not criticize Chile, even if your host is doing so.

▶ PROTOCOL

Greetings

- Men will shake hands when greeting someone. Women will often pat each other on the right forearm or shoulder instead of shaking hands. If they are close, women may hug or kiss each other on the cheek.
- At a party, greet and shake hands with each person individually. Do not ask a person his or her occupation directly, but wait for the information to be volunteered.

Titles/Forms of Address

- Do not address a Chilean by his or her first name unless invited to do so. Older executives may wish to use their last names at work. Generally, younger Chileans are more comfortable using first names.
- Persons who do not use professional titles should be addressed as "Mr.," "Mrs.," or "Miss," plus their surname. In Spanish, these are:
  Mr.= *Señor*
  Mrs. = *Señora*
  Miss = *Señorita*
- Most Hispanics have two surnames: one from their father, which is listed first, followed by one from their mother. Only the father's surname is commonly used when addressing someone; for example, Señor Juan Antonio Martinez García is addressed as Señor Martinez and Señorita Ana María Gutierrez Herrera is addressed as Señorita Gutierrez. When a woman marries, she usually adds her husband's surname and goes by that surname. If the two people in the previous example married, she would be known as Señora Ana María Gutierrez Herrera de Martinez. Most people would refer to her as: Señora de Martinez or, less formally, Señora Martinez.
- Most Chileans do not use a professional title. Those who do expect to be addressed with that title followed by their surname. Physicians always are called "Doctor."

Gestures

- The Chilean people converse at a closer distance than many Asians, North Americans, or Northern Europeans are used to—often with a hand on the other person's lapel or shoulder. Restrain yourself from trying to back away; a Chilean will probably step forward and close the distance.
- Maintaining eye contact is necessary to show interest and sincerity—something that North Americans may find difficult when speaking to a person at such close quarters.
- At a meal, keep your hands above the table at all times.
- Do not raise your right fist to head level; this is a Communist sign.

Gifts

- Gifts are not expected in business until the relationship is a close one.
- When visiting a Chilean home, send flowers in advance (avoid yellow roses, which signify contempt) or bring wine or liquor. Other popular gifts include leather appointment books, quality pens or cigarette lighters, perfume, and local crafts from home.
- If you receive a gift, open it promptly in the presence of the giver and extend thanks.
- Give gold jewelry to a girl on her fifteenth birthday. This birthday (called the *quinceaños*; the party is called a *quinceañera*.) is a very important celebration in Chile; to be invited to one is a privilege.

Dress

- Business: Dress is generally equivalent to that in Europe (meaning it is more conservative than in the USA). Men may wear a dark blue or gray suit, a light shirt, and a conservative tie. Bright colors and flashy fashions are not appropriate, nor is wearing anything on the lapel. Women should wear a suit and heels.
- Casual: When not doing business, pants or good jeans and a shirt are appropriate. Shorts will rarely be seen in public. Chile experiences temperature extremes from the beaches to the mountains. You will need warmer clothes at higher altitudes.

Colombia

Republic of Colombia
Local short form: Colombia
Local long form: Republica de Colombia

Cultural Note

Colombians have distinctive methods for indicating height and length:

To indicate the height of an animal, Colombians hold one hand horizontally at the appropriate height, as if they were resting their hand on top of the animal's head. However, to describe the height of a person, the hand is held vertically (palm out, thumb on top), as if it were touching the back of the person's head. To describe a person's height using a horizontal hand is to dismiss him or her as an animal.

North Americans often indicate length by holding both hands out with the index fingers extended. This means that the length is the distance between the two fingers. However, two pointing fingers is an obscene gesture in Colombia. Colombians indicate length by extending their right arm and placing their left hand at the point on the arm where the distance from the fingertips on the right hand to the point marked by the left hand is equal to the length being indicated.

▶ WHAT'S YOUR CULTURAL IQ?

1. To date, Gabriel García Márquez is the only Colombian author to win a Nobel Prize for literature. With which of the following Latin literary styles is he associated?
   a. *Nueva sensibilidad* (new sensibility)
   b. Modernism (modernism)
   c. Nudísts (beat poetry)
   d. *Reálism magic* (magic realism).

   ANSWER: d. This style, favored by García Márquez and others, intertwines dreams and mythic archetypes with reality.

2. TRUE or FALSE? Although Colombia is named after Christopher Columbus, he never set foot on Colombian soil.

ANSWER: TRUE. The first Europeans to reach Colombia were led by Alonso de Ojeda in 1499.

3. Believing Colombia to be the site of El Dorado (the lost city of gold), the Spanish quickly explored and conquered the country. While all of the following resources were eventually found in Colombia, the Spanish only discovered one of them in substantial quantities. Which one was it?
   a. Salt
   b. Emeralds
   c. Gold
   d. Silver

ANSWER: a) The Chibcha Indians led the Spanish to an amazingly productive salt mine at Zipaquirá. This hugely productive mine is so large that it now contains an underground cathedral!

▶ TIPS ON DOING BUSINESS IN COLOMBIA

- Colombia has a reputation (which may or may not be deserved) as the most dangerous nation for foreigners to visit in Latin America. The danger to foreigners comes not from narcoterrorists but kidnappers, who hold businesspeople for ransom.
- While foreigners are not usually in danger from narcoterrorists, you must be sure that you are not doing business with a Colombian company that has ties to the narcotraffickers. The United States of America (and other countries) maintains a list of companies with links to narcotics trafficking. It is illegal for U.S. citizens to work with them.
- Colombians are known for having long greeting rituals. Every conversation seems to begin with long inquiries as to the health, welfare, location, and status of the speakers and their relatives. Visitors who attempt to cut this greeting are considered impolite.
- While there are relatively few businesswomen in important positions in Colombia, foreign businesswomen usually find Colombian businessmen receptive.

- Traditional Colombian cuisine is very starchy. While your gracious Colombian hosts will encourage you to eat more, overeating is considered gauche by the upper classes.

▶ COUNTRY BACKGROUND

Demographics

The population numbers more than 43 million (2006 estimate). Mestizos constitute the largest single group at some 58 percent of the population. Colombia's power elite is concentrated among persons solely of European descent; these whites make up only 20 percent of the population. The remainder consists of 4 percent of African descent (living on the north coastal areas), 14 percent mulatto, and 3 percent-mixed African-Amerindian. Pureblooded Amerindians now constitute only 1 percent of the population.

An estimated 55 percent of Colombians live below the poverty level.

History

At the time of Christopher Columbus's discovery of the New World, Colombia was home to several Amerindian peoples. None of these native peoples could overcome the Spanish conquistadores, who arrived in the early 1500s.

Colombia became part of the Spanish viceroyalty of New Granada, which encompassed present-day Colombia, Ecuador, Panama, and Venezuela. Bogotá was designated the capital of the entire viceroyalty in 1717. Along with other colonies, Colombia sought independence from Spain at the beginning of the nineteenth century. In 1810, under its first president, Simón Bolívar, Colombia defied Spanish authority, and full independence was proclaimed in 1813.

Bolívar also founded Colombia's Conservative Party; his rivals founded the Liberals. This rivalry contributed to Colombia's eight civil wars. These two parties continue to this day, and have frequently alternated as the party in power.

Gran Colombia broke up in 1830 into Ecuador, Venezuela, and Colombia. Panama became Colombia's northernmost province.

Panama remained a part of Colombia until 1903, when it broke away with the support of the United States of America.

After the assassination of a Liberal leader, the most violent of the Colombian civil wars erupted in 1948. Known as La Violencia, 300,000 Colombians died in the fighting. With the country on the verge of breaking apart, members of both the Liberal and Conservative parties supported a military coup by General Gustavo Rojas Pinilla, Colombia's only military junta of the twentieth century. He remained in power from 1953 to 1957.

Elections returned in 1957, although the choice was limited to approved Liberal and Conservative candidates. For the first time, women were allowed to vote in Colombia. Over the next sixteen years, the two major parties shared political power, with the presidency alternating between the Liberals and the Conservatives. All other political parties were suppressed, contributing to the eventual growth of guerrilla movements. This sharing of power is known as the National Front; they renewed their power-sharing agreement in 1974.

During the 1980s, the rise of the narcotraficantes, with their enormous wealth and power, threatened to undermine the authority of the Colombian government. Guerrillas, such as the M-19 group, also fought the government.

In 1984, the narcotraficantes finally went too far when they assassinated Justice Minister Rodrigo Lara Bonilla. In response, the Colombian government finally began to extradite Colombian narcotraficantes wanted for trial by the USA. These drug lords, who become known as Los Extraditables, alternated violence with bribes to avoid being extradited. They even offered to pay off Colombia's entire U.S. $13 billion foreign debt. (The offer was declined.)

In November of 1985, the M-19 guerrillas occupied the Colombian Palace of Justice in Bogotá. Government troops defeated the occupiers, but the fighting caused the death of over 100 people, including eleven justices of the Colombian Supreme Court. Following this event, paramilitary death squads were formed to execute government opponents.

Open elections were finally held in 1990, allowing the participation of candidates from outside the National Front. Some former guerrillas were elected, and violence by many guerrilla organizations ceased. The last of the well-known narcotraficantes, Medellín Cartel leader Pablo Escobar, was killed in 1993. The new Cartel leaders learned to keep a lower profile, and were less likely to assassinate government officials.

Type of Government

The Republic of Colombia is a unitary, multiparty republic with two legislative houses: the Senate and the House of Representatives. There is also a judiciary branch. The president is elected to a single four-year term and cannot succeed himself. The president is both chief of state and head of the government.

The rule of government in Bogotá does not reach all of Colombia. For the past few decades, armed guerrilla groups have set up de facto governments in large areas of the Colombian countryside. For current government data, check with the Embassy of Colombia, at *www .colombiaemb.org*.

Language

The official language of Colombia is Spanish (which they call *Castellano*, not *Español*). Colombians have many regional terms, which are collectively known as *colombianismos*.

English is not widely spoken, although some international business executives speak it.

Colombia has a substantial Amerindian population, and the country's rugged geography resulted in the evolution of many isolated linguistic groups, many of whom speak only their indigenous languages. An estimated half-million Colombians speak an Amerindian tongue as their first language.

Counting Spanish, the Amerindian tongues, and various imported languages—such as Creole and Romany, the language of the Rom (Gypsies)—linguists have identified ninety-eight languages in Colombia. Of these, twenty are now considered extinct.

There are two distinct Sign Languages for the Deaf: Colombian Sign Language, which developed in 1929, and a sign language used only on the Caribbean island of Providencia. Providencia is a long way from the Colombian mainland; in fact, it is closer to Nicaragua than Colombia. Interestingly, most of the 3,000 people on Providencia seem to have some fluency in this sign language, although there are less than a few dozen deaf people on the island.

For data on the various languages of Colombia, see Ethnologue at *www.ethnologue.com.*

The Colombian View

The vast majority (90 percent) of Colombians are Roman Catholic. The constitution guarantees freedom of religion. Protestant groups are making inroads, especially Pentecostalists.

If geography is destiny, then Colombia's geography accounts for much of the country's uniqueness. Colombia borders Venezuela, Brazil, Peru, Ecuador, and Panama. It is the only South American country to have coasts on both the Caribbean and the Pacific. Furthermore, Colombia's mountainous interior isolates regions from each other. One has to expect diversity in such an environment.

While the United States of America has a history of intervention throughout Latin America, its effect on Colombia is unique. The USA prompted the removal of Panama from Colombia in 1903 to facilitate the building of the Panama Canal. Today, the United States is increasingly involved in Colombian interior affairs as the central government attempts to regain control of the countryside and reduce narcotics trafficking. Consequently, Colombians see the USA as both a savior and a demon.

As for Colombia's drug trade, smuggling didn't start with marijuana and cocaine. The illegal export of Colombian emeralds and exotic birds has been occurring for decades. Smuggling occurs in the other direction as well. Onerous taxes (as high as 36 percent) on imported goods have made it profitable to smuggle consumer goods into Columbia.

☑ Know Before You Go

As previously noted, the major hazard to foreign visitors is kidnapping. (Many Colombians have been kidnapped and held for ransom as well.) Colombia is one of the countries where you should secure kidnap insurance before your visit.

Street crime, such as pickpocketing, is common in Colombian cities. Such crimes are usually nonviolent, except when an unwary traveler is drugged. Burundanga is a drug derived from a common Colombian tree. A full dose renders a person unconscious. Burundanga has no taste or odor and can be added to almost anything you put in your mouth: candy, chewing gum, drinks, and even cigarettes. To avoid being drugged, avoid accepting anything from someone you do not know.

Volcanic eruptions occur in the highlands. There are also periodic earthquakes and droughts.

Due to vehicle emissions, the air quality in Bogotá is sometimes hazardous.

The highlands of Colombia are elevated enough to cause altitude sickness. Altitude sickness can strike anyone, even if you have never experienced it before. There is no sure prevention except gradual acclimation to high elevation: once you get to 6,000 feet above sea level, spend at least two nights there. Repeat this acclimation period at each increase of 3,000 feet. Alcohol consumption tends to make the symptoms worse. Sunburn is also a danger at high altitudes, because there is less atmosphere to protect you from the sun.

While they are not the pastimes of the upper classes, Colombians have a penchant for diversions that can cause injury or property damage. Urban Colombians like to set aloft hot air balloons made of paper; they often catch fire from the lit candle inside, raining down flaming debris. *Papeletas* are small, triangular bags filled with gunpowder, used in various games; although banned in some cities, they are still omnipresent.

▶ CULTURAL ORIENTATION

Cognitive Styles: How Colombians Organize and Process Information

Colombia is a diverse nation with many cultural and linguistic groups. The following information applies to the majority culture.

In Colombia one perceives an openness to discuss any topic, but do not expect attitudes to change based upon these discussions. Colombians process information on a subjective, associative level unless they have extensive higher education. They tend not to abstract to higher principles, but rather treat each situation as a unique experience.

Negotiation Strategies: What Colombians Accept as Evidence

Feelings are the primary source of truth. Colombians' interpersonal reality is such that they will give you the "truth" as they think it should be or as you would like it to be. Thus, their use of facts is nebulous. For the majority of Colombians, there are no ideologies strong enough to make faith a source of the truth.

Some sociologists believe that Colombians have a high level of uncertainty avoidance, although it is not out of line with other Latin American countries. This makes Colombians averse to risk and hesitant to accept change.

Value Systems: The Basis for Behavior

The effects of the drug cartels cut across all levels of Colombian society. The following three sections identify the Value Systems in the predominant culture—their methods of dividing right from wrong, good from evil, and so forth.

Locus of Decision-Making

There are informal, yet very powerful decision-making groups called *roscas*. Individuals make their own decisions but are influenced by their need to satisfy their families or groups. Kinship plays a major role in one's business associations because traditional elements of trust and mutual dependence among relatives are very strong, no matter how distant the relationship. The collectivist mindset is very much in evidence.

Sources of Anxiety Reduction

It is an individual's role in the social structure and the presence of the extended family that gives a sense of stability to life. This also brings anxiety, as one must be a success in the eyes of both the extended family and society. There is a strong need for consensus in the group, but values differ with the situation, and the rules are learned only by experience.

Issues of Equality/Inequality

The economic and political elite are generally European in heritage. They handle most of the business, commerce, and industry. Society is very class-conscious and is stratified by skin color and class membership, with limited vertical mobility. Colombian women are among the most politically active in Latin America, in spite of cultural restrictions on their social and work behavior.

On the other hand, Colombians still have one of the highest masculinity index levels in Latin America, which tends to ossify gender roles.

▶ BUSINESS PRACTICES

Punctuality, Appointments, and Local Time

- Business hours are generally 9:00 A.M. to 5:00 P.M., Monday through Friday.

    Store hours vary, but are usually from 9:00 A.M. to 12:30 P.M. and then from 2:00 P.M. to 7:00 P.M., Monday through Saturday.

- As a foreigner, you are expected to be punctual. Be on time for all business appointments.

- Colombians are not known for punctuality. They may arrive at a business meeting fifteen or twenty minutes late, yet feel they are on time. Do not expect them to apologize for being late.

- Even foreigners are expected to be late to social occasions. Arrive fifteen to thirty minutes late for a party; some Colombians will be a full hour late.

- Like many Europeans and South Americans, Colombians write the day first, then the month, then the year (e.g., December 3, 2010, is written 3.12.10 or 3/12/10).

- Schedule appointments at least one week before your arrival in Colombia. Do not depend upon regular mail service to arrange appointments; use the phone, e-mail, fax, or registered mail.

- Unless you are traveling only to the coastal lowlands, it is best to arrive a day early so that you can adjust to the high altitude. This is especially true in the capital, Bogotá, which is 8,600 feet (2,600 meters) above sea level.

- For a listing of official holidays in Colombia, visit *www.kissbow orshakehands.com.*

- Colombia is five hours behind Greenwich Mean Time (G.M.T. – 5), which is the same as U.S. Eastern Standard Time.

Negotiating

- Inland Colombians are among the most formal and traditional of Latin Americans. Only along the coast does a more relaxed attitude prevail.
- It will be difficult, if not impossible, to conduct business without hiring a local contact. This contact not only will introduce you to the Colombians you must deal with, but often will pick you up at the airport and reserve a room for you at a hotel as well.
- In most situations with the governments, you will need to speak Spanish or have an interpreter. However, many businesspeople speak English.
- Never change the members of your negotiating team. Such a change could bring the negotiations to a halt. Colombians feel that they are negotiating with people, not a corporation.
- Expect delays. You should allocate a week in Colombia to accomplish something that would generally take several days in other countries.
- Avoid discussing politics, terrorism, or illegal drugs.
- Avoid unfavorable comparisons between your native country and Colombia.
- Colombians are very proud of their nation and its achievements. It is a good idea to be informed about Colombian culture, literature, and history, or, at least, to show curiosity about such things.
- Business cards printed in your native language on one side and the translation in Spanish on the other are most effective. These should be presented with the Spanish side facing your Colombian colleague.

Business Entertaining

- Lunch is the main meal of the day and is a popular choice for a business meal.
- Colombians have a tradition of hospitality and frequently invite guests to their homes.
- Let the host be the first to make a toast; then you might wish to make one.

- Theoretically, the person who has initiated the invitation will pay for a meal in a restaurant. In practice, you may have to fight for the check even when you issued the invitation.
- Leave a small amount of food on your plate to demonstrate that you have had enough to eat.

Cultural Note

Dinner is normally eaten between 7:00 and 9:00 P.M., but a dinner party will begin and end later. Guests will not arrive until at least 8:00 P.M., and people will sit down to dinner from 10:00 P.M. to midnight. Many people eat something before going to a dinner party so that they will not starve (or be drunk) before dinner begins. A dinner party will end soon after the meal, but a cocktail party (with dancing) may go on until 5:00 A.M. Expect formal dress for either event.

⊙ PROTOCOL

Greetings
- The standard greeting is the handshake. It is also used when departing.
- Among close friends, women may clasp forearms or kiss each other on one cheek. Men embrace and slap each other's back; this manly hug is called the *abrazo*.
- Colombians often complain that North Americans and Europeans don't know how to greet someone. Colombians take a long time in greetings; they feel that this conveys respect for the other person. After the handshake (or hug), Colombians ask numerous polite questions. North Americans typically progress beyond the greeting phase after one or two questions. Expect inquiries as to your health, your trip, your relatives, and any friends or acquaintances you have in common. Don't rush! Rushing is interpreted as callousness or disrespect.

Titles/Forms of Address
- Do not address a Colombian by his or her first name unless invited to do so. In general, only children, family members, and close friends address each other by their first names.

- The only professional title in common use is "Doctor" (*Doctora* for women). However, it is often applied to any accomplished or educated person, whether or not he or she has a Ph.D. Indeed, the poor often refer to any upper-class person as "Doctor."
- See Appendix A for basic information on titles.

Gestures
- Colombians stand somewhat closer together when conversing than do North Americans. However, Colombians engage in less physical contact during conversations than some South Americans.
- The formality of inland Colombians extends to their mannerisms; they do not engage in expansive gestures and animation. Residents of the coastal regions tend to be more expressive and less formal.
- It is considered impolite to yawn in public.
- Colombians indicate that someone is stingy by tapping their fingers on their elbow.
- The North American "okay" gesture (thumb and forefinger curled into a circle) has a different meaning in Colombia. A Colombian places the circle over his nose to indicate that someone is homosexual.
- Bare feet are acceptable only at the beach. Slippers or sandals should be worn at all other times, even when going to or from the bathroom.
- In a restaurant, some Colombians summon a waiter by raising their hands over their head and clapping. Others use a hissing sound. Neither method is considered courteous, and both should be avoided by foreigners.

Gifts
- If you are given a gift, you should be very effusive in your thanks.
- When invited to a home for a meal, bring flowers, pastries, or chocolates. Avoid lilies and marigolds, which are used at funerals.
- You may give perfume to women.
- If you know you will meet a business associate's family, it is a good idea to bring a gift for the children.

- Although gifts are always appreciated, a wrapped gift is generally not opened in the presence of the giver, because Colombians feel that this would make them appear greedy. Indeed, the gift may never be mentioned again. You can be sure, though, that it was noted and appreciated.
- Other good gifts are fine wines and liquors. Do not bring foreign beer; Colombia brews fine local beers.

Dress

- In general, formality increases as you move inland. The coastal resort areas are the most casual, and shorts may be worn in public there.
- On the coast, where it is hot, some men will wear a guayabera shirt to work, and women will wear sleeveless dresses. Foreigners, however, are expected to dress more formally for business meetings.
- Inland, it is important to adopt conservative business attire. Men should wear a jacket and tie even in hot weather. Suits in dark colors are preferred. Expect to wear the jacket and tie to social occasions as well.
- Women should dress conservatively and modestly. A suit or dress is appropriate for business, while a cocktail dress will be required for most social occasions.
- Although Colombia is an equatorial country, the high elevations of some cities result in cool weather. Wool sweaters or jackets are needed in Bogotá and sometimes in Medellín.

Cultural Note

Colombia is divided by three mountain ranges, and this has led to the development of strong regional movements. When these movements fail to find common ground with the government in Bogotá, guerrilla movements (usually left-wing) evolve. Some guerrilla movements accept government amnesty and become political parties, such as the April 19 Movement Democratic Alliance (a.k.a., M-19). Others continue to fight the government. The end of the Cold War also ended foreign subsidies for Marxist guerrillas; therefore, some have increasingly turned to kidnapping and drug smuggling to earn funds. However, there is no mistaking the guerrillas for the drug cartels; the late Pablo Escobar failed to convince anyone that his Medellín drug cartel was a political organization.

Costa Rica

Republic of Costa Rica
Local long form: Republica de Costa Rica

Cultural Note

To preserve its unique natural resources, the government of Costa Rica has set aside 21 percent of its land area as protected areas. This is a larger percentage than any other nation in the world, and is one reason that Costa Rica is a favorite destination for ecotourists.

▶ WHAT'S YOUR CULTURAL IQ?

1. Which of the following is *not* true about Costa Rica?
   a. Costa Rica is currently the wealthiest country in Central America.
   b. Coast Rica abolished its army in 1948.
   c. The people of Costa Rica's are the best educated in Central America.
   d. Costa Rican President Oscar Arias received the 1987 Nobel Peace Prize for his work in negotiating a peace plan in neighboring Central American nations.

   ANSWER: a. Actually, the wealthiest nation in Central America is Panama, where the economy is buoyed by fees from the Panama Canal. Costa Rica comes in second, although its wealth is distributed much more evenly.

2. TRUE or FALSE? Ticos (as Costa Ricans are called) worry about losing their sovereignty to foreign influences; some accuse the USA of running a "parallel government" within Costa Rica.

   ANSWER: TRUE. The U.S. Agency for International Development (among other U.S. organizations) is so omnipresent in Costa Rica that it has been accused of being a "parallel government."

3. The name Costa Rica means "Rich Coast." TRUE or FALSE: On his fourth and final expedition to the New World, Christopher Columbus gave Costa Rica its name because of the gold he acquired here.

ANSWER: TRUE. However, the gold artifacts Columbus got from the local Amerindians were not mined locally. Costa Rica has no gold; the artifacts had been imported, presumably from Mexico. Far from being a prosperous place, the Spanish who settled there found a coast so pestilent that they settled in the central highlands, where agricultural riches finally came their way, centuries later.

⊙ TIPS ON DOING BUSINESS IN COSTA RICA

- Although the official language is Spanish, the large numbers of North Americans in Costa Rica have made English a virtual second language.
- Even though almost all Costa Rican business executives speak English, all written materials should be translated into Spanish.
- While it is often pointed out that peaceful Costa Rica has no army, it has plenty of other law enforcement personnel. These range from the police to the Civil Guard to the commandos of the Immediate Action Unit.
- Costa Ricans call themselves *ticos* (the feminine form is *ticas*).
- Face-to-face contact is preferred over telephone calls. Traditionally, Costa Ricans kept phone calls short. This is changing as cell phones become more common, and upper-class youths utilize them constantly.

⊙ COUNTRY BACKGROUND

Demographics

Costa Rica has a population of just over 4 million (2006 estimate). Some 95 percent of Costa Ricans are of European descent (including some 7 percent mestizo—mixed European and Indian blood), 3 percent black or mulatto, 2 percent East Asian (primarily Chinese), and 1 percent Amerindian. About 51 percent of Costa Ricans live in urban centers.

Tradition says that the national nickname of *ticos* (for women, *ticas*) came from the Costa Rican tendency to add *tico* as a diminutive or affectionate suffix, as in *momentico* (a short moment) or *chiqitico* (very small).

Costa Rica did import small numbers of black slaves from Jamaica, mostly to work on plantations. A small black population still lives in the Caribbean-coast province of Limón. Some of them still speak a Jamaican dialect of English rather than Spanish.

Note that most Costa Rican Amerindians dislike the term *indio* (Spanish for Indian), preferring to be called *indígena* (which means indigenous person). Although they number only some four or five thousand, the indígenas have 22 reservations in Costa Rica.

History

Christopher Columbus led the first European expedition to visit Costa Rica in 1502. He collected several gold decorations from the friendly Amerindians. Believing that the gold was mined locally (it was not), the Spanish named the region Costa Rica (Rich Coast).

After several failed attempts, the first successful Spanish outpost was established under Juan Vásquez de Coronado in 1562. To avoid the disease-ridden coastal regions, he selected the central highlands for the site of his new city, which was named Cartago. The Spanish found few surviving Amerindians to enslave or marry, so Costa Rica never developed a significant mestizo population. In 1821, all of Central America declared its independence from Spain. Costa Ricans were so remote that the news took a month to reach them. The Mexican empire claimed all of Central America, but Costa Rica was too far south—Mexican troops never arrived there. Costa Rica declared its independence from Mexico in 1832 and became the southernmost part of the new Central American Federation.

The Central American Federation collapsed in 1838; Costa Rica became an independent republic, and was one of the five successor states. Export of Costa Rican coffee began around this time.

Costa Rica soon established a tradition of democracy and peaceful transition from one government to another. When former president Juan Rafael Mora tried to seize power in 1860, his coup failed and he was executed. The voting franchise was extended from wealthy landowners to poor male farmers in 1889.

Rafael Angel Calderón Guardia, elected president in 1940, ran a reformist administration supported by the Communists and opposed by the Conservative landowners. When he ran for re-election in 1948, Calderón was declared the loser in a disputed election. The Conservative candidate, Otilio Ulate, was proclaimed the winner. The dispute escalated into civil war, and some 2,000 Costa Ricans were killed.

Peace was restored in 1949, and Otilio Ulate became president. A new constitution extended the vote to all citizens over eighteen, including blacks and women. The Costa Rican Army was dissolved. Peace is maintained by the Civilian and Rural Guard. Since 1949, Costa Rica has run free and democratic elections.

In 1987, Costa Rican president Oscar Arias received the Nobel Peace Prize for his work in negotiating a peace plan in neighboring Central American nations. Some believe this regional peace plan also had the effect of reducing the influence of the United States of America in Central America.

Type of Government

The government is a unitary multiparty republic, composed of a president, a unicameral legislative assembly made up of deputies, and the Supreme Court of Justice. The president is both the chief of state and the head of the government. The president and his deputies may only hold one successive four-year term of office. Judges are elected to eight-year terms. A fourth branch of government, the Supreme Electoral Tribunal, oversees the electoral process.

The people of Costa Rica are politically active and proud of their government. Elections, with voting mandatory for anyone over eighteen years old, are likened to a party, with festivities and celebrations lasting many days. Governments swing from moderately conservative to moderately progressive, as the political parties traditionally alternate power with each election.

For current government data, check with the Embassy of Costa Rica at *www.costarica-embassy.org*.

Language

Spanish is the official language of Costa Rica. Caribbean Creole English is spoken by 2 percent of the population, descended from Caribbeans who were imported to work on the railroads. English has become Costa Rica's second language and is widely understood, especially in urban centers and among the young. Nevertheless, materials should be translated into Spanish, rather than presented in English.

Linguists have identified eleven languages in Costa Rica, one of which is now extinct. The largest Amerindian language, Bribri, has only 6,000 native speakers.

For data on the various languages of Costa Rica, see Ethnologue at *www.ethnologue.com.*

Cultural Note

It has been over a decade since the USA, Canada, and Mexico entered into the North American Free Trade Agreement (NAFTA). In December 2003, the USA negotiated a similar trade pact with Central American nations. The signatories to this deal, tentatively known as CAFTA, include Guatemala, Nicaragua, El Salvador, and Honduras. However, to the surprise of many, Costa Rica decided to opt out of the agreement. It's not that Costa Rica opposes trade (one of their official government slogans is *"Exportar es Bueno"*); their government actively promotes trade and investment, yet it declined to join a free-trade agreement with the United States of America. Costa Rica's rejection of the CAFTA agreement illustrates the diversity of Latin America: every Latin American is not alike, and obstacles may appear where you least expect them. On the positive side, Costa Rica allows foreigners to own businesses without taking a Costa Rican citizen as a partner. (A somewhat unusual circumstance in Latin America).

The Costa Rican View

Costa Rica has retained Roman Catholicism as its national religion. Some 86 percent of Costa Ricans identify themselves as Catholics. As in other Latin American countries, there is rapid growth of Protestant religions. Over 9 percent of Costa Ricans are Protestants, and more than half of them belong to Pentecostal churches.

Costa Ricans welcome all affluent foreigners, although they have an ambivalent relationship with citizens of the USA. Costa Ricans are also convinced (with reason) that they live in the best and most stable country in Central America, and do not encourage poor immigrants from neighboring nations. Many social ills, from petty crime to the perceived loss of civility, are attributed to Central American immigrants.

Costa Rica has a tradition of egalitarianism. "Sharing the wealth" is not just a social custom but a government mandate. Costa Rica's relative prosperity and ethnic homogeneity allows such egalitarianism, as does a commitment to widespread education. Nevertheless, there is a Costa Rican upper class, consisting of wealthy landowners. Three-quarters of the pre-1970 presidents descended from just three of the original colonizers of Costa Rica.

Costa Rica's institutes of higher education award degrees in many fields—including law. Costa Rica has a higher number of lawyers per capita than any other country in Central America.

☑ Know Before You Go

Costa Rica has four volcanoes, two of them active, which rise near the capital of San Jose in the center of the country. One of the volcanoes, Irazu, erupted between 1963 and 1965.

There are occasional earthquakes, hurricanes along the Atlantic coast, and flooding during the rainy season. Visitors need to be prepared for the hot, humid climate.

Cultural Note

The two-wheeled wooden oxcart has been designated as the national labor symbol of Costa Rica. European settlement began in the highlands, away from the malarial coasts, so the oxcart became the main mode of transportation. An oxcart transported the first coffee crop for export in 1843, marking the end of Costa Rica's international isolation.

Costa Ricans like to paint their oxcarts in bright colors with geometric designs. Ticos consider the painted oxcart a form of national folk art.

▶ CULTURAL ORIENTATION

Cognitive Styles: How Costa Ricans Organize and Process Information

Costa Ricans love to use language and are open to discussions on any topic. However, they have very strong beliefs and are not easily persuaded to another's point of view. They are primarily associative in their thinking and look at each situation as a unique happening. They are intuitive and use rules only as guidelines.

Negotiation Strategies: What Costa Ricans Accept as Evidence

Facts are usually interpreted through subjective feelings, though Costa Ricans will sometimes use faith in a humanitarian ideology as a source of the truth. Frank criticism is rare because the use of tentative language is much more conducive to saving face. The truth is what is believed at the moment.

Value Systems: The Basis for Behavior

This is a very humanitarian, fiercely democratic culture with a belief in peace through negotiations. The following three sections identify the Value Systems in the predominant culture—their methods of dividing right from wrong, good from evil, and so forth.

Locus of Decision-Making

Costa Rican culture is traditionally collectivist as opposed to individualist. While each individual is independent, there is a strong sense of responsibility to the family or group. Favored treatment is given to kin. Upward mobility often means using the group for individual advancement. A person trusts only those who appreciate his or her uniqueness. Costa Ricans have a strong self-image but loathe arrogance and expect people in high places to display humility.

Sources of Anxiety Reduction

Family lineage is important to who you are; it determines your identification and status. Success is in the eyes of the extended family. There is a strong work ethic, but progress toward the goal of the project is not as important as working on the project. Costa Ricans prefer to think small, go slowly, and avoid risks, anxiety, or overwork. They generally try to avoid precise commitments, although they may make them vocally to avoid hurting your feelings.

Sociologists have determined that Costa Ricans typically display what is called a "high uncertainty avoidance." This leads them to establish strict rules and policies, both in their legal system and in societal norms. Such cultures are highly risk-averse and generally resist change.

Issues of Equality/Inequality

Costa Ricans believe strongly in the philosophy of the equality of all people because each one is a unique individual—more so than any other Latin American culture. Wealth and family lineage are the primary determinants of social position. Costa Ricans' "power distance ratio" has been measured as half that typical among Latin cultures. That means that there is a strong emphasis on the equality and dignity of work regardless of your social class.

Machismo, while extant, is also lower in Costa Rica than in its neighbors. The masculinity index of Costa Ricans has been quantified as less than half the amount typical for Latin cultures. This is indicative of low levels of gender discrimination. Women maintain their own identity apart from that of their husband in all legal and business matters.

⊙ BUSINESS PRACTICES

Punctuality, Appointments, and Local Time

- Business hours are generally 8:00 A.M. to 5:00 P.M. Monday through Friday and 8:00 to 11:00 A.M. Saturday. Businesses usually close for lunch from 11:00 or 11:30 A.M. to 1:00 P.M., daily.
- Costa Ricans are by far the most punctual people in Central America.
- All foreign businesspeople are expected to be on time for appointments.
- Costa Ricans allow themselves only a limited time for their midday break, so everyone is expected to be on time for a business lunch.
- In Costa Rica, as in many European and South American countries, the date is written day first, then the month, then the year (e.g., December 3, 2010, is written 3.12.10 or 3/12/10).
- Good times to do business in Costa Rica are February to March and September to November. The rainy season runs from May

through November (with rain heaviest on the Caribbean coast). The most popular vacation times are December and January and around the Christmas and Easter holidays.

- Make appointments in advance, and reconfirm before arrival.
- In the public sector, the fiscal year is the same as the calendar year.
- For a list of Costa Rica's official holidays, visit *www.kissbowor shakehands.com*.
- Local time is six hours behind Greenwich Mean Time (G.M.T. – 6); this is one hour behind U.S. Eastern Standard Time (E.S.T. – 1).

Negotiations

- Decision-makers are readily accessible and will be frank and open during discussions. Business takes place on a personal basis in Costa Rica. It is important to establish a relationship with your Costa Rican counterpart before proceeding to business issues.
- There is a strong sense of personal honor and social equality on the part of the Costa Rican businessperson. More so than anywhere else in Central America, every person is assumed to have value and dignity. Therefore, avoid any behavior that would demean another person, especially in public.
- Decisions are made by consensus of all involved, not just by top officials. This may slow the process down; avoid showing impatience. Being impatient lowers your credibility and puts you at a disadvantage.
- Precisely because persons at all levels of a company have input, remember to be polite to everyone you meet.
- Foreign investment—notably from the United States of America and Mexico—is aggressively competitive in Costa Rica. Contacts are very important to doing business. Remember to treat your business counterparts with the same respect with which you would treat a valued client at home.
- Time estimates and deadlines may not be strictly observed. Also, late payments are very frequent. Be prepared to travel to Costa Rica several times to finalize plans. Be tolerant of delays, and remain flexible by building these factors into your own plans.

- Women in business will meet with greater acceptance in Costa Rica than in other Latin American countries. Women have been elected to the vice presidency in Costa Rica.
- Costa Ricans are much more formal and serious than their neighbors. Informality, casual dress, and the use of obscenity are negative traits that Costa Ricans associate with other Central Americans.
- Have business cards, proposals, and other material printed in both English and Spanish. While most executives speak English well, technical workers may not.
- While it is not technically necessary for foreigners to offer a partnership to a Costa Rican citizen, you should have local legal representation and use a local advertising agency. Some foreign businesses offer partnerships to Costa Ricans to make use of their local connections.

Business Entertaining

- Most business entertaining takes place in the evening, since lunch is the main meal of the day. Spouses are welcome at business dinners.
- Good topics of conversation are children, families, and the beauty of Costa Rica. The Costa Rican people enjoy discussing politics, particularly with foreigners. Costa Rica's history of stable democracy provides a good topic for conversation. Foreigners should have some knowledge of the political history of Central America in order to speak intelligently on the subject.

⊙ PROTOCOL

Greetings

- Men will shake hands with other men in greeting. Women will often pat each other on the right forearm or shoulder instead of shaking hands.
- Women who are close friends may hug or kiss each other on the cheek. However, Costa Rican men do not usually hug other men. The hearty male *abrazo* (backslapping embrace) seen in other Latin American countries is rare in Costa Rica.

- In rural areas, some men will nod instead of shaking hands.
- Costa Ricans who are used to greeting North Americans may offer a firm handshake, but many handshakes may tend to be gentle. Adjust your grip to the other person's handshake.
- Do not refer to the people as *ricans*, as this word has a bad connotation. The people of Costa Rica are referred to as ticos.
- At parties, it is customary to be introduced to and shake hands with everyone in the room.

Titles/Forms of Address

- You should address most people you meet by their title and their surname. Only children, family members, and close friends address each other by their first names.
- When a person has a title, it is important to use it. Usually the title alone is preferred; no surname is necessary. A Ph.D. or a physician is called "Doctor." Teachers prefer the title *Profesor*, engineers go by *Ingeniero*, architects are *Arquitecto*, and lawyers are *Abogado*.

Gestures

- Making a fist with the thumb sticking out between the middle and index fingers is obscene. This gesture is known as the "fig."
- Most North American gestures will be understood in Costa Rica.
- Don't rest your feet on any furniture except items expressly designed for that purpose.

Gifts

- Costa Ricans will exchange gifts frequently for all kinds of special occasions. Because of the large number of U.S. citizens in Costa Rica and the lack of import restrictions, U.S. goods are freely available there.
- If you are invited to a home for dinner, bring flowers, chocolates, Scotch, or wine.
- Baskets of assorted delicacies are very popular. Do not bring calla lilies; they are associated with funerals.
- For more guidelines on gift giving, visit *www.kissboworshake hands.com*.

Dress

- Business: Men should wear a conservative dark suit. During business meetings, expect to keep your jacket on even in the heat. Costa Rican men in the hot coastal areas sometimes do without a jacket, but foreigners should bring a jacket and remove it if their counterpart does not wear one. Women should wear a dress or skirt and blouse.
- Historically, trousers were never worn by businesswomen, but this is changing.
- Casual: Shorts are worn only on the beach. Revealing clothing for women is not acceptable. Bring a sweater or jacket to wear at night in the higher elevations.
- Bring multiple changes of clothes. Because of the heat, people in Costa Rica bathe frequently—often more than once a day.

Cultural Note

Costa Rica's egalitarianism manifests itself in extensive squatters' rights. Squatters cannot be evicted if they are allowed to remain for three months. If they remain for ten years, squatters can even claim title to the land. This makes it difficult for absentee landowners to maintain ownership of their property.

Ecuador

Republic of Ecuador

Cultural Note

Ecuador is South America's second largest producer of oil. The drop in oil prices since 1982, plus an earthquake in 1987 that crippled the country's main oil line, forced Ecuador to temporarily suspend interest payments on its foreign debt. Ecuador resigned from OPEC in 1992, stating that the cartel failed to benefit smaller oil producers.

▶ WHAT'S YOUR CULTURAL IQ?

1. Which of the following islands are administered by Ecuador?
   a. Easter Island
   b. Galápagos Islands
   c. Malvinas Islands
   ANSWER: b. Ecuador administers the Galápagos Islands. (Chile has Easter Island, and Argentina claims the Malvinas Islands—but they are occupied by the United Kingdom, which calls them the Falkland Islands.)

2. Until the discovery of oil, Ecuador was primarily an agricultural nation. TRUE OR FALSE: Since the Second World War, coffee has been Ecuador's primary cash crop.
   ANSWER: FALSE. Ecuador has never been one of South America's top coffee producers. Until the 1920s its major agricultural export was cacao (the source of chocolate). But after an infestation of insects damaged cacao production, bananas became Ecuador's most important crop.

3. Which South American country invaded Ecuador in 1941?
   a. Brazil
   b. Colombia
   c. Peru

ANSWER: c. Peru invaded Ecuador in 1941 and annexed almost half of Ecuador's territory. Ecuador has resented Peru ever since, and these sentiments have boiled over several times at the ill-defined border. Military on both sides of the border attacked each other in 1981 and again in 1995.

⊙ TIPS ON DOING BUSINESS IN ECUADOR

- Do not discuss other Latin American countries with Ecuadorians. In 1941, Ecuador lost half its land to Peru, (a decision supported by the USA, Argentina, and Brazil). This made Ecuador one of the smallest nations in South America, and has resulted in strained relations between Ecuador and Peru ever since. The most recent border war between the two countries flared in 1995, and was resolved in 1999.

- Obviously, Ecuador is located directly on the equator—make allowances for the climate in your wardrobe.

- The Galápagos Islands are a major ecotourism site for Ecuador. A visit to the islands—which were claimed by Ecuador in 1832— shows interest in their natural resources (besides oil).

- There are differences between Ecuadorians who live in the interior, and those on the coast. The inhabitants of Quito (known as *Quiteños*) tend to be formal, conservative, and very Catholic. People on the coastal city of Guayaquíl tend to be more liberal and serene.

- Visiters may encounter problems with the legal system. It is complex, politicized, unevenly applied, and slow-moving. Reforms were made in 1996 to try and make improvements.

⊙ COUNTRY BACKGROUND

Demographics

The population numbers around 14 million (2006 estimate). The breakdown of the ethnicity of Ecuadorians is a highly charged political issue. The best current evaluation estimates that 40 percent of the population is Amerindian and another 40 percent is mestizo (mixed European and Indian blood). Persons descended solely from white

Europeans account for just 15 percent. The remaining 5 percent consists of a small black minority, most of who live along the north coast of Ecuador. The population is evenly split between urban and rural residents.

History

Archaeological evidence indicates that Ecuador has been continuously occupied for some 5,000 years. The powerful Inca empire reached its height in this area just prior to Columbus's discovery of the New World.

The Spanish conquistadores' arrival came at a time when the Incas were weakened by a brutal civil war. The Spanish conquest of Ecuador was complete by 1534. Ecuador became part of the Spanish viceroyalty of Peru. The colony got off to a poor start when the conquistadores began assassinating one another. This precedent for political change accompanied by violence has been repeated many times in Ecuador.

Along with other colonies, Ecuador sought independence from Spain at the beginning of the nineteenth century. Independence was declared in 1809, but was not secured until 1822. At first, Ecuador joined with Colombia, Panama, and Venezuela to form the Republic of Greater Colombia. But this turbulent union soon fell apart, and Ecuador became an independent nation in 1830.

Ecuador suffered through both political unrest and border disputes with both Colombia and Peru. Revolts and dictatorships became common; rarely did one freely elected government succeed another.

Political instability continued throughout the twentieth century. Peru invaded in 1941, and annexed almost half Ecuador's land. The two countries still dispute their borders.

Ecuador's turbulence is reflected in the leadership of José María Velasco Ibarra, who was elected president five times between 1944 and 1972, yet was allowed to complete only one full term in office!

Despite this instability, Ecuador often managed to be better off than its neighboring countries, both politically and economically.

Ecuador underwent its most recent coup in 2000.

Cultural Note

Dinners at Ecuadorian homes last long into the night. Expect drinks and appetizers around 8:00 P.M., with dinner served around 11:00 P.M. or midnight. Your hosts may be dismayed if you leave as early as 1:00 A.M.

Parties at Ecuadorian homes also begin late and end around 4:00 or 5:00 A.M. Guests may sometimes be served breakfast before they leave.

Type of Government

Ecuador has endured frequent civilian and military dictatorships over its history. Ecuadorian political parties have often had difficulties with disorganized platforms (or lack of platforms), charismatic leaders who do not follow specific programs, and small factions within the parties. Ecuador suffered a coup in January 2000, when a huge demonstration in Quito occupied the National Assembly building (the police and the military refused to stop them). President Jamil Mahaud was forced to flee. A military triumvirate, which was running the country, backed Vice President Gustavo Noboa and he succeeded to the presidency.

The Republic of Ecuador is a unitary multiparty republic. It has a single legislative house, the National Congress. The president is both the chief of state and the head of the government, and serves a single four-year term.

According to Ecuador's current constitution, the president may not be re-elected, and legislators must sit out a term before running again for a two-year term. Voting is compulsory in Ecuador from age eighteen to sixty-five for all literate citizens.

For current government data and guidelines for doing business in Ecuador, check with the Embassy of Ecuador at *www.ecuador.org*.

Language

The official language of Ecuador is Spanish. Many businesspeople speak English.

Ecuador has a large Amerindian population, many of whom speak only their indigenous languages. Quichua is the most common Amerindian language, numbering approximately 1.5 million speakers of its various dialects.

Counting all the varieties of Quichua, a total of twenty-three languages have been identified in Ecuador by *www.ethnologue.com*; one of those is now extinct.

The Ecuadorian View

There is no official religion in Ecuador, and the constitution guarantees freedom of religion. The vast majority (93 percent) of Ecuadorians are Roman Catholic; various Protestant groups have made inroads in the past few decades.

Ecuador is subject to the hazards typical of the Andes: earthquakes, volcanoes, and mudslides. Some sociologists believe that this is one source of many Ecuadorians' fatalistic viewpoint.

Ecuador is unusual in that Amerindians form a bloc as large as any other ethnic group. In the past, Amerindians formed the lowest level of Ecuadorian society. In the past few decades, increasing militancy and political activism has raised the prestige of Ecuador's indigenous people.

Once reason for increased political activity by Ecuador's poor (Amerindians and mestizo alike) is the perceived failure of Ecuador's oil exports to improve their lives.

☑ Know Before You Go

Ecuador is subject to earthquakes and volcanoes, as well as severe weather due to fluctuations in the El Niño Current. The latter caused massive flooding and mudslides in 2002.

As a result of Ecuador's wars with Peru, there are as many as 100,000 land mines along the country's border. Since 1995, the mines have caused over sixty casualties (both civilian and military). Persons traveling along the border should use extreme caution.

Rebel groups from Colombia sometimes retreat into Ecuadorian territory. Some of these rebel groups kidnap foreigners and hold them for ransom.

Altitude sickness can strike anyone, even if you have never experienced it before. There is no sure prevention except gradual acclimation to high elevation: once you get to 6,000 feet above sea level, spend at least two nights there. Repeat this acclimation period at each increase of 3,000 feet. Alcohol consumption tends to make the symptoms worse. Sunburn is also a danger at high altitudes, as there is less atmosphere to protect you from the sun.

Cultural Note

Ecuador prospered under the viceroyalty. Some of the finest Spanish empire art came from here, with native craftsmen fulfilling church commissions in the style which came to be known as the Quito school.

▶ CULTURAL ORIENTATION

Cognitive Styles: How Ecuadorians Organize and Process Information

In Ecuador there is a basic tendency to accept information on any topic for discussion. However, Ecuadorians are not easily moved from their positions. They arrive at their beliefs through association and experiential thinking. They generally look at each particular situation rather than using universal rules or laws to guide their behavior.

Negotiation Strategies: What Ecuadorians Accept as Evidence

A person's feelings about a topic or situation are the primary source of the truth. Faith in an ideology of class structure may influence the truth. Typically, an argument based entirely on quantifiable data is not convincing to the majority of Ecuadorians.

Value Systems: The Basis for Behavior

Rigid class distinctions are supported by a strong tradition of social distance between the upper class and the common people. The following three sections identify the Value Systems in the predominant culture—their methods of dividing right from wrong, good from evil, and so forth.

Locus of Decision-Making

There is a preoccupation with each individual's status. This lends itself to the belief in *personalismo*—an exaggerated attention to one's own personal position with relatives and society. Self-identity is based on the social system and the history of the extended family. Kinship and friendship play a major role in business associations.

Ecuadorians have been measured to have a low individualism ranking. This indicates a collectivist culture in which a person's group identity is paramount.

Sources of Anxiety Reduction

One's role in the social structure and the presence of the extended family and kinship groups give a sense of stability to life. The Catholic Church has a strong influence on personal and social behavior. There is a strong work ethic, but progress toward the goal of the project is less important than working on the project.

Issues of Equality/Inequality

The Sierra elite (conservative) consider themselves the upper class by birth and intermarriage, so there is a power struggle between the Sierra and Costa (liberal). Ecuadorians have displayed a higher power distance rating than is average for Latin Americans, meaning that there are extreme contrasts between rich and poor. There is still a belief that powerful people are entitled to special privileges that come with an important office—although this is changing among the young. Machismo is widespread. The man is still the head of the household, and the woman is responsible for managing it.

Cultural Note

Individual honor is so highly prized in Ecuador that defamation is a criminal offense punishable by up to three years in prison. This sometimes results in reporters taking a rather nonconfrontational viewpoint on potentially controversial topics.

The media is also required by law to give the government free air time, therefore many government-produced programs that feature the president and top officials are broadcast.

▶ BUSINESS PRACTICES

Punctuality, Appointments, and Local Time

- Business hours generally are 9:00 A.M. to 1:00 P.M. and 3:00 to 6:00 P.M., Monday through Friday. (However, many executives arrive late, so do not schedule appointments for earlier than 10 A.M.)

- As a foreigner, you are expected to be punctual to all business appointments.
- Be aware that Ecuadorians do not always stress punctuality among themselves. If Ecuadorians arrive at a meeting fifteen or twenty minutes late, they still feel they are on time. There have been recent government efforts to force Ecuadorians to be more punctual.
- Remember that many South Americans write the day first, then the month, then the year (e.g., December 3, 2010, is written 3.12.10 or 3/12/10). This is the case in Ecuador.
- Make appointments about two weeks in advance.
- It is best to arrive in Quito a day before you begin work, because it takes time to adjust to the high altitude.
- Ecuador is five hours behind Greenwich Mean Time (G.M.T. – 5), which is the same as U.S. Eastern Standard Time.

Negotiating
- Ecuadorians are more relaxed and informal in business settings than some other Latin Americans.
- It will be difficult to conduct business without hiring a local contact, who can be either a business consultant or an Ecuadorian lawyer.
- When dealing with the government, you will need to speak Spanish or have an interpreter. However, many executives in the private industry will speak English.
- Business cards printed with English on one side, and the translation in Spanish on the other are most effective. These should be presented with the Spanish side facing your Ecuadorian colleague.
- Never change the members of your negotiating team. Such a change could bring the negotiations to halt. Ecuadorians feel they are negotiating with people, not a corporation.
- Expect delays and many contract iterations.
- Avoid discussing politics, especially Ecuador's relations with Peru. (The two countries have had many disputes.)

- Ecuadorians are sensitive to foreign attitudes of superiority; be careful not to give that impression. Don't compare how things are done in Ecuador to how things are done "back home."
- It is a good idea to be informed about local culture and history, or at least to show curiosity about Ecuador.
- For a list of the holidays of Ecuador, visit *www.kissboworshake hands.com.*

Business Entertaining

- Lunch is the main meal of the day, and is the most popular for business meetings.
- Let the host be the first to make a toast; then you can follow his or her lead.
- It is considered rude to suggest an ending time for a social gathering.
- It is acceptable to order a cocktail before the meal.
- Wine may be served with the lunch. Keep in mind that Ecuadorians will be accustomed to a heavy meal with alcohol at midday.
- Ecuadorians are very friendly; if you establish a good relationship, you may be invited to your associate's home or farm. Never decline an offer like this—it is an honor.
- Women should note that while it is acceptable to drink wine, Ecuadorians are not accustomed to seeing a woman drink whiskey or other hard liquor.
- If a businesswoman wishes to pay for an Ecuadorian man's meal, she should make arrangements ahead of time. If the check is presented at the end of the meal, the man will probably refuse to let her pay.

⊙ PROTOCOL

Greetings

- The standard greeting is the handshake, both for men and women and between the sexes.
- The handshake is also used when departing.

- Among close friends, women kiss each other on one cheek. Men embrace; generally, men only honor elders (of either sex) with a kiss on one cheek.

Titles/Forms of Address

- Do not address an Ecuadorian by his or her first name unless you are invited to do so. Younger executives may move to a first name basis quickly, but it is better to err on the side of formality.
- For further information on the proper titles and forms of address in Ecuador, please consult Appendix A.
- Be sure to use an Ecuadorian's professional title, if he or she has one.

Gestures

- Ecuadorians stand closer together when conversing than do North Americans and northern Europeans. There is a good deal more contact, including touching on the arm, shoulder, and lapel. Try not to back away; an Ecuadorian is likely to move forward to restore what he or she feels is the proper distance.
- Instead of using head motions to indicate "yes" or "no," it is safest to indicate consent or disagreement verbally. Not all Ecuadorians may be able to interpret your physical signals.
- As in most of the world, it is considered impolite to yawn in public or to point at others.
- Nervous, repetitive movements (toe tapping, knee jiggling, thumb twiddling, and so forth) should be minimized. Ecuadorians find them disturbing.
- In a restaurant, some Ecuadorians summon a waiter by raising their hands over their head and clapping. This is not considered courteous, and it should be avoided by foreigners.

Gifts

- If you are given a gift, you should be effusive in your thanks.
- When invited into a home for a meal, bring flowers, pastries, or chocolates. Avoid lilies and marigolds, which are used at funerals.
- Fine wines and liquors are also good gifts.

- Be sure to select name-brand gifts.
- If you know you will meet a business associate's family, it is a good idea to bring gifts for the children.
- For further guidelines on gift giving, visit *www.kissboworshake hands.com.*

Dress

- In general, formality increases as you move inland. The coastal resort areas are the most casual, and shorts may be worn in public there (although bikinis are rarely seen, even on the beach).
- On the coast, where it is hot, some men will wear a guayabera shirt to work, and women will wear sleeveless dresses. Foreigners, however, are expected to dress more formally for business meetings.
- Inland, it is important to adopt conservative business attire. Men should wear a jacket and tie even in hot weather. Suits in dark colors are preferred. Jackets and ties can be worn to social occasions as well.
- Women should dress conservatively and modestly. A suit, dress, or designer pantsuit is appropriate for business. A cocktail dress will be required for most social occasions.

Cultural Note

In an effort to stabilize the economy and slow inflation, Ecuador adopted the U.S. dollar as its national currency in 2000.

El Salvador

Republic of El Salvador
Local long form: Republica de El Salvador

Cultural Note

Many organizations that have supported the poor against the ruling elite of El Salvador have been subject to intimidation. Lutheran Bishop Medardo Gómez left El Salvador in 1989 after death threats. The U.S. Peace Corps pulled its workers out in 1979. And among traditionally Catholic nations, El Salvador probably has the worst record for the murder of clergy. In addition to the well-known murders of Archbishop Romero in 1980 and six Jesuit priests in 1989, at least 600 other Catholic clergy or lay workers died or "disappeared" during the 1980s.

▶ WHAT'S YOUR CULTURAL IQ?

1. Which of the following nations has the highest population density?
   a. El Salvador
   b. Guatemala
   c. Honduras
   ANSWER: a. Many El Salvadorans leave their crowded country to seek work elsewhere... which is one of the reasons El Salvador has had tense relations with its neighbors.

2. El Salvador experiences which of following?
   a. Earthquakes
   b. Hurricanes
   c. Volcanic eruptions
   d. All of the above
   ANSWER: d. El Salvador was hit by a devastating earthquake in 2001. Although the Pacific side of Central America is sheltered from hurricanes, large storms such as Hurricane Mitch in 1998 can cross over. And, while volcanic eruptions are rare, they do occur—the fertility of El Salvador's soil is due to its volcanic origins.

3. The assassination of Catholic Archbishop Oscar Arnulfo Romero made news around the world. TRUE or FALSE? Archbishop Romero was awarded the Nobel Peace Prize for his attempts to mediate between the Salvadoran government and the guerrillas. ANSWER: FALSE. Archbishop Romero had been nominated for the Nobel Peace Prize, but had not won it at the time of his assassination in March 1980.

▶ TIPS ON DOING BUSINESS IN EL SALVADOR

- Since its founding, El Salvador has been dominated by an oligarchy. The original Fourteen Families *(Los Catorce)* who ran the country for their benefit have expanded into about 250 families, but they continue to dominate the Salvadoran economy.

- While there have been efforts to start businesses among poorer Salvadorans, doing business in El Salvador usually means doing business with the oligarchy.

- Salvadorans have learned the dangers of depending upon a single crop. In the 1920s, 95 percent of El Salvador's export earnings came from coffee. But the demand for coffee plummeted during the Great Depression. Since then, El Salvador's agricultural exports have been expanded to include bananas and sugar cane. When the banana harvest was badly damaged by Hurricane Mitch in 1998, sugar cane and coffee became Salvador's most important crops.

- El Salvador is still recovering from its civil war. Although fighting ended with the 1992 peace accords, an estimated 70,000 Salvadorans lost their lives, and more than 750,000 fled the country.

- It is important for foreigners to stay out of Salvadoran politics. The Salvadoran Constitution prohibits foreigners from participating in domestic political activities, including public demonstrations. Violators are deported.

▶ COUNTRY BACKGROUND

Demographics
El Salvador's population of 6.8 million (2006 estimate) is composed of three ethnic groups: Mestizo (a mixture of European and

Indian) 90 percent, Amerindian 1 percent, and European 9 percent. Many Salvadorans work outside the country, especially in the USA. Remittances by citizens living abroad are an important part of the Salvadoran economy.

History

El Salvador was one of the homes of the Mayan people, who went through a "Golden Age" around 200 B.C., building large cities and temples. For reasons still unknown, the Mayan civilization declined around A.D. 900, and the great cities were abandoned.

In 1519, Hernando Cortés led the first European expedition to subdue Mexico. After fighting his way through Guatemala, Pedro de Alvarado (one of Cortés's lieutenants) entered El Salvador in 1524. He spent several years conquering the resisting Amerindians.

The Spanish founded San Salvador in 1528. Although the region has no mineral wealth, the rich volcanic soil drew many Spanish colonists.

Mexico declared itself independent from Spain in 1821. Mexico also claimed all of Central America as part of the new Mexican empire. In 1823, the five Central American states (Guatemala, El Salvador, Honduras, Nicaragua, and Costa Rica) created the United Provinces of Central America, independent from Mexico.

Following years of internecine fighting, the United Provinces of Central America broke up in 1838. However, El Salvador hoped for a reconciliation, and did not officially call itself a Republic until 1856.

Gerardo Barrios became president of El Salvador in 1859. During his four-year term, he established the Salvadoran coffee industry. Most of the succeeding presidents were members of the Fourteen Families (Los Catorce).

Due to the Great Depression, coffee prices plummeted in 1931. A disputed Presidential election plunged the country into chaos. The minister of war, General Maximilano Hernández Martínez seized power, ruling as dictator until 1944.

A new Salvadoran Constitution was adopted in 1950, which provided some improvements in human rights and the welfare of the poor.

In 1969, El Salvador and Honduras engaged in a brief conflict known as the "Soccer War."

In the 1980s, violence by both guerrillas and the government escalated. Some priests in the Catholic Church adopted "Liberation Theology," calling for aid to the poor and opposition to the government. Death squads executed many Salvadorans. Aid from the United States of America poured in to combat Communist guerrillas.

In 1980, Catholic Archbishop Oscar Arnulfo Romero, a nominee for the Nobel Peace Prize, was assassinated while celebrating Mass. That same year, four churchwomen from the USA were raped and killed. Both actions were traced to government death squads.

In the 1989 national elections, the Communist FMLN was allowed to participate for the first time. But the presidency was won by Alfredo Cristiani of the Rightist ARENA Party. Violence resumed, and six Jesuit priests at the University of Central America were executed by government death squads.

In 1990, the United States of America mediated peace talks while cutting its aid to the El Salvador government. All parties signed a peace treaty on January 16, 1992. The war cost the lives of at least 70,000 Salvadorans.

Type of Government

The Republic of El Salvador is a multiparty republic with a unicameral legislative house, the Legislative Assembly. The president is the chief of state and the head of the government.

In recent years, the right-wing ARENA party has led the national government, while the left-wing FMLN party has run many local governments.

For current government data, check with the Embassy of El Salvador at *www.elsalvador.org*.

Language

Ethnologue, at *www.ethnologue.com*, has identified six languages used in El Salvador. The official language of the country is Spanish.

English is understood in tourist centers and by many upper-class businesspeople, some of whom have been educated in the USA.

Cultural Note

Bananas are a staple of the Salvadoran economy, but their future is in doubt. The current variety familiar to Western consumers, the Cavendish, is threatened by fungal diseases. These same diseases wiped out the former leading banana variety, known as the Gros Michel, in the 1960s. Some scientists predict that the Cavendish variety will also be eliminated within a decade. Efforts are underway to develop genetically modified bananas, and El Salvador will be a likely market for such fungus-resistant bananas.

The Salvadoran View

El Salvador has no official religion. Although the Salvadorans have traditionally been Roman Catholic, various Protestant sects have gained ground in recent years, and now constitute some 10 percent of the population.

In the 1950s, some Roman Catholic clergy embraced what is called "liberation theology" and a "preferential option for the poor." This meant that the Catholic Church could not endorse a government that kept the vast majority of Salvadorans living in poverty. Such elements of the Church became, in the eyes of some Salvadorans, "enemies of the state." This led to the growing popularity of Evangelical Protestantism as an alternative faith, especially among the privileged classes. Many businesspeople in El Salvador are now members of Neo-Pentecostal groups, which equate wealth with God's favor.

Cultural Note

The ubiquitous drink among the Salvadoran poor is *boj,* a sweet sugar cane liquor. Legend says that a devil pricked his finger and let a drop of his blood mix with the liquor—the better to seduce a pretty harp player. When Salvadorans get in a drunken fight, it is often blamed on the "blood of the devil" that they consumed.

About half of El Salvador's population continues to live in extreme poverty. Although the civil war has been over since 1992, animosity remains between the Salvadoran poor and the upper class. Aside from government employees, relatively few Salvadorans can be considered middle class.

Visitors to El Salvador—whether businesspeople or foreign officials—are viewed with suspicion by many poor Salvadorans. Historically, foreigners have only brought prosperity to the upper classes.

☑ Know Before You Go

El Salvador is categorized as a developing nation; aside from international hotels, facilities for foreign visitors may be limited.

Street crime and kidnapping are major problems in El Salvador. A new National Civilian Police force (PNC) has been established, but its effectiveness is widely criticized.

El Salvador has been called the Land of the Volcanoes. It is subject to occasional highly destructive earthquakes and volcanic eruptions. Although the country does not have a Caribbean coastline, hurricanes and tropical storms sometimes cause damage—such as Hurricane Mitch did in September 2001.

Due to deforestation, heavy rains sometimes cause cataclysmic mudslides. The mudslides caused by Hurricane Mitch destroyed thousands of homes.

Malaria is endemic. A mosquito-borne epidemic of dengue fever broke out in 2000.

Antipersonnel mines, left over from the civil war, are still found in rural areas. These include mines the government bought from the United States of America, and improvised explosive devices deployed by the rebels. Explosives are stored in military bases, some of which are located in residential areas. In May 2000, there was an accidental explosion at a military storage facility in San Salvador, which caused injuries and damage to some 700 nearby houses.

▶ CULTURAL ORIENTATION

Cognitive Styles: How Salvadorans Organize and Process Information

In El Salvador there is great skepticism about information supplied by outsiders or those on the opposite side of an issue. They may discuss it but not act on it. Children are brought up to be subjective and associative.

The elite are educated in the USA and so may be objective and abstractive. Even so, Salvadorans approach each issue from a personal perspective and seldom resort to universal rules or laws to solve problems.

Negotiation Strategies: What Salvadorans Accept as Evidence

Personal feelings about a situation or issue are the most important source of truth. Some Salvadorans may be influenced by faith in a religious or political ideology. However, few Salvadorans will make a decision based entirely on objective facts. All information presented by foreigners is subject to great skepticism. Some sociologists believe that Salvadorans are very averse to risk and slow to accept change.

Value Systems: The Basis for Behavior

This is a culture dominated both politically and economically by a landed oligarchy that is backed by the military. The following three sections identify the Value Systems in the predominant culture—their methods of dividing right from wrong, good from evil, and so forth.

Locus of Decision-Making

The oligarchy is the seat of decision-making. Individuals are responsible for their decisions, but the best interests of the family, group, organization, or nation are dominating factors. Self-identity is based on the social system and the history of the extended family. Expertise is less important than the ability to be a member of the group. Salvadorans have been charted as having a low individualism rating, reflecting a collectivist society in which the group is more important than the individual.

Sources of Anxiety Reduction

Salvadorans find stability in their role in the social structure and their extended families. Family lineage establishes social position. Generations of poverty have given the Salvadoran poor (which is the majority of the population) a sense of fatalism and helplessness. Natural disasters such as hurricanes and earthquakes only add to those attitudes. Despite this, Salvadorans endure. The Catholic Church is not as strong in El Salvador as in other Central and South American countries, but its rituals give structure to society. Protestantism has grown very rapidly, especially among the upper classes.

Issues of Equality/Inequality

El Salvador has a tradition of economic and social inequality and political authoritarianism. The middle class is very small and there are extreme contrasts between rich and poor. In the past, changes in the system have usually been accomplished via revolution or military coup. The culture of machismo is very evident. Women may be able to fight side by side with their men in the war, but when they return home, they lose that level of equality.

▶ BUSINESS PRACTICES

Punctuality, Appointments, and Local Time

- Business hours are generally 8:00 A.M. to noon and 1:00 to 6:00 P.M., Monday through Friday. Many businesses are also open 8:00 A.M. to noon on Saturday.
- Punctuality, although not strictly practiced by Salvadorans, is appreciated in business circles and expected from foreigners.
- As in most of the world, Salvadorans write the day first, then the month, then the year (e.g., December 3, 2010 is written 3.12.10 or 3/12/10).
- Make appointments far in advance of your trip by telephone, and follow up by e-mail. Confirm appointments prior to your arrival.
- The best times to visit El Salvador are February through June and September through November. Common vacation times are the two weeks before and after Christmas and Easter, and the month of August. The rainy season lasts from May to October; expect rain every afternoon. This season also tends to be warmer and more humid than the dry season.
- Local time is six hours behind Greenwich Mean Time (G.M.T. − 6); this is one hour behind U.S. Eastern Standard Time (E.S.T. − 1). El Salvador does not observe daylight saving time.

Negotiating

- Business is conducted only after a relationship of trust has been established. Spend time forming a friendship before switching to business conversations.

- Negotiations tend to proceed at a much slower pace than in Europe or North America. Be calm and patient with any delays. Several trips may be necessary to complete a transaction.
- Contacts are very important in establishing business relationships. They can be found through embassies, banks, shipping corporations, legal firms, and so forth.
- Be careful not to use the term "Americans" to refer to citizens of the USA. Central and South Americans—in fact, all Latin Americans are also Americans—and they are sensitive to U.S. executives monopolizing the term.
- Salvadorans tend to speak softly. Match your volume to that of your Salvadoran counterpart.
- Personal honor and saving face are very important to people in El Salvador. Therefore, never criticize or embarrass someone in public.
- Although the situation is changing, there are not many women in upper levels of business in El Salvador. A visiting businesswoman should act professionally, be exceedingly competent, and convey that she is representing her company.
- Business is discussed in an office or over a meal. It is not discussed around family or in most social situations.

Business Entertaining
- If you are invited to a Salvadoran home, be sure to compliment the hostess (and her cook) on the food and gracious hospitality.
- Good topics of conversation are sports, family, work, and El Salvador's natural beauty.
- Topics to avoid include political unrest, violence, religion, and the United States of America's intervention in Latin America. Remember that El Salvador has gone through twelve years of civil war, and emotions still run high.
- The main meal of the day is at noon. This will probably include black beans, tortillas or meat, and fruit and vegetables.
- The specialty dish of El Salvador is the *pupusa*, a small corn tortilla filled with soft white cheese, pork, or beans.

- In a private home, each person serves himself or herself. It is rude to take food and leave it on your plate uneaten.

▶ PROTOCOL

Greetings
- Men shake hands with each other in greeting. Women will often pat each other on the right forearm or shoulder instead of shaking hands. Women who are close may hug or kiss each other on the cheek. Sometimes only a nod of the head is given.
- While Salvadoran men are willing to shake hands with women, the woman must first extend her hand. Foreign men should wait for a Salvadoran woman to extend her hand.
- Only Salvadorans familiar with North American habits will shake hands with a firm grip. Do not be surprised to receive a limp handshake; adjust your grip. Salvadoran handshakes may also last longer than the brief handshakes common in North America.
- At parties and gatherings, it is customary to greet and shake hands with everyone in the room individually.
- Keep the vocal component of your greeting soft. Many Salvadorans dislike loud people.

Titles/Forms of Address
- Most people you meet should be addressed by their title or by their surname.
- When a person has a title, it is important to use it. Usually the title alone (without the surname) is preferred. A Ph.D or a physician is called "Doctor." Teachers prefer the title *Profesor*, while engineers go by *Ingeniero*, architects are *Arquitecto*, and lawyers are *Abogado*.
- For further information on the proper titles and forms of address in El Salvador, please consult Appendix A.

Gestures
- The Salvadoran people converse at a closer distance than do North Americans or northern Europeans. Restrain yourself from trying

to back away; a Salvadoran will probably step forward and close up the distance.

- Because so many Salvadorans have spent time in the United States of America, most U.S. gestures are recognized.
- It is considered impolite to point your finger at anyone.
- To beckon someone over, extend the arm and wriggle the fingers with the palm down. Only summon close friends with this gesture.

Gifts

- If invited to a Salvadoran home, it is appropriate to bring a gift of candy or flowers.
- Avoid giving white flowers, which are associated with funerals.
- For more guidelines on gift giving, visit *www.kissboworshake hands.com.*

Dress

- For business, men should wear a conservative, lightweight suit. Women are seen in suits, but not as often as skirts and blouses, or dresses.
- For casual situations, men should wear pants and a shirt in cities and a sweater in the cooler highlands. Women should wear a skirt and blouse. Short pants and jeans are not appropriate; women in revealing clothing may offend some people.

Cultural Note

During the civil unrest of the 1980s, hundreds of thousands of Salvadorans fled to the USA. Since the U.S. government was then publicly aiding the government of El Salvador, most Salvadoran refugees were denied asylum. This gave rise to the sanctuary movement, in which a network of U.S. churches and synagogues sheltered Salvadoran refugees, hiding them from U.S. immigration authorities. Today, there may be as many as 1 million Salvadorans living—legally or otherwise—in the USA.

Guatemala

Republic of Guatemala
Local long form: Republica de Guatemala

Cultural Note

The resplendently plumed quetzal bird is the national symbol of Guatemala. Its name is used for the county's currency as well as its second largest city. However, due to widespread environmental devastation, it is difficult to see a live quetzal in the wild. Aside from a few reserves, most of the mountain forests which were the quetzal's habitat have been decimated.

▶ WHAT'S YOUR CULTURAL IQ?

1. Which civilization achieved supremacy in what would become Guatemala and southern Mexico around 800 B.C.?
   a. The Olmecs
   b. The Mayans
   c. The Toltecs
   ANSWER: a. The Olmecs were the first identifiable civilization that ruled Guatemala prior to the Mayans. After the great Mayan cities were mysteriously vacated in approximately A.D. 900, the Toltecs were one of their successors.

2. TRUE or FALSE? Two Nobel Prizes have been awarded to Guatemalans.
   ANSWER: TRUE. The 1967 Nobel Prize for literature was awarded to Miguel Ángel Asturias, while the 1993 Nobel Peace Prize went to Rigoberta Menchú Tum.

3. TRUE or FALSE? The Guatemalan civil war was the longest-running insurgency in Central America in the twentieth century.
   ANSWER: TRUE. By the time a treaty was signed in 1996, the war had lasted thirty-six years.

▶ TIPS ON DOING BUSINESS IN GUATEMALA

- The inhabitants of Guatemala refer to themselves as *guatemaltecos.*
- In Guatemala—as elsewhere in Latin America—successful business relationships hinge on friendly social relationships. Guatemalan decision-makers are free to base their decisions on gut instincts. If they dislike you—or even if you just made a poor first impression—they may not do business with you.
- Unlike members of the Latin upper class elsewhere, Guatemalan executives tend to be open and blunt-spoken. Also, foreigners are frequently surprised at the accessibility of the decision-makers. Even high-ranking leaders in business and government tend to be willing to see foreign salespeople.
- Rather than establishing joint ventures in Guatemala (a highly complex process), many firms prefer to find a local distributor. Another popular method is to set up a franchise.
- Price is the single most important factor in a purchasing decision. After sale service is also a high priority. Guatemala is a small market, and a negative reputation (especially for such things as service) spreads quickly.

▶ COUNTRY BACKGROUND

Demographics

With more than 12 million inhabitants (2006 estimate), Guatemala is the most populous country in Central America (excluding Mexico, which is usually considered part of North America). The population is approximately 55 percent Ladino (mestizo, which is Amerindian and European mixed) and 43 percent Amerindian (or predominantly Amerindian). The remaining 2 percent includes whites, blacks, and a substantial Chinese population.

History

Guatemala was home to the Mayan people, who developed a highly advanced civilization. In 1519, Hernando (Hernán) Cortés led the first European expedition to subdue Mexico. A lieutenant of Cortés, Pedro de Alvarado, made the first Spanish inroads into Guatemala in 1524.

Independence from Spain was declared in 1821; in 1823, representatives of the five Central American states (Guatemala, Honduras, El Salvador, Nicaragua, and Costa Rica) founded the United Provinces of Central America, independent from Mexico.

Following years of internecine fighting, the United Provinces of Central America was dissolved in 1838. Guatemala became a solitary independent state, led by Rafael Carrera. A semiliterate mestizo farmer, Carrera seized power during an Amerindian uprising. He remained dictator until 1865, and undid all the reforms enacted by the leaders of the United Provinces.

Justo Rufino Barrios, hailed as the "Great Reformer," became president in 1873. He encouraged European immigration, coffee growing, and reduced the power of the Catholic Church. He died in 1885 while trying to forcibly reunite the United Provinces.

Manuel Estrada Cabrera came to power in 1898 in a rigged election for the presidency. He managed to hold on to power until 1920. It was Cabrera who gave huge concessions to the foreign plantation owners, especially the United Fruit Company. He was ousted in a bloody coup in 1920.

Juan José Arévalo was elected president in 1944. Calling himself a "Spiritual Socialist," he enacted reforms and granted political liberties. He also survived twenty-five coup attempts by Conservative forces during his six-year term in office!

Colonel Jacobo Arbenz Gúzman was elected president in 1951. He continued Arévalo's reforms, including the expropriation of land from foreign owners, such as the United Fruit Company. Angered, the United States of America supported a 1954 coup to overthrow him. The conservative oligarchy took power. There would not be free and fair elections in Guatemala until the 1990s.

After 1960, guerrilla movements began to grow in force, finally erupting into full-scale terrorist activities concentrated in Guatemala City. Many leading political figures, including the U.S. ambassador, were killed. By 1966, Guatemalan military and death squads begin to make thousands of Guatemalan citizens "disappear."

General Efraín Ríos Montt seized power in 1982. His sixteen-month dictatorship was marked by a scorched-earth campaign against rebels. His ruthlessness restored a measure of order, and was popular with the oligarchy. He seized power a second time in 1989.

Jorge Serrano was elected president in 1991. His inauguration marked the first time in fifty-one years that one freely elected civilian government followed another in Guatemala. In 1993, faced with public unrest and official corruption, Serrano dissolved the Congress and Supreme Court. His attempt to seize dictatorial powers failed, and he was forced to flee into exile.

In 1992 the Nobel Peace Prize was awarded to Rigoberta Menchú Tum for her work with Guatemala's Mayan Indians. In 1996, after five years of negotiations, President Alvaro Arzu signed a peace treaty with URNG guerrilla front leader Rolando Moran and Amerindian peace activist Rigoberta Menchú. This marked the official end to Guatemala's thirty-six-year civil war.

In December of 2003, President Óscar Berger Perdomo won a run-off election.

Type of Government

Guatemala has had a difficult political history since its independence from Spain in 1821. It has seen dictators, revolutions, and violent transfers of power. Since 1986, however, the country has been under civilian rule. The Republic of Guatemala has a unicameral legislative house, called the Congress of the Republic. The president is both chief of state and head of the government.

Voting is compulsory for all literate persons in Guatemala over the age of eighteen.

For current government information, check with the Embassy of Guatemala at *www.guatemala-embassy.org*.

Language

Spanish is the official language. Many Amerindian languages and dialects are used in the interior of the country. Not all are mutually intelligible. Ethnologue, at *www.ethnologue.com*, has identified fifty-six separate languages in Guatemala, two of which are extinct.

The Guatemalan View

Guatemala has no official religion. Until the 1950s the majority of the people were Roman Catholic. Recently, Evangelical Protestantism has made the greatest number of converts amongst a traditionally Catholic population. Estimates show that a quarter of Guatemalans are now Protestants. Evangelical Protestants have even been elected president of Guatemala. Televangelists have also become popular.

The Guatemalan ruling elite has come to embrace the "prosperity theology" of some Neo- Pentecostal sects. As elements of the Catholic Church became associated with the betterment of the poor, Catholicism lost popularity among the wealthy. (Indeed, those Catholics whose "liberation theology" allied them with guerrillas came to be considered enemies of the state.). Some of Guatemala's Amerindians retain their traditional religious beliefs. In its long civil war, Guatemalans have suffered enough to acquire a sense of fatalism and helplessness.

Cultural Note

Precise population figures are impossible to determine, and reports of the proportion of Indians are often politically motivated. Guatemalan officials state that Amerindians now constitute less than half the population. On the other hand, supporters of Amerindian movements estimate that as many as 70 percent of Guatemalans are indigenous.

It is clear that Amerindians are demanding a greater voice in decision-making. The issues in dispute include land reform and more cultural recognition on behalf of the Amerindians. There is no unanimity among the leaders on what to call themselves; many accept the traditional term *indígena* (indigenous person). Others prefer the term *Maya*, despite the fact that Guatemala was home to many tribes; the Mayans were simply the best-known Amerindian people.

The old term *indio* (Indian) is now generally considered insulting.

The economy is agricultural. The main crops (which are also exported) are sugar cane, corn, bananas, coffee, beans, and livestock.

☑ Know Before You Go

Guatemala is subject to violent earthquakes and volcanic eruptions. The country's Caribbean coast is vulnerable to hurricanes and tropical storms. Mudslides often follow heavy rains.

The history of Guatemala's various capitals shows the country's propensity for natural disasters. The first capital of Guatemala was Santiago de los Caballeros de Guatemala. Founded in 1527, it was destroyed by mudslides in 1543. (It was later rebuilt under the name Ciudad Vieja.) Next, nearby Antigua became the capital, until it was leveled by an earthquake in 1773. The current capital, Guatemala City, was founded in 1776. While it has endured its share of disasters, it has survived.

Street crime remains a problem. As a result of years of civil war, Guatemala is awash with weapons. Not only does this mean that criminals are liable to be armed, but there have been a substantial number of land mines in the countryside. Although Guatemala tried to clear all land mines and unexploded ordnance by 2004, persons traveling in areas that were planted with mines should use extreme caution.

Guatemala is a major transit country for drug smuggling.

▶ CULTURAL ORIENTATION

Cognitive Styles: How Guatemalans Organize and Process Information

Guatemalans love to converse. Foreigners can easily construe the acceptance of information by Guatemalans where no such acceptance exists. Guatemalans process information subjectively and associatively rather than objectively or abstractively. They look at the particulars of each situation, rather than appeal to a rule or law to solve problems.

Negotiation Strategies: What Guatemalans Accept as Evidence

Subjective feelings are much more important than objective facts in determining the truth. There is some faith in the ideology of the Church (Protestant and Catholic) in providing the truth, but Guatemalans are more apt to trust in the ideology of their ethnic heritage.

Value Systems: The Basis for Behavior

The value systems of the indigenous Indians are very different from those of the ruling class.

Locus of Decision-Making

The individual is responsible for his or her decisions, but these must be viewed in the context of the needs of the family, group, and organization. In Guatemala, "friends do things for friends"—thus it is necessary to develop friendships with business associates. In the workplace, your ability to get along with colleagues can be more important than your expertise.

Sociologists have proposed that Guatemala has one of the highest scores in terms of power/distance in Latin America. This translates into a large gap between authoritarian figures and their subordinates. Not surprisingly, economic power (in the form of business ownership) in Guatemala is concentrated in less than 1 percent of the population.

Sources of Anxiety Reduction

Wealth and family ties give the individual status and security. Trust and loyalty are centered on close kin. The Catholic Church has little influence in the government, but its precepts permeate the population and give structure to life. Often, it seems more important to make a pronouncement than to actually carry out the action. Progress in any endeavor takes a long time, which protects those who are threatened by change.

Guatemala has been ranked as having the lowest score in Latin America for individuality. This indicates a highly collectivist culture in which loyalty to one's group is paramount.

Issues of Equality/Inequality

Deep-seated social, economic, and political inequality exists, particularly between the mestizos and the Mayans. These ethnic relations have been changing and are dynamic, ranging from cordial and tolerant to open hostility and violence. Changes in the political system are often made by revolution or military coups. Women are still considered subordinate (they did not receive the right to vote until 1945, and under current law, only women may be charged with adultery).

▶ BUSINESS PRACTICES

Punctuality, Appointments, and Local Time

- Business hours are generally 8:00 A.M. to noon and 2:00 to 6:00 P.M., Monday through Friday.

- Punctuality, although not strictly adhered to in daily living, is expected from foreigners and in business situations.
- There are many Asian-owned manufacturing companies in Guatemala. A company that runs along Asian management lines will consider punctuality extremely important.
- Guatemalans, like many Europeans and South Americans, write the day first, then the month, then the year (e.g., December 3, 2010, is written 3.12.10 or 3/12/10).
- Make appointments as far in advance by telephone or e-mail.
- The best times to visit Guatemala are February through July and September through November. Common vacation times are the two weeks before and after Christmas and Easter, Independence Day (September 15), and the month of August.
- For a list of the official Guatemala holidays, visit *kissboworshake hands.com*.
- Local time in Guatemala is six hours behind Greenwich Mean Time (G.M.T. − 6); Guatemala is in the same time zone as U.S. Central Standard Time (E.S.T. − 1).

Negotiating

- Contracts are done among Guatemalans only after a relationship has been established. Spend time forming a friendship before jumping into business discussions. Business tends to take place at a slower pace than in Europe or North America. Be patient with delays. Several trips may be necessary to accomplish a transaction.
- There is a strong sense of personal honor on the part of the Guatemalan businessperson. Therefore, do not criticize a person in public or do anything that will cause him or her embarrassment.
- The majority of Guatemalan *maquiladoras* (manufacturing plants) are Asian-owned (primarily by South Koreans). Among Asians (as among Guatemalans), it is very important to avoid humiliating a person in public.
- Business is discussed in an office or over a meal in a restaurant. It is not discussed in a home or around family.
- Guatemalans find loud voices annoying. Speak in soft, well-modulated tones (especially in public).

- Contacts are very important in establishing business relationships. Your embassy may have a foreign commercial service officer who can provide you with contacts in your industry segment. Banks, accounting or legal firms, shipping and export corporations can also expand your network.
- Women executives are still the exception in Guatemala. Visiting businesswomen should act extremely professional and convey that they are representing their company, rather than speaking for themselves personally.

Business Entertaining

- Business breakfasts or lunches are preferred to dinners.
- An invitation to a Guatemalan home is offered for the purpose of getting to know you personally. This is not the time to discuss work. Spouses are usually invited to such gatherings. Good topics of conversation are Guatemalan tourist sites, your family, hobbies, travel, and so forth. Topics to avoid include political unrest and violence.
- If you speak to a married couple, the man will generally be the one who will converse or answer your questions.
- The main meal of the day is eaten at noon. This will probably include black beans, tortillas or meat, and fruit and vegetables.
- Meals are eaten "family style," with each person serving herself or himself. It is rude to take food and leave it on your plate uneaten.

Cultural Note

Do not be surprised if some Guatemalans claim that the military is defending Guatemala's "territorial integrity" against incursion from neighboring Central American nations. It is true, however, that Guatemala has Latin America's longest-running guerrilla opposition. Neither of these topics are appropriate dinner conversation.

⊚ PROTOCOL

Greetings

- Men always shake hands when greeting. Women sometimes shake hands with men; this is done at the woman's discretion.

- The handshake is usually accompanied by a verbal greeting, such as ¡Buenos días! (good morning/day), ¡Buenas tardes! (good afternoon), or ¡Buenas noches! (good evening).
- Do not expect firm grips when shaking hands; if you can, modify your own handshake to mirror your Guatemalan associate's.
- Close male friends may hug or pat each other on the back in greeting. Women will often pat your right forearm or shoulder instead of shaking hands. If they are close friends, they may hug or kiss each other on the cheek.
- At parties or business gatherings, it is customary to greet and shake hands with everyone in the room.

Titles/Forms of Address
- Most people you meet should be addressed by their title alone, without their surname.
- Traditionally, only children, family members, and close friends address each other by their first names.
- Younger businesspeople will quickly move to a first-name basis with their peers.

Gestures
- Guatemalans wave goodbye using a gesture that looks like someone fanning themselves: hand raised, palm toward the body, and a wave of the fingers back and forth, with the fingers together as if encased in a mitten.
- To beckon someone, extend your arm (palm down) and make a slight scooping motion toward your body (more with the fingers than the wrist).
- The "fig" gesture (thumb-tip protruding from between the fingers of a closed fist) is considered obscene in Guatemala. (However, in some parts of South America it is considered a "good luck" gesture.)
- The "okay" sign (thumb and forefinger forming a circle) is considered obscene.
- Make eye contact while speaking with Guatemalans.

Gifts

- If invited to a home, it is appropriate to bring flowers or candy, and something for the children.
- Always take a more personal gift with you after an initial visit.
- Do not bring white flowers; they are reserved for funerals.
- If you will be returning to Guatemala, you may ask your counterpart if there is something that you can bring from your home country.
- For further guidelines on gift giving, visit *www.kissboworshake hands.com.*

Cultural Note

Remember that Guatemala is in a tectonically active zone, with frequent earthquakes and occasional volcanoes. Easily breakable gifts may not be the best choice.

Dress

- For business, a lightweight suit is appropriate for men; women should wear a suit, dress, or skirt and blouse.
- When dressing casually, men should wear pants and a shirt in cities and a sweater in the cooler highlands; women should wear a skirt and blouse. Short pants and jeans are not appropriate for cities and more rural areas. Women in pants are becoming more common, but still may offend some people.

Cultural Note

Military clothing is illegal; it can neither be worn nor brought into the country.

Honduras

Republic of Honduras
Local short form: Honduras
Local long form: Republica de Honduras

Cultural Note

During the 1980s, anti-Communist Honduras was seen as a pivotal outpost of stability in Central America. Consequently, Honduras was the recipient of massive financial and military aid from the United States of America. Since 1990, Honduras has tried to reduce its dependence on the USA by encouraging investments from other nations with tax advantages and cheap labor. A large number of foreign-owned manufacturing plants *(maquiladoras)* have been built, with owners in Hong Kong, Singapore, Taiwan, and especially South Korea.

▶ WHAT'S YOUR CULTURAL IQ?

1. Of the many Amerindian groups of Honduras, the Lenca were the only tribe to mount a serious offense against the Spanish. TRUE OR FALSE: Modern Hondurans honored the Lenca chief Lempira by naming their national currency after him.
   ANSWER: TRUE. Chief Lempira led 30,000 Lenca warriors against the Spanish in 1537. Unable to defeat him in battle, the Spanish seized and executed Lempira while under a flag of truce. By 1539, the Spanish had suppressed the Lenca revolt.

2. U.S. citizen Sam (the Banana Man) Zemurray is considered the man responsible for turning Honduras into the archetype of a banana republic. Zemurray did more than buy land to grow bananas—he deposed Honduran governments at will. TRUE OR FALSE: Zemurray hired a U.S. mercenary with the unlikely name of General Lee Christmas to persuade recalcitrant Honduran politicians.
   ANSWER: TRUE. Lee Christmas even became commander in chief of the Honduran Army.

3. Competition for control of the banana market was fierce. Which company eventually won out to become the leading banana producer in Honduras?

a Sam Zemurray's Cuyamel Fruit Company
b The United Fruit Company (which became United Brands)
c The Vaccaro Brothers (which became Standard Fruit)

ANSWER: b. United Fruit became the leader after buying out Zemurray's company in 1929. This made United Fruit the primary target during the 1954 general strike that united Hondurans against the foreign corporations which all but ran their country. Coffee has since replaced bananas as Honduras' chief agricultural export.

▶ TIPS ON DOING BUSINESS IN HONDURAS

- Hondurans are status conscious. At least one member of the negotiating team should be from senior management. Emphasize qualifications, titles, degrees, etc.—stay in good hotels, and eat at fine restaurants.
- If you work in Central America, be aware that Honduras has had antagonistic relations with its neighbors. In 1969, Honduras fought a short war with neighboring El Salvador. It became known as the Soccer War because the precipitating incident was an attack on Honduran soccer fans at a World Cup qualifying game in San Salvador. However, the actual cause was the influx of Salvadoran immigrants living and working in Honduras. Tiny El Salvador is overpopulated, while large Honduras has a much lower population density. But both countries are very poor, and Hondurans perceived illegal Salvadoran immigrants as stealing jobs and vital resources from Hondurans. The fighting ended within 100 hours, but the two countries did not sign a peace treaty until 1980.
- While Honduran law does not require that a foreign firm use a local agent, hiring one is recommended. However, be judicious because Honduran representatives of foreign companies often sell products made by competitors. Also, if things do not work out with your agent, it can be difficult to terminate him or her.
- Price remains the primary motivator for purchases, but Honduran consumers also list customer service as important. The lack

of reliable local service will impact your sales. This is hinged to the perception that once a product is purchased, it can not be returned.

- As one of the poorest countries in the Western Hemisphere, Honduras is hoping for expanded trade privileges under the Enhanced Caribbean Basin Initiative and the Free Trade Zone of the Americas. Growth remains dependent on the economy of its major trading partners, on commodity prices (particularly coffee), and on the reduction of Honduras' high crime rate.

▶ COUNTRY BACKGROUND

Demographics

The population of Honduras is over 7.3 million (2006 estimate). The ethnic makeup is 90 percent mestizo (a mixture of Indian and European heritage), 7 percent Indian, 2 percent black, and 1 percent white. There is a small population of Arabs and Lebanese, who are disproportionately represented in Honduran business.

Honduras has the highest rate of deaths due to AIDS in Central America. This results in lowered life expectancy and higher infant mortality rates.

History

The Mayan Indians achieved an advanced level of civilization in Honduras. But the Mayan empire had passed its peak before the arrival of Europeans. Christopher Columbus arrived in Honduras in 1502, but no Spanish outpost was immediately established.

The Spanish found their first permanent outpost in 1525 at Trujillo. It became the first capital of Honduras, but it was hot and malaria-ridden.

In 1537, the Spanish established a new capital at Comayagua in the cooler interior highlands. In the same year, 30,000 Lenca warriors nearly drove the Spanish out of Honduras. The Lenca are the only Amerindian tribe to mount an effective opposition to the Spanish.

Subsequently, control of Central America (including Honduras) was centralized in Guatemala by the Spanish Crown.

Both gold and silver were discovered near Tegucigalpa in the 1570s. Until the ore ran out, Honduras was the wealthiest nation in Central America. Amerindians were enslaved on a massive scale to work the mines and plantations.

The Mexican Revolution of 1821 eliminated Spanish authority in the region. Honduras (along with the rest of Central America) declared its independence from Spain. The new Mexican empire claimed sovereignty over all of Central America, but Mexican troops never reached as far south as Honduras.

In 1823, Honduras joined the new Central American Federation, which was led by a Honduran, General Francisco Morazán. But the federation suffered factional disputes and soon dissolved. Honduras declared its independence on November 5, 1938. Honduras became one of the five independent successor states of the federation.

Cultural Note

Honduras's capital and largest city is Tegucigalpa (colloquially known as *Tegus*, pronounced "TEY-goose"). Many Honduran corporations have their offices in Tegucigalpa. However, Honduras' boom town is its second largest city, San Pedro Sula. Before Hurricane Mitch in 1998, San Pedro Sula was the fastest-growing city in Central America.

The United Kingdom ceded the island of Roatan (formerly Ruatan) to Honduras in 1860. U.S. mercenary leader William Walker, who had previously conquered Nicaragua, tried to capitalize on the situation by leading the English-speaking residents of Roatan against Honduras. When this scheme was thwarted by British warships, Walker decided to invade the Honduran mainland instead. He landed his small force of men at Trujillo and captured the local fort, but British marines forced Walker to surrender. The British turned Walker over to the Hondurans, who executed him.

Honduras became a major exporter of bananas in 1910, when Sam (the Banana Man) Zemurray, a naturalized U.S. citizen, bought 15,000 acres of Honduran land near the Caribbean coast. The very next year, Zemurray helped to overthrow an unfriendly Liberal Honduran government. He then hired mercenary Lee Christmas to enforce his will. Lee Christmas later became commander in chief of the entire Honduran Army.

A general strike was called against the largest banana producer, the United Fruit Company, in 1954. Some concessions were granted, but the strike's greater significance was in the unified opposition of Central Americans to the foreign corporations that had controlled their economies for decades.

Type of Government

The Republic of Honduras is run by a president (who is both chief of state and head of the government), a Council of Ministers, and a unicameral National Congress. Voting is compulsory over the age of eighteen.

Since independence from Spain in 1821, Honduras has experienced great political instability. There have been nearly 300 civil wars, rebellions, and changes of government—almost half of them during this century. However, in comparison to the turbulence of its Central American neighbors, the political situation has been relatively stable.

For current government data, check with the Embassy of Honduras at *www.hondurasemb.org*.

Cultural Note
The name "Honduras" comes from the Spanish word *la hondura* (depth), which is a reference to the deep water off the country's Caribbean coast. The Hondurans refer to themselves as *hondureños*.

Language

Spanish is the official language, although several Amerindian dialects are also spoken in remote areas. Many Hondurans have a basic understanding of English, and it is widely understood in urban and tourist centers. A form of Creole English is the main language in many communities on the Caribbean coast, but this may be unintelligible to foreign English speakers.

Ethnologue.com has identified eleven distinct languages in Honduras, all of them still extant.

The Honduran View

The Roman Catholic Church has a strong cultural influence in Honduras, with 97 percent of the population following its teachings. Various Protestant sects account for the remainder.

Ever since the country's mines ran out 200 years ago, wealth has always come from outside Honduras. Although Hondurans love their beautiful country, many long to leave it. They often seek prosperity and security elsewhere.

A sign on the jail in Trujillo reads *"La Ley es Duro, pero es la Ley"* (The law is hard, but it is the law). This aphorism says much about the attitudes of average Hondurans toward their government. The law is seen as a harsh master from which there is neither appeal nor escape—rather than as an even-handed form of protection for every citizen. The upper classes may view the law differently.

Cultural Note

Honduras is one of the poorest and least-developed countries in Central America. However, the people are warm and hospitable. They are proud of their heritage and value the ties of the family. It is common to find an extended family of grandparents, uncles, aunts, and children all living in one house. Among working Hondurans, over 60 percent are engaged in agriculture.

☑ Know Before You Go

The greatest hazard for a visitor comes from erratic drivers and street crime. The prevalence of crime and corruption are a serious drawback to conducting business in Honduras.

Violent earthquakes, volcanoes, and mudslides occur periodically. The Caribbean coast of Honduras is particularly prone to hurricanes and tropical storms. In 1998, Hurricane Mitch devastated Honduras' second largest city, San Pedro Sula.

Unlike most of its neighbors, Honduras never planted antipersonnel mines on its territory. However, during the Nicaraguan civil war, combatants planted over 50,000 mines on both sides of the border. Since 1990, over 200 civilians have been injured by mines near the Honduras-Nicaragua border.

A 2001 survey reported no mines on the border between Honduras and El Salvador.

Along the Honduras–El Salvador border there are still some disputed areas, as well as in some small islands in the Caribbean. Law enforcement agencies report that Honduras is a transshipment point for illegal drugs.

▶ CULTURAL ORIENTATION

Cognitive Styles: How Hondurans Organize and Process Information

Honduras is a relatively open society that readily accepts change. Negotiations may take a long time to complete. Education is by rote, so information processing is subjective and associative. Hondurans become personally involved with all problems, seldom using universal rules or laws to make decisions.

Negotiation Strategies: What Hondurans Accept as Evidence

Subjective feelings are the primary source of truth, ameliorated by faith in the Church or the cultural heritage. Objective facts are seldom seen as a useful basis for the truth.

Value Systems: The Basis for Behavior

The pluralistic atmosphere of Honduran social and political life stems from a more homogeneous mestizo society, which developed without extensive, institutionalized slavery.

Locus of Decision-Making

People gain their identity from family lineage and their role in society, so the individual's capacity to make decisions is compromised by his or her need to satisfy family and social groups. A person's ability to maintain a harmonious group is more important than his or her expertise. A small elite group, mostly foreigners, control the majority of economic resources. They are relatively weak politically, because they have not formed a cohesive group.

Sources of Anxiety Reduction

The Catholic Church gives social structure to life through its precepts and holidays, though it is not a strong political force. A person's role in the social structure and the presence of a strong extended family gives him or her a sense of security. Hondurans are always busy, but progress is not necessarily the primary goal. This laid-back behavior helps to reduce anxiety.

Issues of Equality/Inequality

Honduras is the poorest country in Latin America. The homogeneity of the mestizo society only makes for a large, poor middle class, with the few rich above and the poorer Miskito Indians in the east at the bottom of the social ladder. Yet Hondurans feel they are all equal because each individual is unique, and there is an inherent trust in people because of the social interrelationships of extended families and friends. Machismo is strong, and there are clear and classic role differences between the sexes.

⦿ BUSINESS PRACTICES

Punctuality, Appointments, and Local Time

- Scheduled appointments may be delayed, and punctuality is not strictly adhered to in daily life. However, punctuality is expected of foreigners.
- Arrive about thirty minutes late for social events.
- In Honduras, as in many European and South American nations, it is customary to write the day first, then the month, then the year (e.g., December 3, 2010, is written 3.12.10 or 3/12/10).
- Personal relationships are extremely important. Be sure to make contacts through appropriate intermediaries.
- The best time to visit Honduras is between February and June. The rainy season lasts from May to November. December and August are popular vacation times.
- Meetings may take place at breakfast, lunch, or dinner. Let your counterpart suggest the time.
- For a list of the official holidays of Honduras, visit *www.kissbow orshakehands.com.*
- Honduras is six hours behind Greenwich Mean Time (G.M.T. – 6), which is the same as Central Standard Time in the USA (E.S.T. – 1).

Negotiating

- Business tends to take place at a much slower pace than in Europe or North America. Be calm and patient with delays. Several trips may be necessary to conclude a transaction.

- Personal friendships are vital to business in Honduras. Hondurans are looking for a long-term relationship based on mutual trust and reliability. It is important to spend time building a relationship before jumping into discussions. Plan to make repeated visits and maintain contact after your trips.
- Try to keep the same person as the lynchpin during all your negotiations. Much of the business relationship will be based on this personal friendship.
- Latin Americans respect the value of individual dignity and honor, regardless of social status or wealth. Never publicly criticize a Honduran, or do anything that would cause him or her humiliation.
- In their desire to please, Hondurans are likely to give you the answer they think you want to hear. Be careful how you phrase your questions. For example, a question such as "Does the market open at 8:00?" will probably be answered "yes," whether this is the truth or not, because this is the answer they think you want. Instead, phrase questions so that they require more detailed answers, such as "What time does this market open?"
- Remember to avoid saying "no" in public while in Honduras. "Maybe" or "we will see" generally means no.
- Because of Hondurans' desire to tell people what they want to hear, get all agreements in writing. A verbal agreement may have been given out of politeness and may not be considered binding.
- When negotiating, emphasize the trust and mutual compatibility of the two companies. Stress the benefits to the person and his or her family and pride. An argument based upon feelings and personal priorities will be more effective than the logical bottom line of a proposal. If there is a disagreement, do not expect a compromise, since this is seen as a show of weakness.
- Decisions are not made quickly. Indeed, snap decisions are suspect; take time before announcing a final decision, even if your mind is already made up.
- Include a margin for bargaining in your initial offer, but do not overinflate your prices. That will erode the level of trust people will have in you. Using powerful graphics will leave a strong impression after your presentation is over.

- Although the situation is changing, women in upper levels of management are an exception. A woman may face some initial lack of respect in Honduras. Since titles and position are valued, a businesswoman should emphasize her qualifications with the firm, and that she has the authority to make decisions for her company.
- Hondurans are proud of their heritage and their individuality. Therefore, be careful of sensitivities in referring to citizens of the United States of America as "Americans." That term applies to all North and Latin Americans.
- Do not be offended if another person is served before you in a line. Preference is given to the elderly and those with higher positions and social status.
- Never overly admire another's belongings. The owner may feel obligated to give them to you.
- Have business cards and other material printed in Spanish as well as your native language. Present your card to a Honduran with the Spanish side up.

Business Entertaining
- Good topics of conversation are Honduran tourist sites, your family and job at home, and sports (especially soccer, the national sport). Topics to avoid are local politics and unrest in Central America.
- The best times for business meetings are breakfast and lunch, the main meal of the day. If you are invited to a home or invited to a meal where spouses are also included, do not expect to discuss business. Instead, socialize and get to know the family. Dinner is eaten between 8:30 and 9:00 P.M. Arrive about thirty minutes late.
- Foreign businesswomen should never invite their male counterparts to a business dinner unless spouses also attend. For business lunches, eat at your hotel and have the bill added to your tab; otherwise your male guest will not want to let you pay.

⊙ PROTOCOL

Greetings
- Men shake hands in greeting.

- Women often pat each other on the right arm or shoulder. If they are close friends, they may hug or kiss each other on the cheek.
- Do not be surprised if handshakes are light, with a relatively weak grip; give the same in return.
- At parties it is customary to greet and shake hands with everyone in the room.

Gestures

- Several gestures are unique to this area. Placing a finger below the eye indicates caution. A hand below the elbow means that a person is stingy. "No" is indicated by waving the index finger. Joining one's hands together shows strong approval.
- Conversations take place at a much closer distance than may be considered comfortable in northern Europe or North America. Pulling away from your counterpart may be interpreted as rejection.
- Honduran men are warm and friendly and make a lot of physical contact. They often touch shoulders, or hold another's arm. To withdraw from such a contact is considered insulting.

Dress

- Business: Men should wear a conservative suit. Women should wear a suit, skirt, and blouse, or a dress. Honduran businessmen commonly wear a guayabera, which is a decorative shirt, rather than a shirt and tie.
- Casual: A light shirt and pants for men and a skirt and blouse for women may be worn in urban areas. Revealing clothing for women and shorts for either sex are not appropriate. Pants for women are not common, and may offend some locals.

Cultural Note

In the 1980s, revolutions in neighboring Nicaragua and El Salvador had wide-ranging effects on Honduras. To suppress leftist governments in these countries, the USA trained anti-Communist Salvadoran and Nicaraguan troops inside Honduras. This training of foreign troops brought in millions of U.S. dollars. Nevertheless, the Honduran people wanted the U.S. and foreign troops off their soil. This sentiment was so strong that Honduran president José Simeón Azcona del Hoyo was forced to ask the United States of America to leave.

Mexico

United Mexican States
Local long form: Estados Unidos Mexicanos

Cultural Note

Mexico remains a very Catholic country; every town and village has a patron saint.

Many Mexicans consider themselves *Guadalupeños,* a nickname for those who believe in the miracle of the Virgin of Guadalupe (the Virgin Mary). She appeared three times to a poor Aztec, Juan Diego, in 1513, and told him to build a church in Tepeyac, where the Aztec goddess Tonantín was worshipped. Today the basilica is visited by more than 1 million pilgrims annually, and images of the Virgin of Guadalupe are everywhere, a symbol of unity between the Aztec and Spanish cultures and of Mexican nationality.

▶ WHAT'S YOUR CULTURAL IQ?

1. Dictator and military leader Antonio López de Santa Anna was famous for:
   a. Losing the Texas War of Independence
   b. Losing the U.S.-Mexican War
   c. Selling a strip of Mexican territory so the United States of America could build a railroad
   d. Seizing the presidency of Mexico no less than eleven times!
   e. All of the above
   ANSWER: e. During Santa Anna's tenure, Mexico lost half its territory to the United States of America. His career was ended by Mexican outrage after he sold southern Arizona and New Mexico to the USA in the Gadsden Purchase.

2. The Mexican Revolution lasted from 1910 to 1920 and cost over 1 million Mexican lives. TRUE or FALSE: The United States of

America supported the rebel Mexican leaders Pancho Villa, Pascual Orozco, and Emiliano Zapata.

ANSWER: FALSE. The USA opposed the radical leaders. Although Villa and Zapata managed to occupy Mexico City, the U.S.-backed Constitutionalists eventually won.

3. Which of the following Mexican authors won a Nobel Prize for literature?
   a. Carlos Fuentes
   b. Jorge Ibargüengoitia
   c. Octavio Paz
   d. None of the above

ANSWER: c. Octavio Paz won the 1990 Nobel Prize for literature. His acceptance speech is available at *www.nobel.se/literature/laureates/1990/paz-speech.html.*

⊙ TIPS ON DOING BUSINESS IN MEXICO

- Elaborate, effusive courtesy is a characteristic of Mexican communications. This formal courtesy can conceal true feelings. It is quite possible for Mexicans to politely say one thing and do the opposite.
- Although the United States of America and Mexico are neighbors, their citizens have different attitudes toward eye contact. In the USA, someone who does not directly meet your gaze is often suspected of being untrustworthy. Mexicans find continued, intense eye contact to be aggressive and threatening. Mexican business executives expect intermittent eye contact.
- The family is the single most important institution in Mexico. Because of this, nepotism is an accepted practice. Mexican executives generally put a higher importance on the best interest of their families than on their place of employment.
- Mexico is the most populous Spanish-speaking nation in Latin America. Only Portuguese-speaking Brazil has more people (or a larger gross national product). This gives Mexico a position of cultural and political primacy throughout Hispanic America.
- Mexico has had a complex historical relationship with many other countries. Much of the southwestern USA was once part of

Mexico. After achieving independence from Spain, the Mexican empire claimed all of Central America down to the Panamanian border. For a brief time, Mexico ruled what is now Costa Rica, Nicaragua, Honduras, El Salvador, and Guatemala.

Cultural Note

The official name of Mexico—Estados Unidos Mexicanos—translates to "The United States of Mexico." Consequently, referring to the United States of America as simply "The United States" can cause confusion. Curiously, the polite Mexican term for a citizen of the United States of America is *norteamericano*, although Mexico itself is technically part of North America. Canadians are called *canadienses* to differentiate them from norteamericanos. The term *americanos*—Americans—is insufficient to designate citizens of the United States of America, as it can apply to anyone in North, Central, or South America.

◉ COUNTRY BACKGROUND

Demographics

The population of Mexico was estimated at 107 million in 2006. The ethnic composition of the country is approximately 60 percent mestizo (a mixture of Indian and European), 30 percent Amerindian, 9 percent white, and 1 percent other. Catholicism has a significant influence on Mexican culture.

The question of how many Amerindians (called indígenos) there are in Mexico is a politically-charged issue. The difference between mestizo and indígeno is often one of language and culture rather than genetics. Mexico's National Indigenous Institute (INI) recognizes less than 10 percent of Mexicans as indígenos, which they define as persons speaking an Amerindian language. However, many Mexicans who no longer speak an Amerindian language nevertheless consider themselves indígenos.

History

The origins of Mexican culture date back to the Mayan and Aztec Indians. Their empires were destroyed by the Spanish conquistadors (assisted by European diseases, superior military technology, and infighting amongst the Amerindian tribes), and Mexico came under colonial rule in 1521.

By the 1700s, Mexico had become the heart of the viceroyalty of New Spain, which encompassed all of Central America down to Panama. One advocate of independence was a parish priest from the Mexican town of Dolores. This priest, Father Miguel Hildalgo, issued a call for independence, known as "the Grito de Dolores" (the Cry from Dolores). Delivered on 16 September 1810, the Grito de Dolores became one of the most famous speeches in Mexican history. Father Hildago led a rebellion against the viceregal forces, but he was captured and executed in 1811. After eleven years of rebellion, Mexican independence was finally achieved in 1821. But the new nation became a monarchy, rather than a republic, angering many of the rebels. A defector from the Spanish viceregency, Colonel Agustín de Iturbide had himself inaugurated as the first emperor of Mexico in 1822. After just nine months in office, Iturbide was forced to abdicate by military leader Antonio López de Santa Anna.

The first Mexican Constitution was approved in 1824, establishing the Republic of Mexico. Guadalupe Victoria became Mexico's first president.

Santa Anna seized the presidency of Mexico in 1833. During the next twenty-two years, Santa Anna occupied the presidency no less than eleven separate times.

In 1836, Texas successfully achieved independence from Mexico, following the defeat of Santa Anna's forces at the Battle of San Jacinto.

When Mexico protested the admission of Texas into the United States of America, the U.S. Congress declared war. By 1848, Mexico's forces were defeated, and the USA annexed the Mexican territory west of Texas. This annexed territory now forms all or part of the states of California, Nevada, Utah, Colorado, Arizona, and New Mexico.

In 1862, Napoleon III of France decided to conquer all of Mexico. Napoleon restored the Mexican monarchy and placed Archduke Maximilian of Austria on the throne. Following the end of the U.S. Civil War, the United States of America was in position to demand the removal of French forces from Mexico under the Monroe Doctrine. The French troops left, but Maximilian refused to abdicate.

Mexican forces under Benito Juárez defeated the remaining imperial forces in May 1867, and Maximilian was executed by firing squad the next month.

In 1876, Porfirio Díaz first came to power in Mexico. For the next thirty-four years, he ruled Mexico either directly as president or indirectly through his proxies. This period was known as the "Porfiriato."

Opposition to the dictatorship of the Porfiriato erupted into strikes in 1910. Rebel leaders Pancho Villa, Pascual Orozco, and Emiliano Zapata all led factions that fought the government. Eventually, Mexico was divided into two camps: the Constitutionalists and the Radicals. Slowly, the Constitutionalists gained the upper hand. By the time the rebellion ceased in 1920, the decade-long revolution had cost the lives of almost one out of every eight Mexicans.

As Mexico's economy continued to grow after World War II, so did the country's population. The population doubled, and the poor left their small farms and moved to the cities. During the presidency from 1988 to 1994 of a Harvard-educated technocrat, Carlos Salinas de Gortari, the Mexican economy improved. Salinas signed the North American Free Trade Agreement (NAFTA), which is known in Mexico as *Tratado de Libre Comercio (TLC)*.

Vicente Fox Quesada was elected president in 2000, ending seventy-one years of national dominance by the PRI (Institutional Revolutionary Party). The July 2006 election was so close, the outcome was disputed. As of this writing, no official winner had been declared.

Type of Government

The United States of Mexico—as Mexico is officially known—is a federal republic. The head of the government is the president, who is elected to a six-year term and cannot be re-elected. During the seventy-one-year rule of the Partido Revolucionario Institucional (PRI) Party, presidents were generally able to handpick their successors. Whether this will continue remains to be seen.

There is a bicameral legislature with a Senate and a Chamber of Deputies, plus a judicial Supreme Court.

For current government data, check with the Embassy of Mexico at *www.embassyofmexico.org*.

Language

Spanish is the official language of Mexico, although ethnologue
.com also lists over 200 Amerindian languages.

In the past, French was the foreign language of choice of the upper
class. English is now the most popular second language, and an English speaker is usually near at hand in most multinational firms.

Cultural Note

Mexicans often speak in a flowery, obsequious manner that should not be interpreted literally.
For example, the phrase *para servirle* literally means "I am here to serve you." Yet a Mexican
can utter such a phrase and have no intention of being helpful at all. Similarly, the response
Mándeme means "Command me"—and can be said by someone who will be as obstructive
as possible.

The Mexican View

There is no official religion in Mexico, but almost 90 percent of
Mexicans are Roman Catholic. Protestants account for around 5 percent, and their percentage is growing—notably among the Evangelical sects.

NAFTA and privatization have changed everyday life in Mexico,
at least for consumers and nonagricultural workers. For example,
after decades of protectionism, foreign consumer goods are readily
available in Mexico.

Young Mexican executives are generally familiar with foreign
business practices and online communications. Most Mexicans are
highly skeptical of authority figures. Politicians and police alike are
often seen as corrupt and self-serving. Outlaws who are honest about
their criminality are sometimes glamorized, especially narcotics traf-
fickers. The Mexican equivalent of gangsta rap is the *narcocorrido*—a
form of popular song about the macho exploits of narcotics traffick-
ers. Translated from the Spanish, one popular lyric goes:

Death does not frighten me, nor being locked up,
Prison is for men, and I am a tested fighting cock.

Mexico is one of the United States of America's most important trade partners. It is the third largest exporter to the USA, and its international trade products include oil exports, tourism, and the products of its many assembly plants (called *maquiladoras*).

☑ Know Before You Go

Currently, the greatest concern of foreign visitors in Mexico is street crime, up to and including kidnapping. Kidnappers range from highly organized groups who target specific individuals, to kidnappers-of-opportunity who grab random, affluent-looking targets.

Mexico City, with nearly 20 million inhabitants, is the second largest urban area in the world. Despite efforts to limit air pollution, the problems with air quality in Mexico City remain.

Mexico has numerous high-altitude sites. Altitude sickness can strike anyone, even if you have never experienced it before. There is no sure prevention except gradual acclimation to high elevation: once you get to 6,000 feet above sea level, spend at least two nights there. Repeat this acclimation period at each increase of 3,000 feet. Alcohol consumption tends to make the symptoms worse.

Sunburn is also a danger at high altitudes because there is less atmosphere to protect you from the sun.

⦿ CULTURAL ORIENTATION

Cognitive Styles: How Mexicans Organize and Process Information

In Mexico, information is readily accepted for purposes of discussion, but little movement in attitude is seen. Mexicans tend to become personally involved in each situation and look at the particulars rather than initially using a rule or law to solve problems.

Negotiation Strategies: What Mexicans Accept as Evidence

Subjective feelings generally form the basis for truth, and this can lead to the truth altering depending on perceptions and desires. Faith in the ideologies of the Catholic Church, though pervasive, does not greatly affect their perception of the truth. Those with a higher education more often use objective facts.

Value Systems: The Basis for Behavior

Mexico's long and unhappy history with the United States of America makes Mexicans suspicious of U.S. businesspeople—and, to a lesser extent, of foreigners from any industrialized country. The following three sections identify the Value System in the predominant culture—their methods of dividing right from wrong, good from evil, and so forth.

Locus of Decision-Making

The individual is responsible for his or her decisions, but the best interest of the family or group is a dominating factor. One must know a person before doing business with him or her, and the only way to know a person in Mexico is to know the family. Expertise is less important than how one fits into the group, so it is extremely important to cultivate personal relations with the right people in the right places.

Sources of Anxiety Reduction

It is one's role in the social structure and the presence of the extended family that give a sense of stability to life. However, families exert pressure on the behavior of their members. Group members are bound by intense friendship and personal relations, and commit themselves to assisting one another in case of need. This network of relatives, friends, and memberships is crucial to class affiliation and social mobility. All of these expect mutual support—a lifelong commitment.

Mexicans have been charted as risk-averse and resistant to change. Their societal norms have not varied significantly in the last decade.

Issues of Equality/Inequality

There are extreme contrasts between rich and poor, but Mexico has the largest upper middle class of all Latin American countries—all interrelated in one way or another. Machismo is very strong, and there is a general belief that if there is an opportunity for sex to occur, it will. Mexicans are also known for their endless variety of sexual double-entendres. Many innocuous Spanish terms have slang sexual meanings.

For women, femininity is stressed in dress, makeup, and behavior. Despite widespread machismo, most Mexicans believe that mothers are the central figure in every family.

⊚ BUSINESS PRACTICES

Punctuality, Appointments, and Local Time

- Business hours are generally 9:00 A.M. to 6:00 P.M., with lunch between 1:00 and 3:00 P.M., Monday through Friday.
- Punctuality, although admired, is not strictly adhered to in daily life. However, it is expected from foreigners and in business circles, so be on time for appointments—but bring some work in case your counterpart is late.
- Punctuality is not expected for parties, dinner invitations, and so forth. Be at least thirty minutes late when invited to a party at a Mexican home. In Mexico City, be at least one hour late; some guests will be two or even three hours late.
- Make appointments approximately two weeks prior to your arrival in Mexico by e-mail or phone, then reconfirm it a week before. Establish your contacts as high up in the organization as possible. Use a local *persona bien colocada* (well-connected person) to make introductions and contacts for you.
- Meetings may take place at breakfast, lunch, or dinner. Let your counterpart select which time.
- Mexico is six hours behind Greenwich Mean Time (G.M.T. − 6), or one hour behind U.S. Eastern Standard Time (E.S.T. − 1).

Negotiating

- The business atmosphere is friendly, gracious, and unhurried.
- The pace will tend to be slower than that of Canada, the United States of America or northern Europe. Decisions are made at top levels, with consultation at lower levels. This may take time. Be calm and patient with delays and build them into your expectations.
- Personal friendships are vital to business in Mexico. Mexicans look for long-term relationships based on mutual trust and reliability, or *personalismo*. It is important to spend time building

these relationships, as your friendship will mean more to your prospects than the multinational firm you represent. Plan to make repeated visits and maintain contact after your trips.

- Be warm and personal, yet retain your dignity, courtesy, and diplomacy. Your Mexican counterparts may initially seem vague, suspicious, and indirect. Overcome this with trust and goodwill.

- Mexicans highly value the individual dignity of a person, regardless of social standing or material wealth. It is important not to pull rank, publicly criticize anyone, or do anything that will cause an individual to be humiliated.

- Mexicans avoid saying "no." "Maybe" or "We will see" may actually mean "no." Get all agreements in writing, as the "yes" may have been said out of politeness and the agreement later reversed.

- When negotiating, emphasize the trust and mutual compatibility of the two companies. Stress the benefits to the person and his or her family and pride. This emotional approach may be more effective than the logical bottom line of a proposal.

- If there is a disagreement, do not overcompromise, because this would show weakness.

- Leave yourself a reasonable margin for negotiating in your prices.

- Use high-end, sharp visuals in your presentations.

- Although the situation is rapidly changing, there are still fewer women in upper levels of management than men. A woman should display her competence in a dignified manner, or she may face some initial lack of respect in Mexico.

- Mexicans are status conscious. At least one member of the negotiating team should be from higher-level management. Stay in prestigious hotels, eat at good restaurants, and mention major achievements (for example, advanced degrees from a prestigious university—if the topic arises).

- One major barrier in negotiations is the issue of financing the cost of foreign goods and services. Be prepared with some creative financing solutions.

- For the official holidays of Mexico, visit *www.kissboworshake hands.com*.

Business Entertaining

- The times for business meetings are breakfast or lunch, the main meal of the day. Business breakfasts are held at a guest's hotel and start at 8:00 or 8:30 A.M., and may last for up to two hours.
- If you are invited to a Mexican home, do not expect to discuss business. Instead, use this time for socializing. Dinner is never eaten before 8:30 P.M. Arrive about thirty minutes late.
- Good topics of conversation include Mexican sights and your family and job at home. Sports are also good topics: football (soccer), baseball, basketball, and bullfighting. Topics to stay away from include historically sensitive issues such as Mexico's territorial losses or the large numbers of Mexicans who work illegally in other countries, especially in the United States of America.
- It is customary for one person to pay the check for a group meal. This is often the oldest person in the group. It is good manners to haggle over paying the bill. Reciprocate by inviting the person out for another meal, insisting ahead of time that this will be your treat.
- You may be invited to a girl's fifteenth birthday party. This is called a *quinceañera*, and is an important occasion.
- It is not wise for foreign businesswomen to invite their counterparts to a business dinner unless other associates or spouses also attend. For business lunches, eat at your hotel and have the bill added to your tab. Otherwise men will resist having you pay.

▶ PROTOCOL

Greetings

- Men will shake hands in greeting. Women will often pat each other on the right forearm or shoulder instead of shaking hands. If they are close, they may hug or kiss each other on the cheek. Men may wait for women to initiate a handshake.
- Be prepared for a hug on the second or third meeting.
- At a party, give a slight nod to everyone as you enter the room. It is customary to greet and shake hands with each individual. Usually your host will introduce you. You are also expected to shake hands with each person when you leave.

Titles/Forms of Address

- Titles are very important in Mexico. Address a person directly by using his or her title only, such as *Profesor*. First names are used only by people on familiar terms. Wait for your counterpart to initiate this switch to first names.
- For further information on the proper titles and forms of address in Mexico, please consult Appendix A.

Gestures

- Conversations take place at a closer physical distance than what may be considered comfortable in the USA or northern Europe. Pulling away from your counterpart may be regarded as unfriendly—and your Mexican associate may step forward and close up the distance.
- Mexican men are warm and friendly and make a lot of physical contact. They often touch shoulders or hold another's arm. To withdraw from such a gesture is considered insulting.
- Mexicans may catch another's attention in public with a *psst-psst* sound. This is not considered rude.
- Men should avoid putting their hands in their pockets. Hands on your hips indicate that you are making a challenge.
- When indicating height, always use the index finger. Only the height of an animal is shown by using the whole hand.
- In a store, pay for purchases by placing the money in the cashier's hand, rather than on the counter.

Gifts

- Giving gifts to executives in a business context is not required at an initial meeting. However, small gifts, such as items with a company logo (for an early visit) or a bottle of wine or Scotch (on subsequent trips) are appreciated. If a gift of greater value is called for, desk clocks, finely made pens or gold cigarette lighters are good choices (smoking is still common in Mexico).
- Small electronics, like MP3 players loaded with your associate's favorite artist, or selections from prominent musicians in your country, make for a thoughtful gift. Make sure the electronic device was made in your country.

- Mexican secretaries expect gifts from foreign businesspeople. A government secretary who performs any service for you is generally given a token gift. For secretaries in the private sector, a more valuable gift should be given on a return visit.
- Gifts are not required from a dinner guest. An extension of thanks and a reciprocal invitation are considered sufficient. However, a gift will be happily accepted if offered. Good choices are candy, flowers (if sent ahead, impress upon the florist that the delivery must arrive early or on time), or local crafts from home.
- Regional viewpoints on the significance of specific flowers vary—check with your hosts or the local embassy to determine appropriate floral arrangements.
- Avoid giving gifts made of silver; it can be associated with trinkets sold to tourists in Mexico.
- Gifts of knives should be avoided in Latin America; they can symbolize the severing of a friendship.
- For more guidelines on gift giving, visit *www.kissboworshake hands.com*.

Cultural Note

Mexicans feel compelled to help someone who asks for assistance. If you become lost in Mexico City, asking for directions can easily become a group event. There are many stories of travelers who ask one person for help, and that individual consults with another Mejicano, who asks a cab driver, etc. The process is only resolved when everyone is satisfied that the lost innocent is safely on his or her way—often with a personal guide.

Dress

- For business, men should wear a conservative dark suit and tie; women should wear a suit, pantsuit, or dress.
- Pants and a light shirt are casual wear for men; women may wear a skirt or nice pants. Jeans are not considered appropriate unless they are tailored and well pressed. Revealing clothing for women and shorts for either sex are still sometimes viewed as inappropriate except at a resort. Men may wish to wear the traditional guayabera, a light shirt worn untucked.

Nicaragua

Republic of Nicaragua
Local short form: Nicaragua
Local long form: Republica de Nicaragua

Cultural Note

Nicaraguans have, without much success, tried to escape the overwhelming influence of the USA. For example, in 1909, leftist Nicaraguan dictator José Santos Zelaya entered into negotiations with the Japanese and the Germans to build a canal in Nicaragua. Not wanting competition against their Panama Canal, the USA helped conservative leaders take power. To keep pro-U.S. conservatives in power, U.S. Marines were stationed in Nicaragua from 1912 to 1933.

▶ WHAT'S YOUR CULTURAL IQ?

1. TRUE or FALSE? The name "Nicaragua" comes from an Amerindian leader who presided over his tribe's conversion to Catholicism in the 1500s.
   ANSWER: TRUE. A chief named Nicaro led the peaceful Amerindian population that lived around Lake Nicaragua.

2. Francisco Hernández de Córdoba established Nicaragua's first two Spanish cities in 1524. These two cities later become rival centers, vying for control of Nicaragua. Which two cities are they?
   a. Bluefields and Granada
   b. Granada and Managua
   c. Managua and León
   d. León and Granada
   ANSWER: d. The rivalry between León, center of the Liberals, and Granada, center of the Conservatives, was so intense that it broke out into civil war several times. A compromise was reached in 1857, when Managua was made the compromise capital. Unfortunately, Managua

is in a seismically active zone; it was severely damaged by earthquakes in 1931 and 1972. (Granada is the oldest city founded by the Spaniards in continental America.)

3. While the canal that links the Atlantic and Pacific Oceans was eventually built in Panama, Nicaragua was also considered as a possible site for a canal. TRUE or FALSE: The U.S. Congress voted for Panama because a Nicaraguan canal would have needed more costly digging of channels.
   ANSWER: FALSE. In 1902, the Congress voted against Nicaragua because they were afraid of Nicaragua's volcanoes. (Nicaragua's Mount Momotombo had a major eruption before the vote.) Actually, the Nicaraguan route would have needed less digging than Panama, not more. Most of the proposed Nicaraguan route used existing rivers and lakes, so only sixteen miles of channels needed to be excavated.

▶ TIPS ON DOING BUSINESS IN NICARAGUA

- Nicaraguans can be fiercely patriotic and somewhat confrontational. They dislike being mistaken for any of their neighbors—especially their prosperous neighbors to the south, the Costa Ricans.
- Nicaraguans are generally informal. Greetings and introductions are gracious, but not highly structured. The general attire also reflects the relaxed character of the people: casual attire, which is appropriate for Nicaragua's hot climate.
- Despite years of political upheaval, Nicaragua has a rich cultural life, spanning writing, art, and theater. Many of Nicaragua's writers have spent years away from their home country, either in exile or to seek broader opportunities. Poetry is especially popular— Nicaraguans often claim that their country has more poets (per capita) than any country in the world.
- Some Nicaraguans—especially the leftist members of the Sandinistas—are virulent anticapitalists. They oppose globalization in all its forms. They have reason to: foreign governments and companies have rarely benefited the Nicaraguan poor.
- Conversely, there are many Nicaraguans who have worked in other countries and are accustomed to foreign ways of doing business. The so-called *Nicas Ricas* (Rich Nicaraguans) earned

U.S. dollars in the Miami area, and constitute a good market for foreign consumer goods.

Cultural Note
The devastating Nicaraguan earthquake of December 1972 killed or injured 10,000, yet it is best remembered by U.S. citizens for the death of Pittsburgh Pirates baseball player Roberto Clemente. The Puerto Rican–born Clemente—the most famous Hispanic athlete of his generation—insisted upon flying to Managua in an overloaded DC-7 full of relief supplies, knowing that only his presence would ensure that the supplies would reach the poor. His plane crashed shortly after takeoff, and the supplies that did reach Managua went directly into the hands of Somoza's National Guard, who sold most of them at a profit.

▶ COUNTRY BACKGROUND

Demographics
Nicaragua's population of over 5.5 million (2006 estimate) is 69 percent mestizo (a mix of European and Indian), 17 percent European, 9 percent black, and 5 percent Amerindian.

History
The original inhabitants of Nicaragua were Amerindians; the coastal tribes were the first to encounter Europeans when Columbus landed in 1502. The Spanish explorer Francisco Hernández de Córdoba (after whom Nicaragua's currency is named) established settlements in 1523. However, full-scale colonization by Spain did not occur until the following century.

Most of Nicaragua eventually came under Spanish imperial rule. In 1821, Nicaragua became part of the United Provinces of Central America, which declared its independence from Spain. Between 1837 and 1838 the United Provinces of Central America broke up. Independent Nicaragua then experienced a period of instability and violence stemming from a rivalry between the Conservatives, based in Granada, and the Liberals, based in León.

Foreign influence—mostly from the USA and Britain—was strong in the new Nicaraguan state. Perhaps the biggest shock to both the Conservatives and the Liberals came in 1855, when a Tennessee adventurer named Walter Walker invaded Nicaragua with a mercenary army. Walker's "Phalanx of Immortals"—all fifty-eight of them—actually conquered the country, and Walker proclaimed himself president of Nicaragua. Neighboring Central American countries marched against him, and Walker was forced to flee in 1857. Control of the country then returned to Nicaraguans.

Subsequently, the Conservatives and the Liberals agreed on Managua as a neutral site for a permanent capital. The Conservatives then took power for thirty years, during which time they persecuted the Liberals and encouraged foreign investment.

The Liberals returned to power after a revolt in 1893 and soon antagonized the United States of America. The Conservatives were returned to power in 1910 when the USA refused to accept the new Liberal candidate for president. U.S. troops—in the form of a 100-man Marine "Embassy Guard"—kept the Conservatives in power. Additional troops were brought in as needed, as when the USA kept order during the 1912 elections (which offered only one presidential candidate, a U.S.-backed Conservative).

When the USA removed its Marines in 1925, civil war immediately broke out. U.S. President Calvin Coolidge found that many of his constituents were against returning the Marines to Nicaragua, so the "Communist threat" was invoked for the first time. Coolidge then sent Henry L. Stimson to Nicaragua as a special envoy to negotiate peace between the warring factions. One Liberal leader, the charismatic General Augusto César Sandino, refused to give up his arms until the U.S. troops left, and he conducted a guerrilla war against both the Nicaraguan National Guard and the U.S. Marines. The six years of fighting that followed proved inconclusive, although it gave the U.S. Marine Air Corps the opportunity to be the first in military history to use aerial dive-bombing tactics.

When the U.S. military finally left, Sandino stopped fighting, only to be assassinated in Managua in 1933. (Almost thirty years later, the Sandinista rebels named themselves after Augusto Sandino.)

With the withdrawal of U.S. forces, National Guard Commander Anastasio Somoza García consolidated his power. Somoza ascended to the presidency of Nicaragua in 1937 and soon became the wealthiest man in Central America. He or his surrogates ruled Nicaragua until his assassination in 1956. The Somoza family continued to dominate the country through the presidencies of his two sons, Luis Somoza Debayle (1956–1963) and Anastasio Somoza Debayle (1967–1979).

In 1979, the Marxist Sandinista National Liberation Front (FSLN), which had been fighting a guerrilla war since 1962, succeeded in taking control of the government. Somoza fled, complaining that the United States of America had let him down.

The pluralistic government gradually became dominated by a single party as the Sandinistas suspended the constitution and elections, and began tightening control. The elections of 1984 brought Sandinista leader Daniel Ortega Saavedra to power.

Once again the USA found a Nicaraguan government unsatisfactory and made an effort to remove it. An anti-Sandinista group called "the Contras" was given massive support, and the U.S. government imposed a trade embargo on Nicaragua. The Contras conducted a guerrilla war against the Sandinista government.

After many years of fighting, the Central American Peace Plan proposed by Costa Rican President Oscar Arias Sánchez was finally adopted. A cease-fire was reached, and free elections were promised if the Contras would disarm. In February 1990, elections took place and Ortega was defeated by Violeta Barrios de Chamorro, wife of the assassinated newspaper editor Pedro Joaquín Chamorro. Mrs. Chamorro's victory started a period of democratization and national reconciliation. After Mrs. Chamorro, a president was elected who was ultimately convicted and imprisoned on charges of fraud, embezzlement, and money laundering—Arnoldo Alemán. In contrast, the current president, Enrique Bolaños, implemented an anticorruption campaign that won him plaudits worldwide.

The Liberal Party returned to power in 2001 following the election of its presidential candidate, Enrique Bolaños.

Type of Government
The Republic of Nicaragua is a unitary multiparty republic with one legislative house, the National Assembly. The president is both

head of state and head of the government. Relations between Nicaragua and the United States of America have been strained virtually from the birth of Nicaragua as an independent country. However, relations improved in 1990 with the election of Mrs. Violeta Barrios de Chamorro. The USA backed her election and ended the trade embargo that had crippled the Nicaraguan economy.

For current government data, check with the Embassy of Nicaragua at 1627 New Hampshire Avenue, NW, Washington DC 20009; telephone: (202) 939-6570; fax: (202) 939-6542.

Language

The official language of Nicaragua is Spanish. The second most common language is Miskito, an indigenous tongue. However, many Miskito Indians now speak Spanish as well. English is spoken by businesspeople and among natives along the Atlantic coast—although their Creole dialect of English may not be intelligible to some English speakers.

Ethnologue.com lists a total of ten languages for Nicaragua, three of which are now extinct.

Nicaraguan Spanish has a number of unique vocabulary words. It is also noted for its forcefulness; words considered profane in neighboring Costa Rica are in everyday use in Nicaragua, even in the mass media.

The Nicaraguan View

There is no official religion. Approximately 85 percent of the population belongs to the Roman Catholic Church. The remainder belongs to various Protestant denominations.

The Nicaraguan economy is predominantly agricultural. Exports include coffee (30 percent), shrimp and lobster, beef, sugar, bananas, cotton, gold, and tobacco. The world price for these exports has a great effect upon the economy of Nicaragua.

Nicaragua's economy is also dependent upon the remittances sent home by Nicaraguans working abroad.

Nicaraguans share a sense of solidarity. This and their tenacious nature has helped them survive their many wars and natural disasters.

Cultural Note

Anti-American sentiment can be so strong that some Nicaraguan writers do not seek translation of their work into English. One of the most innovative poets in Central America is Carlos Martínez Rivas. Rivas allegedly hates being translated, describing the process as "a form of assassination."

☑ Know Before You Go

The greatest hazard for a visitor comes from erratic drivers and street crime. The prevalence of crime and corruption is a serious drawback to conducting business in Nicaragua.

Travel in remote areas in the northern and central departments is strongly discouraged because of violent crime.

Violent earthquakes, volcanoes, and mudslides occur periodically. The Caribbean coast of Nicaragua is particularly prone to hurricanes and tropical storms. In 1998, Hurricane Mitch devastated much of this coastline.

Both sides planted antipersonnel mines during the Nicaraguan civil war. Between 1979 and 1990, and estimated 135,000 mines were laid. As of 2001, the Nicaraguan–Costa Rican border was declared free of mines. However, that leaves more than 70,000 mines on the Nicaraguan-Honduran border and at thirty-nine sites inside Nicaragua. Land mines will remain a hazard for years to come. New mine victims are reported every year.

Law enforcement agencies report that Nicaragua is a transshipment point for the illegal drug and arms trade.

⊙ CULTURAL ORIENTATION

Cognitive Styles: How Nicaraguans Organize and Process Information

Nicaraguans are a proud people and are circumspect in their evaluation of external information. Since most of their learning is by rote, they tend to think subjectively and associatively. They look at most situations from a personal perspective and seldom rely on rules or laws to resolve their problems.

Negotiation Strategies: What Nicaraguans Accept as Evidence

A variety of beliefs and/or ideologies—from the Catholic Church to the Sandinista movement—influences many Nicaraguans' perception of the truth. Usually, feelings rather than facts determine the outcome. It is quite acceptable for a Nicaraguan (even a politician or business executive) to make a decision on the basis of "gut instinct." Objective facts are seldom the sole source of evidence.

Cultural Note

The family (including the extended family) is very important, and constitutes the foundation of social life. It is not uncommon for uncles, aunts, cousins, and grandparents to live together in one house or compound.

Value Systems: The Basis for Behavior

The shooting war may be over, but Nicaragua is still struggling with political conflict. This heightens their awareness of their value systems. The following three sections identify the Value Systems in the predominant culture—their methods of dividing right from wrong, good from evil, and so forth.

Locus of Decision-Making

Individual decisions always involve the needs of the family and public group. A person's self-identity is based on his or her place in the family and performance in the group, so Nicaraguans are never completely free of these influences. Expertise is always subordinate to personal connections and one's ability to be part of the team. A small percent of the population controls most of the resources, but there are various factions within this elite group.

Sources of Anxiety Reduction

All classes depend upon an extended family organization—a wide range of relatives who are available for help and support. For the lower classes this is the primary social and psychological support system in the face of constant economic need. The Church has little political power, but its precepts and social structure permeate all of life and bring some stability to it.

Issues of Equality/Inequality

A tiny oligarchy, full of factions, sits at the top of a small middle class and a huge lower class. There are extreme contrasts between the rich and the poor, but everyone is trying to gain or maintain power.

Machismo is very strong. Even the female guerrilla fighters were subordinate to men when they returned home. The women's movement received a small boost when Señora Violeta Barrios de Chamorro was elected president.

Cultural Note

The Nicaraguans call themselves *Nicas* or *Pinoleros.* Other commonly used terms are *costeños* (coastal dwellers—usually referring to residents of the Atlantic coast of Nicaragua); *evangélicos* (Protestants—not necessarily a member of an evangelical or charismatic sect); and *pañas* (Spaniards, from Españoles—referring to the Spanish-descended minority, which rules Nicaragua).

◉ BUSINESS PRACTICES

Punctuality, Appointments, and Local Time

- Business hours are generally 8:00 A.M. to 6:00 P.M., Monday through Friday, and 8:00 A.M. to noon on Saturday.
- While punctuality is admired, it is not strictly observed. Punctuality is, however, expected from foreigners.
- In Nicaragua as in most of the world, the date is written with the day first, then the month, then the year (e.g., December 3, 2010, is written 3.12.10 or 3/12/10).
- Make appointments several weeks in advance of your trip by telephone or e-mail.
- The best times to visit Nicaragua are February through July and September through November. Common vacation times are the two weeks before and after Christmas and Easter, and August.
- For a list of Nicaragua's official holidays, visit *www.kissbowor shakehands.com.*

- Local time in Nicaragua is six hours behind Greenwich Mean Time (G.M.T. − 6), or one hour behind U.S. Eastern Standard Time (E.S.T. − 1).

Negotiating

- Business will take place at a much slower pace than in North America or northern Europe. Be patient with delays, and allow for them in your time estimates.
- Business is conducted with friends in Latin America. Expect to spend a substantial amount of time building a relationship before jumping into negotiations.
- Contacts are very important in business, so try to establish them before your visit, and have them arrange introductions for you with major clients. You can find business contacts (*enchufados*) through embassies, banks, and the International Chamber of Commerce.
- Business is discussed at an office or over a meal in a restaurant. It is not discussed in a home or around family. If you are invited into a Nicaraguan home, this is a social event, not a business opportunity.
- Personal honor and "saving face" are very important to Nicaraguans. Therefore, never criticize someone, be too authoritarian, or do anything that will embarrass an associate in public.

Business Entertaining

- Due to years of civil warfare, Nicaragua lacks an extensive tourist infrastructure. Travelers checks are accepted at major hotels and may be exchanged for local currency at authorized exchange facilities. Credit cards are now accepted at many—but not all—restaurants and hotels.
- The main meal of the day is at noon. This traditionally includes beans, tortillas or meat, and fruit and vegetables.
- Business breakfasts or lunches are generally preferred to dinners.
- International hotels are usually the best place for a foreign executive to host a meal or banquet.

- Good topics of conversation are Nicaraguan sights, family, job, and sports—especially baseball. Baseball is a national obsession, and the careers of Nicaraguan players in the U.S. major leagues are avidly followed.
- Topics to avoid include the political unrest and religion.

Cultural Note

The father of Nicaraguan poetry is Rubén Darío. Not only is he Nicaragua's greatest poet, he was credited with revitalizing Spanish poetry in the late nineteenth century. The multilingual Darío attributed his success to this technique: he started by thinking in French, and then wrote in Spanish. A Web site dedicated to the work of Rubén Darío is accessible at *www.dariana.com/tribute.html.*

⊙ PROTOCOL

Greetings
- Men shake hands in greeting. Women will often pat each other on the right forearm or shoulder instead of shaking hands. Women who are close friends may hug or kiss each other on the cheek.
- Close male friends may engage in an *abrazo*, a brief embrace.
- At parties, it is customary to greet and shake hands with everyone in the room individually.

Titles/Forms of Address
- Traditionally, only children, family members, and close friends addressed each other by their first names. This has changed.
- When a person has a title, it is important to use it along with the surname. A Ph.D. or a physician is called "Doctor." Teachers prefer the title *Profesor*, engineers go by *Ingeniero*, architects are *Arquitectos*, and lawyers are *Abogados*.
- For further information on the proper titles and forms of address for Latin-American countries, please consult Appendix A.

Gestures
- Making a fist with the thumb between the index and middle fingers is considered obscene. (This gesture is known as "the fig.")

- The "come here" gesture is done two ways: the palm is down, and makes a scooping gesture with the fingers or the entire hand; or the palm is up, and faces in while waving, which looks almost like a person fanning himself or herself.
- Do not photograph individuals or religious ceremonies without prior approval; some people object to having their picture taken.

Cultural Note

Under the Chamorro administration, the use of the Sandinista form of address *compañero* (comrade) was banned among government personnel. Officials were to be addressed as *señor* or *señora* (or Doctor, for those with a degree).

Gifts

- Business gifts are generally not given to executives on the first trip to Nicaragua. At the end of your trip, you may ask if, when you return to Nicaragua, there is anything you can bring from your home country.
- Since baseball is one of Nicaragua's most popular sports, baseball-related gifts are prized.
- Secretaries and receptionists can be very influential, so it is useful to give them a small present. A small, brand-name accessory (for example, a scarf) is usually a good choice.
- If you are invited to a home, bring flowers or candy.
- Ask a local florist which types of flowers are appropriate. In general, white flowers are reserved for funerals.
- Further guidelines on gift giving can be found at *www.kissbowor shakehands.com*.

Dress

- Nicaraguans tend to wear comfortable clothes; however, foreign businessmen should start by wearing a conservative dark suit and tie. If your Nicaraguan counterpart suggests you dress more casually, you may do so. They may suggest going without a jacket in the heat.
- Dress for women is conservative.

- Lightweight clothing is appropriate for casualwear. Men should wear pants and a shirt in cities. Women can wear pants, a dress, or skirt and blouse.
- Men may wish to wear the traditional guayabera, a light shirt worn untucked.

Cultural Note

In his book *El Nicaraguense* (The Nicaraguan), the late poet Pablo Antonio Cuadra described his countrymen this way:

"The Nicaraguan is an imaginative, fantastic individual who frequently achieves baroque extravagance. But when faced with real life... he displays a disconcerting sobriety."

"The Nica, in singular terms, is a braggart. In plural, he's self-critical, and his self-criticism is expressed with a great deal of mockery."

The latter characteristic is very evident. Mockery and humor are widespread in Nicaragua. The pretentious and self-important are lampooned and deflated. Some observers consider this mockery a national defense mechanism. Faced with poverty, war, natural disasters, and rapacious leaders, the Nicaraguan's recourse is to laugh.

Panama

Republic of Panama
Local short form: Panama
Local long form: Republica de Panama

Cultural Note

Panamanians are sensitive about the influence of the United States of America on their country. Be careful not to remark how "Americanized" the people are, nor should you refer to U.S. citizens as "Americans," since everyone from North, Central, and South America is an American.

⦿ WHAT'S YOUR CULTURAL IQ?

1. Panamanians enjoy many sports. In which one have they produced fourteen world champions?
   a. Soccer
   b. Baseball
   c. Cockfighting
   d. Boxing
   ANSWER: d. Many Panamanians are avidly interested in boxing. Their fourteen world boxing champions include Roberto Duran.

2. TRUE or FALSE? In 1501, Spanish navigator Rodrigo de Bastidas led the first European expedition to reach Panama.
   ANSWER: TRUE. Rodrigo de Bastidas beat Christopher Columbus to Panama; Columbus arrived later, on his fourth and final voyage to the New World.

3. TRUE or FALSE: Alone among Spain's former colonies, Panama remained prosperous after Spain gave up claims to Latin America.
   ANSWER: FALSE. Panama's importance declined when Spain lost her colonies in South and Central America. Revenues sagged. It took the 1848 discovery of gold in California to revive

Panama's fortunes. As a result, thousands of U.S. citizens from the East Coast traveled to California via Panama (rather than making the long, dangerous land journey across the United States of America).

▶ TIPS ON DOING BUSINESS IN PANAMA

- Panamanians prefer to maintain an image of harmony in public. People are criticized in private, out of hearing of others. Do not criticize or disagree with other members of your negotiating team in public.

- Panama City is often referred to simply as "Panama" by the locals. If you are confused, ask "*¿La nación o la ciudad?*" (The country or the city?).

- White, urban Panamanians hold most of the country's wealth and power. They have the inelegant nickname los rabiblancos (white-tails). Many of them speak English as well as Spanish. They are a separate group from the rural landowners, who never achieved the political influence that is characteristic of agricultural barons elsewhere in Central America.

- Many Panamanians have nicknames. Even powerful politicians are often referred to by their nicknames. Dictator Manuel Antonio Noriega was known as la Piña (the Pineapple) due to his pockmarked complexion. His successor as president, the pleasant and rotund Guillermo Endara, was called Pan de Dulce (Honey Bun)!

- There is wide ethnic diversity in Panama; your firm will be marketing to Hispanic, Antillean blacks, tribal Indians, Chinese, Arabs, Lebanese, North Americans, etc. Their festivals, music, and handicrafts reflect these cultures. Music alone ranges from the tamborito, a traditional folk dance, to a high energy salsa popularized by Ruben Blades.

Cultural Note

Although its distribution of wealth is very unequal, Panama remains the wealthiest Central American nation, in large part due to the Panama Canal and investment from the USA. (Mexico is wealthier, but it is considered part of North America, not Central America.)

▶ COUNTRY BACKGROUND

Demographics

Panama's population of approximately 3.2 million people (2006 estimate) is one of the smallest in Central America. It is 70 percent mestizo (a mix of Indian and European), 14 percent West Indian, 10 percent European, and 6 percent Amerindian.

Over a quarter of the people engage in agriculture, growing crops such as bananas, shrimp, coffee, sugar, rice, corn, sugarcane, and livestock.

History

Panamanian history has been heavily influenced by its unique location.

Columbus reached Panama in 1502 on his fourth and final voyage to the New World. In 1513 Vasco Núñez de Balboa crossed the width of the isthmus, and proved it could provide a path for transport of goods between the Pacific and Atlantic. Subsequently, Panama became a transshipment point; Spain brought its silver and gold up to Panama via ship, then portaged overland via the Camino Real (Royal Road) and loaded it back onto ships bound for Spain. An alternate name for the cross-country trail was the *Camino de Cruces* (Road of the Crosses)—named for all the graves.

Four hundred years later, the completion of the Panama Canal changed the nature of world trade. As a result, Panama has been heavily influenced by Spain and the USA, as each controlled this route of access.

The Spanish included Panama as part of the viceroyalty of New Grenada. Most of Central America declared its independence from Spain in 1821. Rather than going it alone, Panama joined the already-independent nation of Colombia. This union (known as "Gran Colombia") was not entirely successful, and many Panamanians sought independence from Colombia.

The first major U.S. investment in Panama was in 1855, when a railroad was built to ferry people and goods between the coasts. This was prompted by the California gold rush of 1849. Thousands of miners traveled from the Atlantic coast of the USA by sea to Panama, traversed Panama, then took a ship from Panama's Pacific coast to California.

Gran Colombia was reorganized in 1886 as the Republic of Colombia. The autonomy that Panamanians enjoyed was lost in the reorganization. The Panamanian independence movement dates its origin to this time.

The French tried and failed to build a canal across Panama in the 1880s. In the wake of the 1898 Spanish-American War, the United States of America became determined to build a canal. The Panama isthmus was the favored site, but Colombia refused to grant the required concessions.

Consequently, the USA supported Panamanian independence, in return for concessions (primarily the establishment of the U.S.-controlled Panama Canal Zone). The canal was finally completed in 1914. The canal returned to Panamanian control on December 31, 1999. In the same year, Panamanians elected their first female president, Mireya Elisa Moscoso Rodríguez. For better or worse, the Panamanian agency charged with running the canal, the Panama Canal Authority, is largely autonomous—beyond the control of elected Panamanian politicians.

Since its independence from Colombia in 1903, Panama has been a republic. The military often dominated the government until 1989, when dictator General Manuel Noriega was overthrown by U.S. forces and civil rule was instituted.

Type of Government

Panama is a multiparty republic, with a president, two vice presidents, a Cabinet, a unicameral Legislative Assembly serving five-year terms, and a Supreme Court. The president is the head of state and the head of the government.

Frequently dominated by its military, the Republic of Panama has had a peaceful transfer of power between civilian governments since General Manuel Noriega was removed in 1989. (However, even during the Noriega era, the appearance of elective government was maintained.)

For current government data, check with the Embassy of Panama in your country.

Language

Spanish is the official language of Panama. Many Panamanians are bilingual in English as well. There are several Amerindian languages. Ethnologue.com has identified fourteen distinct languages in current use in Panama. (Two of these are languages of Chinese immigrants.)

The Panamanian View

Traditionally a Roman Catholic country, Protestantism has made significant gains in the recent past. Around 80 percent of Panamanians identify themselves as Roman Catholics. Protestants now make up about 15 percent, more than half of them belonging to Pentecostal groups. There are also small numbers of Muslims, Hindus, and others.

Panama has no official religion.

The family remains the single most powerful social unit. Nepotism is considered proper at all levels of society.

Attitudes toward the United States of America—known as *El Gigante del Norte* (the Giant to the North)—are complex. Some Panamanians blame the United States' long domination of Panama for all their country's problems. Nevertheless, many Panamanians view the USA as their best opportunity for education and advancement; thousands of Panamanians live in the USA.

Historically, the Central American upper class associated wealth with vast land ownership. This is less true in Panama, where wealth came not from agriculture but from involvement in transport between the oceans. That was true even during the days of Spanish rule, long before the canal opened.

☑ Know Before You Go

Aside from street crime, the greatest hazard to visitors comes from the heat and humidity.

Panamanian drivers also represent a danger. Many drivers ignore traffic signs in Panama.

If you go swimming in either the Atlantic or Pacific Ocean, be aware that there are dangerous riptides off many Panamanian beaches.

Despite the current government's best efforts, Panama is still listed as a major cocaine transshipment point and primary money-laundering center for narcotics revenue; money-laundering activity is especially heavy in the Colon Free Zone; official corruption remains a major problem.

Cultural Note

Two concepts are helpful in understanding Panama. The first is *personalismo*, which can be defined as the trust you put in an individual and his or her personal sense of integrity (as opposed to putting that trust in a business or government). The second is *machismo*, the belief that males should be dominant (a concept that is gradually changing).

◉ CULTURAL ORIENTATION

Cognitive Styles: How Panamanians Organize and Process Information

Perhaps because Panama has long been a transit port for goods and people from many nations, Panamanians are open to information of many kinds. Panamanians are also very politicized, which shades how they view this information. For example, members of anti-American or antiglobalization parties may resist any data from the United States of America. Panamanians typically process information subjectively and associatively. Their personal involvement in a problem may make it unlikely that they will apply rules or laws to solve it.

Negotiation Strategies: What Panamanians Accept as Evidence

Truth is found in the immediate feelings of the person involved. However, this truth may be influenced by a strong faith in the ideologies of nationalism. Unless they have been educated abroad, older Panamanians will seldom let objective facts stand in the way of their desires. Younger Panamanians may view matters less subjectively.

Value Systems: The Basis for Behavior

The following three sections identify the Value Systems in the predominant culture—their methods of dividing right from wrong, good from evil, and so forth.

Locus of Decision-Making

The individual makes the decisions, but always in light of their effect on the family or group to which he or she belongs. It is difficult for Panamanians to make a negative decision. Personal relationships are everything, and Panamanians strive to maintain them at all costs. A small, elite oligarchy is now in power, and they have historically made decisions favorable to the interests of the USA.

Sources of Anxiety Reduction

The extended family is the surest defense against a hostile and uncertain world. There is a strong work ethic, but levels of production are not highly evident. This is a laid-back society that does not let time dictate its behavior. Panamanians are followers of strong leaders. The rituals and precepts of the Catholic Church give structure to societal behavior.

Panamanians have been charted as having a relatively low individualism index. This indicates a collectivist society in which groups look out for the welfare of each individual member.

Issues of Equality/Inequality

There is a large gap between rich and poor, a fairly large middle class, and a large lower class. Panama has been listed as being tied with Guatemala for the highest power distance in Latin America. This indicates a great difference between the wealthy and the poor, as well as widespread acceptance of this situation. However, younger Panamanians no longer believe that the powerful elite are entitled to unlimited privileges. There is an inherent trust in people, so one needs to cultivate friendships. Machismo is strong. Most Panamanian men believe that the ideal focus for a woman is a home, family, and children.

▶ BUSINESS PRACTICES

Punctuality, Appointments, and Local Time

- Business hours are generally 8:00 A.M. to 6:00 P.M., Monday through Friday.

- Punctuality, although not strictly adhered to in daily living, is expected in business circles—particularly with foreigners.
- If you are invited to a party, never be on time. For dinner parties, it is appropriate to arrive up to one hour late if there are several guests, and up to thirty minutes late if you are alone. At large parties, you may arrive up to two hours late.
- Remember that many Europeans and South Americans write the day first, then the month, then the year (e.g., December 3, 2010, is written 3.12.10 or 3/12/10). Although Panamanians are familiar with the day-month-year format of the USA, they will generally write it in the conventional form for South America.
- Make appointments as far in advance of your arrival in Panama as possible. Confirm your arrival via phone or e-mail at least one week ahead of time.
- For a list of the official holidays of Panama, visit *www.kissbowor shakehands.com.*
- Local time is five hours behind Greenwich Mean Time (G.M.T. – 5), or the same as U.S. Eastern Standard Time.

Negotiating

- Contract negotiations proceed at a much slower pace than in northern Europe or North America. Be patient with delays, and be prepared to travel to Panama more than once to finalize a transaction.
- Business is conducted among friends in Panama. Therefore, spend time establishing a relationship with your counterpart before jumping into business discussions. Emphasize the personal compatibility of the two companies and develop a high level of trust, rather than focusing solely on the logical bottom line.
- Although more women are moving into higher managerial positions, they are still relatively rare. Women should emphasize the fact that they are part of a team from a company that is strongly committed to doing business in Panama.
- Have business cards and other material printed in Spanish as well as English.
- Adjust your starting price to allow a margin for bargaining.

- Latin Americans tend to be status conscious. At least one member of the negotiating team should be from a high level of management.
- Panamanians believe in the intrinsic worth of the individual and treat one another with respect and dignity, regardless of a person's social standing or material wealth. Therefore, it is very important not to publicly criticize a person.
- To avoid embarrassment, Panamanians rarely disagree in public. This can extend to a foreign businessperson trying to close a deal; a Panamanian may tell a foreigner "yes" simply to be polite. Lukewarm affirmatives, like "maybe" or "we will see," are polite ways of saying "no." A "yes" is not final until a contract is signed.
- A familiarity with Panamanian history, sites, culture, and art will impress your counterparts.
- Senior officials and the elderly are given preferential treatment. They should be greeted first, and may be served before you in a line.

Business Entertaining

- Always stay at the best hotels and entertain your guests at premier restaurants. Ask your client's secretary about any preferences the client may have for restaurants or clubs.
- Good topics of conversation include sports, travel, and local cultural events. Avoid supporting claims that "the Canal was run better by the USA," even if they are made by a Panamanian.
- Foreign businesswomen should always include spouses in invitations to business dinners.
- In order to pay for either a lunch or dinner with male clients, women should arrange to take care of the bill privately with the waiter. If the check is brought to the table, the men will strongly resist letting a woman pay. Give the waiter your credit card beforehand or, if you are hosting a dinner at your hotel, arrange to have the charge added to your hotel bill.

Cultural Note

Citizens of the United States of America working in Panama have often remained separate from Panamanians in business and social networks. In order to encourage better cultural and business ties, businesses should plan and support fully integrated functions.

▶ PROTOCOL

Greetings
- Men usually shake hands in greeting. Women will often pat each other on the right forearm or shoulder instead of shaking hands. If they are friends, they may hug or kiss each other on the cheek.
- At parties, it is customary to greet and shake hands with each person in the room.

Titles/Forms of Address
- Titles are very important in Panama and should be used whenever possible. When addressing someone directly, use the title alone and do not include a last name (Profesor, Doctor, and so forth). The title *Licenciado* is used for anyone with a bachelor's degree.
- Traditionally, first names were used only by persons on a familiar basis; however, younger executives may move to the use of first names with business associates from North America.
- For further information on the proper titles and forms of address for Latin-American countries, please consult Appendix A.

Gestures
- Because of the long-standing presence of the USA in Panama, most North American gestures (and insults) are understood.

Gifts
- Gifts are not required in a business setting. However, after the first few meetings, you may want to bring a gift from your home state, such as a local craft or illustrated book. Other good gifts include the latest electronic gadgets or expensive liquor.
- Gifts are appropriate if you are invited to a Panamanian home or if you are visiting rural areas. Some good options are chocolates, wine, Scotch, or local crafts from home.
- Gifts are not expected, however, and it is enough to extend your thanks and to invite your hosts to a meal in return.
- For more guidelines on gift giving, visit *www.kissboworshake hands.com*.

Dress

- In theory, men should wear a conservative business suit for work.
- In practice, jackets and ties are often dispensed with in Panama's hot, humid weather. Panamanian businessmen in higher positions wear suits; others wear *camisillas* (a lightweight, open-necked shirt that is not tucked inside the trousers).
- Women should wear a skirt and blouse or a dress.
- Pants, including jeans, and a shirt are appropriate casualwear in the city.
- Shorts are not often worn by either sex, and women should avoid any revealing clothing. A woman wearing pants in a rural area may draw some attention.

Cultural Note

When the United States of America and the United Kingdom invaded Iraq in 2003, Panamanians could have told them what the immediate aftermath would be: civil disturbances and looting would cause more damage than military actions. This is what happened in Panama when the USA invaded to arrest General Manuel Noriega in 1989. The sudden disappearance of civil authority offered an opportunity for the poor to acquire goods.

Paraguay

Republic of Paraguay
Local long form: Republica del Paraguay

Cultural Note

Try to avoid offering any political opinions. At least, wait until your Paraguayan counterpart has voiced his or hers, then choose a position that does not disagree. "Going along" has been the key to success in Paraguay for many years. Paraguay has not been known for its political tolerance. Paraguayans in positions of authority have never had to be tolerant; under the Stroessner regime political dissidents were harassed or thrown in prison.

▶ WHAT'S YOUR CULTURAL IQ?

1. TRUE or FALSE? Paraguay is the only landlocked country in South America.
   ANSWER: FALSE. Paraguay is landlocked, but so is neighboring Bolivia.

2. Which neighboring countries did Paraguay fight in the War of the Triple Alliance?
   a. Argentina
   b. Brazil
   c. Uruguay
   d. All of the above
   ANSWER: d. Paraguay unwisely fought all three of these countries from 1864 to 1870. As a result, Paraguay lost half of its adult men and much of its territory—including its border with Uruguay.

3. Paraguay had the unsavory reputation as a refuge for exiled or fleeing criminals. If you hear German spoken in Paraguay, who is likely to be speaking it?

a. Escaped Nazi war criminals
b. Mennonite farmers
c. German and Austrian tourists
d. All of the above
e. None of the above

ANSWER: b. Today there are thousands of peaceful Mennonite farmers in Paraguay. Most of the few Nazi war criminals in Paraguay have died off.

▶ TIPS ON DOING BUSINESS IN PARAGUAY

- Paraguay is the only South American nation with two official languages: Spanish and Guaraní. Guaraní, an indigenous language, is the most commonly spoken tongue spoken outside the capital, Asunción. Most executives speak Spanish, if not English.
- However, every politician and civil servant in Paraguay is required to be fluent in Guaraní. If you expect to deal with the government, you may find a Guaraní interpreter to be of use.
- Paraguay once had the reputation as a haven for Nazi war criminals hiding from justice. Today, most German speakers in Paraguay are peaceful Mennonite farmers. There are thousands of Mennonite estancias (ranches) in rural Paraguay.
- The police and intelligence services of many major nations take interest in persons who travel to and from Paraguay. The tri-border area—where the borders of Paraguay, Brazil, and Argentina meet—has been known for decades as a haven for counterfeiters and smugglers.
- Lately, the region's Muslim community has been named by the U.S. State Department as supporters and financiers of terrorism. Traveling to this area may get your passport flagged by the intelligence services of your home country.
- A common drink in Paraguay is mate (pronounced "mah-tay")—a drink prepared from the yerba mate leaf (*Ilex paraguayensis*), and is also known as Paraguayan tea. Paraguayans of every social and economic class drink it. It is not alcoholic, but, like coffee and tea, it contains caffeine.

▶ COUNTRY BACKGROUND

Demographics

Most of the 6.5 million Paraguayans (2006 estimate) do not live in the cities. Although the population is concentrated in 40 percent of the land area of the country, this rural dispersion makes it difficult to provide social services. Health services in the cities are adequate, but malaria remains a serious problem.

Today, 95 percent of the population is mestizo (mixed European and Guaraní Indian ancestry), making Paraguay the most homogeneous nation in South America. The minority population is very small, consisting mostly of Italian, German, and Japanese settlers.

History

The city of Asunción, which today is the capital of Paraguay, was founded in 1537. For a time, Asunción was the capital city of the Spanish colonial provinces of Paraguay and Río de la Plata (encompassing most of the bottom third of South America). To the disappointment of the Spanish colonizers, Paraguay lacked the gold and silver they sought. Consequently, Paraguay remained undeveloped and attracted relatively few Spaniards. Most of the Spaniards who came married Indian women; the arable land was divided into huge plantations.

Jesuit missionaries, however, did venture into Paraguay. They instituted a major social experiment, establishing a series of self-sufficient missions among the Indians, the famous *reducciónes* (reductions). This pitted the Jesuits against the Spanish-descended settlers, who wanted cheap Indian labor for their plantations. Unfortunately, the Jesuits were expelled from the continent in the 1700s; the reducciónes failed, and the Indians fled into the jungle or were sold into slavery. (This saga was portrayed in the 1986 film *The Mission*.)

In 1811, Paraguay became the first nation in South America to gain its independence from Spain. This was accomplished without violence; Spain did not consider remote, agricultural Paraguay worth fighting for.

From 1814 to 1840, Paraguay's elected "supreme dictator," Dr. José Gaspar Rodríguez de Francia, cut the nation off from the outside world. Paraguay became totally self-sufficient, and intermarriage with the Indians was encouraged. As a result, Paraguay evolved into a highly nationalistic, ethnically homogeneous state.

At the time of its independence, Paraguay was about a third larger than it is today. Part of its land was lost when it became involved in territorial wars with all of its neighbors. Had Argentina and Brazil been able to agree upon a partition, Paraguay would have ceased to exist. As it was, the wars of 1865 to 1870 and 1932 to 1935 devastated the population. An astonishing 80 percent of the men in Paraguay were slain in the first war alone.

In 1954, General Alfredo Stroessner took control of Paraguay in a coup. His reign lasted until another coup, led by General Andrés Rodríguez Pedotti, ousted him in February 1989. Rodríguez was elected president of Paraguay in May 1989, and he restored some civil and political rights. Despite occasional irregularities—including coup attempts, resignations, and the assassination of a vice president in 1999—Paraguay has maintained an elective government ever since. However, the threat of another coup will be present as long as economic instability continues.

Type of Government

Technically a constitutional republic, Paraguay has a powerful executive branch and has usually been under the thumb of one strongman after another. However, Paraguay has managed a relatively peaceful transition of power from one elected president to another since 1989. The president is both the chief of state and head of the government.

The government is divided between the executive branch (headed by a president who is elected for a five-year term), an independent judiciary, and a two-house legislature. Voting is mandatory for all citizens between the ages of eighteen and sixty.

For current government data, check with the Embassy of Paraguay at *www.paraguayembassy.com*.

Language

Paraguay is unusual in that it has two official languages: Spanish and Guaraní (a language of most of the indigenous Amerindian population). While most writing is done in Spanish, there is some literature in the Guaraní language.

For data on the various languages of Paraguay, see Ethnologue at *www.ethnologue.com.*

The Paraguayan View

Roman Catholicism is the state religion of Paraguay and is adhered to by about 89 percent of the populace. The state pays all Church salaries and controls all Church appointments. However, religious freedom is guaranteed, and the remainder are primarily members of Mennonite and other Protestant denominations. Protestantism has been gaining in popularity. There is also a small community of Muslim immigrants.

Cultural Note

As in other countries, members of various religious groups in Paraguay have been accused of misdeeds. A notorious 1976 international report called "Genocide in Paraguay" accused fundamentalist Christian missionaries of assisting the Paraguayan government in repressing Indian groups.

More recently, there have been allegations that members of Paraguay's Muslim community support terrorists.

☑ Know Before You Go

Despite widely publicized political violence, the primary hazard for foreign visitors in Paraguay is automobile accidents. Roads vary in quality.

For visitors traveling outside the cities, the environment can be hazardous, especially the heat of the desertlike Chaco region. Poisonous snakes are common in the Chaco.

Earthquakes do occur on occasion. Hurricanes and tornadoes are uncommon. Malaria remains a hazard in many areas.

Paraguay suffered a hoof-and-mouth disease outbreak in 2001, which was of major concern in a beef-exporting nation. The country was declared free of the disease in 2003.

⊙ CULTURAL ORIENTATION

Note: The people of Paraguay have not been studied as extensively as have the people of their neighboring countries. Further research is needed.

Cognitive Styles: How Paraguayans Organize and Process Information

Historically, strict government controls have insulated the people from most outside information. Paraguayans process information subjectively and associatively. This makes their solutions subjective and particular to each situation, rather than rule-based or law-based.

Negotiation Strategies: What Paraguayans Accept as Evidence

Paraguayans generally find truth in the subjective feelings of the moment. This truth may be influenced by faith in the ideologies of nationalism and religion. Objective facts are not used to prove a point. (However, this is not true for young Paraguayans educated abroad.)

Value Systems: The Basis for Behavior

Paraguay has the most homogeneous population (95 percent mestizo) in Latin America. The following three sections identify the Value Systems in the predominant culture—their methods of dividing right from wrong, good from evil, and so forth.

Locus of Decision-Making

The male is the decision-maker, but he keeps the interests of the family or group in mind. An individual's self-identity is based on his or her family genealogy and position in the social system. Decisions will always favor friends or family over expertise. There has always been a strong leader (usually a dictator) to make the decisions for the nation.

Sources of Anxiety Reduction

Family and kin, not the community, are the center of the social universe. They give stability and security to the individual. Godparents are a very important part of the web of kinship. Paraguayans like to follow strong leaders, and their nationalism gives them a sense of security. Catholicism is an essential component of social life, with its rituals, fiestas, and holidays all providing continuity and stability.

Issues of Equality/Inequality

There is a tradition of authoritarian rule and a concomitant lack of democratic institutions. There is an extreme contrast between the elite (educated, prosperous, and city-based) and the poor. The basic social dichotomy is between small farmers and a narrow stratum of elite families who control all the resources. Machismo is strong.

⊙ BUSINESS PRACTICES

Punctuality, Appointments, and Local Time

- While punctuality is not a high priority for Paraguayans, foreigners are expected to be on time.
- Despite their formality, business meetings rarely start on time. It would be unrealistic to expect your Paraguayan counterparts to be prompt. Mornings are best for appointments.
- Paraguayans, like many Europeans and South Americans, write the day first, then the month, and then the year (e.g., December 3, 2010, is written 3.12.10 or 3/12/10).
- The best time of year to conduct business in Paraguay is from June through October. Little business is accomplished during the two weeks before and after Christmas and Easter, or during Carnival. December through February is vacation time in Paraguay, as is May, around Paraguay's Independence Day.
- For a list of the official holidays of Paraguay, visit *www.kissbowor shakehands.com.*
- The country of Paraguay is three hours behind Greenwich Mean Time (G.M.T. – 3), making it two hours ahead of U.S. Eastern Standard Time (E.S.T. + 2).

Negotiating

- The pace of business negotiations in Paraguay is usually much slower than in North America.

- Most Paraguayan men dislike confronting or offending women. Including a female representative on your team can be beneficial in negotiations.
- Personal relationships are far more important than corporate ones in Paraguay. Each time your company changes its representative in Paraguay, you will virtually be starting from scratch. A new relationship must be built up before business can proceed.
- Do not assume that each portion of a contract is settled as it is agreed upon. Until the entire contract is signed, each portion is subject to renegotiation.
- While many of the executives you meet will speak English, check beforehand as to whether or not you will need an interpreter.
- All printed material you hand out should be translated into Spanish. This goes for everything from business cards to reports to brochures. You are not expected to translate material into Guaraní.
- Paraguayans are great sports fans. Talking about sports is generally a good way to open a conversation. Football (called *fútbol* here, and soccer in the U.S.) is the most popular sport. U.S.-style football is *fútbol americano*. Basketball, volleyball, and horseracing are also popular.
- Most people in Paraguay are very proud of their country's massive engineering projects, especially their hydroelectric dams. The Itaipu Dam, a joint project of Paraguay and Brazil, is the world's largest. Inquiring about such projects is a good topic of conversation.

Business Entertaining

- Many people still go home for lunch. However, with enough notice, Paraguayan executives may consider a business lunch.
- Most business entertaining is done over dinner, which is held late, often at 9:00 or 10:00 P.M. Indeed, most restaurants will not serve dinner before 9:00 P.M.
- Dinner is considered a social occasion; do not try to talk business unless your counterpart brings it up.
- Paraguayans love to have long dinners under the stars. Many restaurants have shows that last until after midnight. There are also several casinos.

- Paraguay is a major cattle producer, so expect a lot of beef to be served in restaurants.

Cultural Note
At a gathering such as a party, it is important to shake hands with everyone, both as you arrive and when you leave.

▶ PROTOCOL

Greetings
- Except when greeting close friends, it is traditional to shake hands firmly with both men and women.
- Close male friends shake hands or embrace upon meeting; men kiss close female friends. Close female friends usually kiss each other.
- Close friends of either sex may walk arm in arm.

Titles/Forms of Address
- Remember that Paraguay has two official languages: Spanish and Guaraní. However, all the businesspeople you meet will be fluent in Spanish, so Spanish titles may be used.
- Most people you meet should be addressed initially with a title and their surname.
- For further information on the proper titles and forms of address for Latin-American countries, please consult Appendix A.

Gestures
- As in much of Latin America, Paraguayans converse at a much closer distance than do most people in North America or northern Europe. Restrain yourself from trying to back away; a Paraguayan will probably step forward and close the distance.
- The traditional thumbs-up gesture means "okay."
- Displaying the thumb and index finger curled into a circle (which means "okay" in the United States of America) should be avoided.

When done with the wrist bent and the other fingers pointed toward the ground, the gesture is obscene.

- Crossing the index and second fingers is also considered an offensive gesture.
- Winking in Paraguay has sexual connotations.
- Tapping one's chin with the top of the index finger means "I don't know."
- A backwards tilt of the head means "I forgot."
- Sit only on chairs, not on a ledge, box, or table. Manners dictate an erect sitting posture; don't slump.
- Do not rest your feet on anything other than a footstool or rail; it is very impolite to place them upon a table.

Gifts

- Gift giving is problematical in Paraguay, because corruption was widespread during the former regime.
- As in any country, any gift given should be of high quality. If the item is produced by your corporation, the corporate name or logo should appear discreetly, not emblazoned over the whole surface.
- Avoid giving knives; they symbolize the severing of a friendship.
- Gifts are not expected when invited to a Paraguayan home. However, a gift of flowers, chocolates, wine, or a single-malt whiskey may be appreciated.
- As in many other Latin American countries, gifts are exchanged not on Christmas but on January 6, (the Epiphany), commemorating the gifts given to the Christ Child by the Three Kings.
- For further guidelines on gift giving, visit *www.kissboworshake hands.com*.

Cultural Note

Realize that Paraguay is a major trading center with plenty of affluent consumers. You may have to get creative to discover an item from your homeland that isn't for sale in Paraguay. In fact, many gifts can often be bought at a cheaper price in Paraguay if you are prepared to bargain with the merchants. Whatever you purchase, make sure it is made in your home country.

Dress

- Business dress in Paraguay is conservative: dark suits and ties for men; white blouses and dark suits or skirts for women. Men should follow their Paraguayan colleagues' lead as to wearing ties and removing jackets in the summer.

- Dress to handle the heat and humidity of Paraguayan summers. Most local people wear cotton. Don't forget that the seasons in South America are the reverse of those in North America.

- Sweaters are recommended during the winter. Although Paraguay never gets very cold, the heating in buildings is often poor.

- Whatever the season, be prepared for sudden changes in weather and temperature.

- Men may wear the same dark suit for formal occasions (such as the theater, a formal dinner party, and so forth), but women are expected to wear an evening gown. The invitation will specify that the affair is formal.

- Both men and women wear pants as casualwear. If you are meeting business associates, avoid jeans and wear a jacket or blazer. Women should not wear shorts.

Peru

Republic of Peru
Local long form: Republica del Peru

Cultural Note

Peru is rich in natural resources, some of which are intriguing to international oil, gas, and space industries. A major natural gas site exists in Camisea (an eastern jungle), and the Peru has the world's highest plains near the equator. The high, clear characteristics of Peru's altiplano would make it an attractive location for potential space observations or launches.

▶ WHAT'S YOUR CULTURAL IQ?

1. TRUE or FALSE: The magnificent ruins called "Machu Picchu" were built (and later abandoned) by the Aztecs before the Spanish reached Peru.
   ANSWER: FALSE. Yes, Machu Picchu (often called "The Lost City of the Incas") was abandoned, but it was built by the Incas, not the Aztecs.

2. The Spanish made Peru the seat of Spanish South America because:
   a. It was the location of South America's biggest silver mine
   b. It is free from earthquakes
   c. It was the seat of the Inca empire
   ANSWER: c. Peru was the center of Tahuantinsuyo, which was what the Incas called their empire (the name means "four corners"). Peru also used to rule Bolivia (where the great silver mine of Potosí is located). Peru is certainly not free of earthquakes; a 1971 quake measuring 7.7 on the Richter scale killed some 70,000 Peruvians.

3. TRUE or FALSE: After Peru's modest reserves of gold and silver were exhausted, and long before petroleum was discovered, Peru's most valuable mineral resource was guano.

ANSWER: TRUE. The guano in Peru's southern provinces became so valuable as a fertilizer that Chile fought two wars with Peru to gain control of it. Chile won both times.

▶ TIPS ON DOING BUSINESS IN PERU

- Peru has historically been a highly stratified society, with a wealthy oligarchy ruling over poor mestizos (persons of mixed European and Amerindian heritage) and even poorer Amerindians. There is also a small community of Japanese immigrants, from which the former president, Alberto Fujimori, descended.
- Peru has had difficult relations with bordering countries. It lost valuable territory to Chile in the last century, and a dispute with Ecuador deteriorated into conflicts in the 1990s. In marketing, or in conversation, be careful not to compare Peru to its neighbors.
- Hiring local agents in Peru may be a successful tactic for doing business; however, it is optional, because Peruvian law does not require companies to employ local representatives. Foreign businesses may sell directly to Peruvian consumers.
- Joint ventures in certain industries (like textiles) have experienced strong growth. Items that can be assembled or finished in Peru have potential, particularly when locally finished goods are cheaper than imports (which are subject to import duties and high shipping costs). Inexpensive goods from Asia have acquired a major share of the Peruvian market.
- Peruvian consumers may tend to distrust the quality of items sold by mail. Traditionally, such products have had problems with after-sale service.
- Historically, Peruvian customers have not been accustomed to flexible return policies and extended warranties. This is changing.

▶ COUNTRY BACKGROUND

Demographics

2006 estimates showed a population of approximately 28 million Peruvians. Approximately 45 percent are Amerindian, 37 percent are Mestizos, 15 percent are white, and 3 percent are other.

History

Peru was a center of the powerful Inca empire until the Spanish conquistador Francisco Pizarro invaded in 1532. Peru then became the richest and most powerful of the Spanish colonies in South America.

Peru declared its independence from Spain in 1821. But the war of independence lasted several years, and a subsequent war with Spain lasted from 1864 to 1866. Independence did not bring a stable government. The first hundred years of Peru's existence is a record of one revolution after another.

Although Peru has had democratically elected governments since 1980, it is still seeking stability and freedom from the threat of revolution. Terrorist activities from two major insurgent organizations, the Sendero Luminoso (Shining Path) and the Túpac Amaru Revolutionary Movement (MRTA) have fortunately subsided.

Alberto Fujimori's election to the presidency was a major departure from conventional political elections in 1989. He made radical changes to the Peruvian economy, and in 1992 he dissolved Congress and suspended the constitution, after which he instituted multiple reforms.

On 17 December, 1996, some twenty members of the Túpac Amaru Revolutionary Movement seized the Japanese Embassy in Lima. Over 400 guests were held hostage. The rebels demanded the release of imprisoned members of their group. Eventually, government forces entered the embassy and all the rebels were shot.

Following the ousting of President Fujimori in 2000 by the Congress, Alejandro Toledo was elected in 2001.

Cultural Note

The odd lines at Nazca (which have been called extraterrestrial maps) have been the center of controversy for years. Although these lines can in fact best be viewed by airplane, there is no proof that the lines are the work of extraterrestrials.

Type of Government

The Republic of Peru is a unitary multiparty republic with a single legislative house, the Congress. The president is the chief of state and head of the government.

For current government data, check with the Embassy of Peru at *www.peruvianembassy.us.*

Language

Peru has two official languages: Spanish and Quechua (an Amerindian language). Besides Quechua, another Indian language, Aymara, is spoken in the southern highlands. Although many businesspeople understand English, all written materials should be presented in either Spanish or Spanish and English.

For data on the various languages of Peru, see Ethnologue at *www .ethnologue.com.*

The Peruvian View

The Spanish brought Roman Catholicism to Peru, and the majority of the population is considered Catholic. A minority belong to various Protestant faiths. Religion plays a significant part in Peruvian life, and often reflects a mix of traditional Amerindian beliefs and Christianity.

Peru's social stratification permeates all facets of life. Unlike the Latin American nations to the south, Peru has a large Amerindian population—far too large to be ignored. This population segment has been marginalized economically, and constitutes some of the poorest people in South America.

Mestizos make up the next level. Traditionally exploited by the ruling class, it was the mestizos who elected Alberto Fujimori as president in 1990.

Peru's most powerful economic class is still primarily "white." The majority of private business transactions will be with members of this class.

Cultural Note

Peru is an ethnically diverse country, whose citizens descended from the Incan empire, Europe, Africa, Japan, and China. Their heaviest cultural influences have been from two major ethnic groups: the Incas and the Spanish. Perhaps because of these combined cultures, and the unique variety of indigenous foods available (from high-altitude vegetables to fresh seafood), Peru's cuisine has received worldwide acclaim from food critics. Peruvian food has been lauded as the next big trend.

☑ Know Before You Go

Peru is subject to earthquakes and volcanoes, as well as severe weather due to fluctuations in the El Niño current.

Street crime remains a problem, in both the cities and rural areas.

Activity by the major rebel groups—the Sendero Luminoso (Shining Path) and the Túpac Amaru Revolutionary Movement (MRTA)—has been drastically reduced from its height in the 1980s and 1990s. Although these groups receive worldwide publicity, their actions do not generally affect the international business traveler. (The 1996 seizure of the Japanese Embassy in Lima by the Túpac Amaru Revolutionary Movement was an anomaly.) However, the remnants of such groups sometimes kidnap foreign travelers in rural areas and hold them for ransom.

The cocaine industry has more influence on international business, due to its high profitability, inherent violence, and government efforts to limit it. Peruvians grow more than half of the world's coca crop. The law enforcement agencies of many nations monitor the Peruvian drug traffic. Consequently, innocent business travelers to Peru may find police attention focused on them.

The greatest threat to foreign travelers in Peru is not cholera outbreaks, terrorism, or earthquakes: it's altitude sickness. Lima is near sea level, but other popular destinations (such as Cuzco and the area around Lake Titicaca) are high enough to cause this illness. Anyone can be struck by altitude sickness, and rest is the only sure cure. Be aware that Peruvian folk remedies for the sickness usually contain coca leaves. (Coca leaves, which are chewed by many Amerindians, are legal in Peru. Cocaine itself is highly illegal.)

Altitude sickness can strike anyone, even if you have never experienced it before. There is no sure prevention except gradual acclimation to high elevation. Once you get to 6,000 feet above sea level, spend at least two nights there. Repeat this acclimation period at each increase of 3,000 feet. Alcohol consumption tends to make the symptoms worse. Sunburn is also a danger at high altitudes, because there is less atmosphere to protect you from the sun.

Land mines are still present in Peru. There are estimates of over 100,000 antipersonnel mines on the Peru-Ecuador border. Mines are also present on the Peruvian-Chilean border. Furthermore, during the days of rebel attacks on electrical power stations, the Peruvian government planted mines around power stations and other critical infrastructures. The heavy rains from El Niño sometimes expose land mines or even wash them out of place. Since 1995, there have been 179 reported casualties due to land mines, and information indicates that the data is underreported. Further information is available at *www.icbl.org*.

⊚ CULTURAL ORIENTATION

Cognitive Styles: How Peruvians Organize and Process Information

The culture of Peru is open to most information, but attitudes are not changed easily. Except for the highly educated, information is processed subjectively and associatively. Personal involvement in problems and solutions is more important than having a rule or law that dictates one's approach to life.

Negotiation Strategies: What Peruvians Accept as Evidence

An individual's personal feelings about a situation are the basis for truth. In Peru, the ideologies that may influence the truth are those of elitism and religion. Faith in either of these may have historically affected the truth. This may be changing in the younger work force, because objective facts are beginning to carry more weight.

Value Systems: The Basis for Behavior

The value systems of Peru were built around ideologies of an elitist system in which each level was controlled by the next step in the hierarchy. Some characteristics are changing, as evidenced in the election of an "outsider" in the late 1990s—Alberto Fujimori.

The following three sections identify the Value Systems in the predominant culture—their methods of dividing right from wrong, good from evil, etc.

Locus of Decision-Making

Individuals are responsible for their own decisions, but the best interests of the families or groups are dominating factors. A small upper class of the elite oligarchy still controls most of the resources of the country. Personal relationships are more important than one's expertise in business associations. A person's self-identity is based on the social system and the history of his or her extended family.

Peru has been charted as having a slightly higher than average index of uncertainty avoidance (for Latin America). This indicates that Peruvians have a low level of tolerance for uncertainty and are generally averse to risk.

Sources of Anxiety Reduction

At every level of society, the family is the cornerstone of relationships. Kinships define the principal areas of trust and cooperation. At the highest levels of society, kinship and marriage reinforce and solidify political and economic alliances.

Issues of Equality/Inequality

All classes have ranks that are stratified along lines of deep-seated inequalities. Education is the gatekeeper to social advancement in the Peruvian elitist system. It appears that the economic ruling class tries to maintain the large gap between the rich and poor. Machismo is strong, but there are indicators that Peruvian women are gaining more liberties.

⊙ BUSINESS PRACTICES

Punctuality, Appointments, and Local Time

- Punctuality is becoming more important in private and public sectors. However, do not be insulted if your Peruvian contact is late.
- Remember that many Europeans and South Americans write the day first, then the month, and then the year (e.g., December 3, 2010, is written 3.12.10 or 3/12/10). This is the case in Peru.
- Make appointments about two weeks in advance. Upon arrival, do not make impromptu calls at business or government offices.
- Appointments should be scheduled in the morning and may involve a lunch invitation, so do not plan more than one meeting each morning.
- The work week is rather long in Peru, since businesses are often open six days a week. People may return home for lunch, so offices sometimes close between 1:00 and 3:00 P.M.
- Government offices and banks generally work different hours in the summer (January to March) and winter (April to December).

- Many Peruvians go on vacation between January and March, as well as two weeks before and after Christmas and Easter. Therefore, try not to schedule major appointments then or during national holidays.
- For a list of the official holidays of Peru, visit *wwwkissboworshake hands.com.*
- Peru is five hours behind Greenwich Mean Time (G.M.T. – 5), or the same as U.S. Eastern Standard Time.

Negotiating
- During negotiations, be prepared to discuss all aspects of the contract concurrently, rather than discussing in a sequential manner. Also accept that seemingly extraneous data may be reviewed and re-reviewed. Try to be as flexible as possible; ask questions and avoid confrontations.
- Include a variety of materials in your presentations (Web-based communications, high-end graphics in printed format, interactive demonstrations, etc.).
- If you plan to invite your prospects to dinner or lunch during the negotiations, ask only the key participants. After the deal is completed, invite everyone who was involved in the project.
- You may be received with exceptional warmth, since Peruvians are open to foreign investment.
- Peruvians may be more comfortable discussing their Spanish heritage than their Indian background; therefore, it may be unwise to inquire about an individual's ancestry.
- Also, avoid making remarks in conversation about the Peruvian government, terrorists, relations with neighboring countries, or politics in general.
- Peruvians value personal relationships, and relate more to an individual business associate than to a corporation. When approaching a prospect in Peru, it is always better to establish the connection through a highly regarded local contact. This representative will be able to navigate through the maze of networks that make up Peruvian business and government.

- Have your business cards and all company materials printed in both Spanish and English.

Cultural Note

Above all else, do not switch your company's players during negotiations. The Peruvian negotiation team might call a halt to the process as a result. Peruvians relate to the person they have come to know, not to the organization.

Business Entertaining

- Entertain at prestigious restaurants, and include spouses in the invitations if it will be a dinner.
- Discussing business over dinner is not common.
- Most dinner invitations will be for 9:00 P.M., which means dinner will probably be served around 10:30 P.M. Arrive around thirty minutes late, and stay about thirty minutes after dinner ends.
- Imported alcohol is very expensive.
- Stay at a first-class hotel, and feel free to use it to host a meeting or luncheon, particularly if you will be looking for wireless connections.
- An invitation to tea at a private residence is usually for 6:00 to 8:00 P.M.

⊙ PROTOCOL

Greetings

- Men and women shake hands both in greeting and in parting.
- Once a friendship has been established, men may greet each other with a hug, and women may kiss one another on the cheek.

Titles/Forms of Address

- Titles are very important in Peru. Address a person directly by using his or her title, such as "Profesor" or "Doctor," and last name or surname. Wait for your counterpart to initiate this switch to first names.

- For further information on the proper titles and forms of address in Peru, please consult Appendix A.

Gestures

- Peruvians communicate in close proximity. When they stand nearby, do not back away; you will offend them. Do not be surprised if your Peruvian associates take your arm as you walk—men sometimes walk arm in arm with other men, as do women with other women.
- To signal "come here," hold your hand vertically and wave it back and forth with the palm facing out, or put your palm face down, and wave the fingers back and forth.
- Crossing your legs by resting the ankle of one leg on the knee of the other is inappropriate; you may cross your legs at the knee.
- When eating out, be sure to rest both hands on the table, rather than leaving one in your lap.
- "I'm thinking" is represented by tapping your head.
- "Go away" is shown by holding your hand flat and flicking the fingers toward the irritation.
- "Pay me" is signified by an eyebrow raise, or by sweeping your hand toward your body.

Cultural Note

In Latin America, giving gifts is a normal part of business protocol. Peruvians sometimes consider it ironic that U.S. businesspeople feel hesitant about giving a well-thought-out gift to a Peruvian prospect or client, yet will insist on being overtly friendly by immediately calling the Peruvian by his or her first name.

Gifts

- Giving a gift is not required at the first meeting. Instead, buy lunch for your prospect to start the relationship. Subsequently consider the individual's tastes for future gift giving.
- Wait until after the formal meeting is over to present a gift. A relaxed social situation is the best time.

- A gift with a significant connection to your home region will be remembered (for example, local folk art, liquor produced in your region, or an illustrated book about your home city).
- Keep company logos small.
- Appropriate gifts are ones that "ground" or "locate" the firm. For example, a company might present gifts that incorporate stone quarried from the state where they are headquartered (like paperweights, lighters, business card holders, etc.)
- Small electronic gadgets, such as calculators, MP3 players, a handheld GPS, cell phones, electronic organizers, or various wireless devices, are appropriate—particularly because import taxes would normally have to be paid on these items. Have items customized with your contact's initials when possible.
- Digital cameras and name brand pens are appreciated, as are ties, scarves, or other accessories in natural fabrics. (It is often too hot for man-made weaves.)
- When invited to a home, bring wine, whiskey or other liquors, or chocolates. Also bring gifts for the children, such as T-shirts or caps with the logos of popular sports teams or prestigious universities, CDs, electronic games, and so forth.
- Sending roses after a dinner is appropriate if they are not red (these have romantic connotations). Any other flower is regarded as cheap.
- Avoid sending thirteen of anything, any purple or black objects (which have connotations of religious ceremonies), knives (which can signify cutting off a relationship), or handkerchiefs (which represent grief).
- If you intensely admire one of a Peruvian's possessions, he or she may feel obligated to present it to you as a gift.
- There are some social idiosyncrasies in Peru related to the "caste" system. Various levels of family history, social standing, and education may influence the gifts exchanged. Be aware of these sociological issues.
- For more guidelines on gift giving, visit *www.kissboworshake hands.com.*

Dress

- For business meetings, men should wear well-tailored suits.
- Female executives generally wear suits, but it may depend upon the environment.
- Foreigners should not wear native Indian clothing, even if they intend to honor the local culture.

Cultural Note

The noted author Mario Vargas Llosa is a cultural icon in Peru. His writings deal with corruption in politics and societal changes. This drew both praise and persecution. He ran for president of Peru in 1990, but lost to Alberto Fujimori, who had 60 percent of the vote.

Uruguay

Oriental Republic of Uruguay
Local short form: Uruguay
Local long form: Republica Oriental del Uruguay
Former: Banda Oriental, Cisplatine Province

Cultural Note

Uruguay is small with few natural resources. However, it hopes to become to South America what Belgium is to the European Union: a regional capital where diplomats from many countries come to conduct business. Uruguay promotes itself as "The Gateway to Mercosur" (a customs union consisting of Argentina, Brazil, Paraguay, and Uruguay, with Chile and Bolivia as associate members). Montevideo, Uruguay's capital, is also the administrative capital of Mercosur.

⊙ WHAT'S YOUR CULTURAL IQ?

1. TRUE or FALSE: The Uruguayan resort of Punta del Este is a favored tourist destination for thousands of Argentines.
   ANSWER: TRUE. It is also a favorite setting for international conferences, such as the Uruguay Round of the General Agreement on Tariffs and Trade (GATT), which led to the establishment of the World Trade Organization (WTO).

2. Which of the following statements are true about the military junta that ruled Uruguay from 1973 to 1980?
   a. The government classified every adult citizen in Uruguay as either A (reliable), B (questionable), or C (subversive).
   b. Thousands of citizens were imprisoned.
   c. Over one-tenth of the population fled into exile.
   d. All of the above.
   ANSWER: d. Life under the junta was brutal, but relatively few citizens disappeared—unlike in neighboring Argentina.

3. Which of the following countries did *not* claim Uruguay for their own?
   a. Spain
   b. Portugal
   c. Brazil
   d The United Kingdom
   ANSWER: d. In fact, the United Kingdom helped negotiate Uruguayan independence when both Brazil and Argentina claimed possession of it.

▶ TIPS ON DOING BUSINESS IN URUGUAY

- Uruguay is considered the most literate nation in South America. Visitors should familiarize themselves with Uruguayan authors such as novelist Juan Carlos Onetti, essayist Eduardo Galeano, and José Enrique Rodó, who is considered the country's most famous author.
- Even if you are fluent in Spanish, you may need some time to adapt to the local dialect. The country has many Italian immigrants, and their language influenced Uruguay's version of Spanish.
- Currently, Uruguay has the highest per capita population of urban dwellers in Latin America. About 87 percent of Uruguayans live in urban zones, the majority of them in or around the capital of Montevideo.
- In 2003, Uruguay had the highest percentage of citizens who used the Internet in Latin America.
- Like the Argentines, the Uruguayans are big fans of the tango. Tango refers to a style of music, not just a dance, and many tango compositions are intended for listening, not dance. Uruguay also has an indigenous form of Afro-Uruguayan music and dance called the candombe.
- A common drink in Uruguay is mate—pronounced "mah-tay." It is a drink prepared from the yerba mate leaf (Ilex paraguayensis), and is also known as Paraguayan tea. Uruguayans of every social and economic class drink it. It is not alcoholic, but, like other types of coffee and tea, it contains caffeine. (See the note under Paraguay for instructions on drinking mate.)

▶ COUNTRY BACKGROUND

Demographics

The ancestry of Uruguay's population of 3.4 million (2006 estimate) is different from most of South America where the majority of the population is mestizo (of mixed Indian and European ancestry). Only 8 percent of Uruguayans are mestizos. An additional 4 percent are descended from African slaves imported by the Spanish.

The Charrúa, the original Indian inhabitants of Uruguay, have largely died out. About 88 percent of Uruguayans are of European descent (primarily Spanish or Italian, with some German and English as well).

History

The first Europeans to settle in Uruguay were the Portuguese, who founded the town of Colonia in 1680. The Spanish established a fort at Montevideo in 1726, and the two groups fought for control. Portugal ceded its claim to Uruguay in 1777. When Napoleon conquered Spain in 1808, Buenos Aires (in Argentina) declared itself in command of the viceroyalty of Río de la Plata, which included Uruguay. However, the Uruguayans had no desire to submit to Argentine domination.

José Gervasio Artigas, a captain of Spanish forces in the interior of Uruguay, gathered an army and fought Buenos Aires for control of the area. His efforts, lasting from 1810 to 1814, came to be known as Uruguay's war of independence. Neither Spain nor Argentina was ever to regain control of Uruguay, and Artigas is now revered as the father of his country.

However, Uruguay still had to defend its independence. The country was occupied by Brazilian troops in 1820; Artigas and many others were forced to flee. But in 1825, some thirty-three exiles—immortalized as the "33 Orientals" or "33 patriots"—returned and led Uruguay in a successful revolt. Uruguay had established itself as an independent country.

Despite this, neither Brazil nor Argentina gave up claims to Uruguay. Renewed warfare threatened to disrupt international trade, so in 1828 British gunboats enforced recognition of Uruguay as an independent buffer state between Brazil and Argentina.

The first Uruguayan Constitution was signed on July 18, 1830; the main downtown avenue in Montevideo is named for this date.

Uruguay developed into one of the most stable and wealthiest nations on the continent. Its political stability earned it the nickname "the Switzerland of South America."

However, in the 1950s, Uruguay began to slip into an economic crisis. High tariffs, low productivity, inflation, debt, corruption, and other problems made life difficult for many Uruguayans. Social unrest increased. A Communist guerrilla group, the Tupamaros, became active in the late 1960s. For a time, their tactics—which included jailbreaks of captured members and kidnappings of corrupt officials—provided an entertaining sideshow for a generally sympathetic populace. The Uruguayan police seemed unable to stop them.

But when the Tupamaros started killing government officials, police, and a U.S. advisor, the situation became much more serious. The military (some of whom trained in the United States) took over antiterrorist activities from the civil police. Political activities were banned in 1970. The military assumed control of more and more government functions until, by 1973, it was essentially running the country. In 1976 the military ousted the last elected president and openly ruled Uruguay.

The years of military rule were brutal. Since the Tupamaros had enjoyed widespread popularity before they turned violent, the junta seemed to regard the entire populace of Uruguay as enemies. Of a total population of fewer than 3 million Uruguayans, some 5,000 were imprisoned, and between 300,000 and 400,000 fled the country.

Initially, the junta's foreign economic advisers brought a measure of prosperity to Uruguay, and some speculators made millions. But soon the economic experiment turned sour, and the economy was in worse shape than before. The military decided to turn the government back to the civilians. General elections were finally held in 1984, and the military stepped down the following year.

Type of Government

The Oriental Republic of Uruguay has celebrated over twenty continuous years of free and fair elections. Uruguay has two legislative houses: a Senate and a Chamber of Representatives. The president is both the chief of state and the head of the government.

The military continues to hover in the background, exerting influence but taking little direct action. However, human rights have been restored, and Uruguay is once again a democracy.

For current government data, check with the Embassy of Uruguay at *www.uruwashi.org*.

Language

Spanish is the official language, but many Italian words are commonly used in Uruguay.

Near the border between Uruguay and Brazil, some Uruguayans speak a Portuguese-influenced dialect called "Fronterizo." The Montevideo accent is considered the most prestigious among Uruguay's regional dialects.

For data on the various languages of Uruguay, see Ethnologue at *www.ethnologue.com*.

The Uruguayan View

Uruguay is one of the most secularized states in Latin America. Church and state are strictly separated, and only 70 percent of the population is classified as belonging to a religion. Most Uruguayans are Roman Catholic; Protestants and Jews each number 2 percent of the population.

Few Uruguayans expect to become wealthy, especially if they stay within their country. Instead, Uruguayans typically search for security rather than take risks to achieve wealth.

Gambling is viewed as a valid means of achieving wealth.

The Uruguayan economy has been sluggish for several generations. This has helped inspire a widespread pessimism toward business success among many Uruguayans. The pro-business stance of the widely hated military junta of the 1970s also made business suspect.

☑ Know Before You Go

Uruguayans obey the rules of the road better than some Latin Americans do, but automobile accidents are still a major hazard, both to drivers and pedestrians. Aside from that, Uruguay is a relatively safe nation, free from most natural disasters. Earthquakes, hurricanes, and tornadoes are uncommon. The country is currently free of malaria.

Uruguay suffered a hoof-and-mouth disease outbreak in 2001, which is of major concern in a beef-exporting nation. The country was declared free of the disease in 2003.

▶ CULTURAL ORIENTATION

Cognitive Styles: How Uruguayans Organize and Process Information

The prevailing culture of Uruguay values moderation and compromise. Uruguayans are open to outside information in discussion of most issues. They are trained to think subjectively and associatively. However, the state-supported Uruguayan educational system (which offers free tuition throughout the university level) does not encourage abstraction. Uruguayans are loyal to groups (primarily the family), and they are likely to chose personal loyalty rather than obey a rule or law.

Negotiation Strategies: What Uruguayans Accept as Evidence

Uruguayans find the truth in the subjective feelings one has on an issue. This is sometimes biased by a faith in humanitarian ideologies. Uruguayans seldom resort solely to objective facts to prove a point.

Value Systems: The Basis for Behavior

The Uruguayans extol humanistic, spiritual, and aesthetic values, but take a pragmatic and materialistic approach to life. Each individual is considered unique yet equal. Traditionally, there has been an inherent trust in people and a belief in social justice, but this belief was undermined during the military junta of 1973 to 1984. Uruguayan society is risk-averse and stable, making it resistant to change.

The following three sections identify the Value Systems in the predominant culture—their methods of dividing right from wrong, good from evil, and so forth.

Locus of Decision-Making

The individual is responsible for his or her decisions. Uruguayans tend to respect individualism while regarding the family as the most important group. There is a tendency to adopt fatalistic attitudes. A person's self-identity is based on his or her role in the social system and the history of his or her extended family. Because expertise is less important than one's ability to fit into the group, kinships and friendships play a major role in business transactions.

Sources of Anxiety Reduction

The primary source of anxiety reduction in Uruguay is the family and an individual's role in it. (Interestingly, the Uruguayan nuclear family is smaller and has fewer kinship relationships than those in any other Latin American country.) There is a high need for personal relationships, as friendship networks are important to security, jobs, and socializing. The Roman Catholic Church is an important part of the national culture, offering another source of structure and security.

Research indicates that Uruguayans (along with Guatemalans) have the highest levels of uncertainty avoidance in Latin America. In theory, this means Uruguayans give higher importance to strict rules and regulations than most Latin Americans do. It also implies a dislike of ambiguity and an aversion to risk.

Issues of Equality/Inequality

There is less inequality of wealth in Uruguay than in many Latin American nations. The small upper class, which is extensively inter-married, controls much of the wealth and commerce. However, the large middle class is very influential. Men hold the dominant positions in society, but women are often involved in national life. They are considered equal in most respects. Women enjoy substantial freedom; they are independent and emancipated. Manual labor, which is disdained by many Uruguayans, helps define the class system.

Cultural Note

The military junta that ruled Uruguay from 1973 to 1984 held some 5,000 political prisoners. Considering the traditional Uruguayan dislike for uncertainty, it is not surprising that the political prisons utilized psychological pressure. Prison rules were changed constantly. One day a prisoner would be punished for leaving the window-shade to his cell open, the next day for leaving it closed, and so on.

▶ BUSINESS PRACTICES

Punctuality, Appointments, and Local Time
- Unlike in the past, punctuality is considered important in business affairs in Uruguay. Promptness is not expected in social events.
- Business meetings may or may not start on time, but, as a foreigner, you are expected to be prompt.
- As in most South Americans countries, dates in Uruguay are written in this order: first the day, then the month, then the year (e.g., December 3, 2010, is written 3-12-10). Dates are usually separated with dashes.
- The best time of year to conduct business is from May through November. Little business is accomplished for two weeks before and after Christmas and Easter, as well as during Carnival. January through April is summer in Uruguay, and one or another of the decision-makers is liable to be off on vacation during this period.
- The country of Uruguay is three hours behind Greenwich Mean Time (G.M.T. – 3), making it two hours ahead of U.S. Eastern Standard Time (E.S.T. + 2).

Negotiating
- The pace of business negotiations in Latin America is moderate to slow—much slower than that in the United States. However, many executives are accustomed to the business techniques of their major trading partners. Some younger Uruguayans will adapt to the negotiating style of their foreign counterparts, speeding up or slowing down in accordance with the foreigner's traditions.
- Most Uruguayan executives will be experienced and sophisticated; they may well have studied overseas.
- Most successful Uruguayan executives put in a long workday.
- Uruguay is a nation of immigrants. While many of the businesspeople you encounter will be of Spanish descent, others will be German, Italian, or Jewish. Although many executives speak English, check beforehand as to whether or not you will need an interpreter.
- All printed material you hand out should be translated into Spanish. This goes for everything from business cards to brochures.

- Uruguayans are great sports fans. Talking about sports is always a good way to open a conversation. Football (which is called *fútbol* here, and soccer in the USA) is the most popular sport. (U.S.-style football is *fútbol Americano*.) Basketball is increasingly popular; the Uruguayan basketball team almost beat the U.S. team at the 2003 Pan-American Games.

- Foreign affairs are of great interest to Uruguayans, especially now that Uruguayan troops have been deployed overseas as part of UN peacekeeping missions.

- Uruguay is a popular tourist spot, so ask about sights to see.

Cultural Note

The flag of Uruguay is quite distinctive. The background is white, the stripes are blue, and there is a sun design in the upper left-hand corner. Although Uruguay is a popular tourist destination, the sun-faced symbol is not intended as a promise of sunny vacations. The symbol is the "sun of May" and represents the sunlight that broke through the clouds to shine upon the first colonists who demonstrated against their Spanish overlords in May 1810.

Business Entertaining

- Uruguayans are comfortable conducting business over lunch. Dinner, however, tends to be a social occasion; don't try to talk business during an evening meal unless your counterpart brings it up.

- Business breakfast meetings, while not unheard of, are rare.

- While you are in Uruguay, your counterpart will probably offer to take you out to—and pay for—lunch and dinner.

- Should you wish to reciprocate, the best choice will be an upscale French, Chinese, or Uruguayan restaurant.

- A good choice of location for a business dinner is the restaurant at an international hotel.

- Uruguay is a major cattle producer, and its restaurants serve some of the best beef in the world.

- Despite the traditional Uruguayan aversion to risk, the country has a number of casinos. Your counterpart may invite you out to one or more.

⊙ PROTOCOL

Greetings

- Except when greeting close friends, it is traditional to shake hands firmly with both men and women.
- Close male friends shake hands upon meeting, but men kiss close female friends. Close female friends usually kiss each other.

Titles/Forms of Address

- For further information on the proper titles and forms of address for Latin-American countries, please consult Appendix A.

Gestures

- While most Latin Americans converse at a closer distance than North American citizens are used to, Uruguayans are generally aware that close proximity makes some people nervous. Consequently, most Uruguayan businesspeople will give foreigners more "breathing room" than they would allow fellow Uruguayans.
- The "thumbs-up" gesture means "okay" in Uruguay.
- Curling the fingers around so that they touch the thumb indicates doubt. This gesture is usually done with the right hand.
- Sit only on chairs, not on a ledge, box, or table.
- Don't rest your feet on anything other than a footstool or rail; it is very impolite to place them on a table.
- Avoid yawning in public. It is a signal that it is time to adjourn.

Cultural Note

Do not ask probing questions about an Uruguayan's family unless prompted to by your host. Remember that the country went through over fourteen years of brutal military dictatorship, during which more than 10 percent of the population fled into exile and one out of every fifty of the remainder were detained for interrogation (or worse).

Gifts

- When you are given notice of an invitation to a Uruguayan home, bring (or have sent before you arrive) flowers or chocolates to your hostess. Roses are the most appreciated type of flower. Don't worry about a gift if an invitation is proffered on short (or no) notice. After business dinners in Uruguay, it is common practice to adjourn to someone's home for coffee. Guests are not expected to stay long if the following day is a workday.

- Gift giving is not a major aspect of doing business.

Dress

- Business dress in Uruguay is conservative: dark suits and ties for men; white blouses and dark suits or skirts for women. Men should follow their Uruguayan colleagues' lead with regard to wearing ties and removing jackets in the summer.
- Uruguayans do not favor the bright colors popular elsewhere in Latin America. Choose subtle colors. Men may wear the same dark suit for formal occasions (such as the theater, a formal dinner party, and so forth), but women are expected to wear an evening gown.
- Both men and women wear pants in casual situations. If you are meeting business associates, avoid jeans and wear a jacket or blazer. Women should not wear shorts.
- Don't wear anything outside that can be damaged by water during Carnival because drenching pedestrians is a favorite Carnival trick of the young.
- Summertime can be humid as well as warm, and winters are rainy and chilly. Bring appropriate clothing—and don't forget that the seasons in the Southern Hemisphere are the reverse of those in the Northern Hemisphere.

Cultural Note

If you graduated from the University of Chicago, leave your class ring at home. Under Uruguay's military junta, the generals took their economic policy from the "Chicago boys"—free-market economic advisers largely trained by Milton Friedman at the University of Chicago. The Chicago boys are not popular; some Uruguayans feel that they treated Uruguay as an economics experiment, enforced by the guns of the military. Opponents of the regime had a saying that "In Uruguay, people were in prison so that prices could be free."

Venezuela

Bolivarian Republic of Venezuela
Local short form: Venezuela
Local long form: Republica Bolivariana de Venezuela

Cultural Note

Venezuelans consider native son Simón Bolívar a national treasure, because he was not only the catalyst for Venezuela's independence from Spain but a liberator for much of South America. There is a Plaza Bolívar in the center of most Venezuela cities, and it is important to behave respectfully in that plaza. Venezuela's currency is named the bolívar. And President Hugo Chávez called his 1998 populist restructuring of Venezuelan government and society his "Bolivarian Revolution."

▶ WHAT'S YOUR CULTURAL IQ?

1. Christopher Columbus was the first European explorer to reach Venezuela in 1498. (He named it Tierra de Gracia). After fighting the fierce native Caribs, the Spanish managed to establish their first mainland outpost at Cumaná in 1523. They hoped that Venezuela was the home of El Dorado (the lost city of gold). All they found were pearls, and those reserves were exhausted within a few decades. Instead, the Spanish colonists turned to farming and ranching. Obviously, they failed to discover Venezuela's oil, but what other mineral resources did they miss?
   a. Iron
   b. Coal
   c. Gold
   d. Diamonds
   e. All of the above
   ANSWER: e. Venezuela has significant deposits of all of these resources.

2. Independence for Venezuela itself was not enough for Simón Bolívar. He attempted to combine which of the following countries into his Confederation of Gran Colombia?

a. Colombia and Panama

b. Ecuador and Venezuela

c. Peru and Bolivia

d. All of the above

ANSWER: d. He failed to keep this super-state together. Except for Panama (which remained part of Colombia), all of the above became independent nations within a few years of the death of El Libertador in 1830.

3. TRUE or FALSE: Baseball is the most popular sport in Venezuela.

ANSWER: TRUE. Unlike most Latin American nations where football (soccer) reigns supreme, baseball is considered the national sport of Venezuela. Professional baseball teams play a four-month season and compete in the Caribbean Series. Many Venezuelans have played professional baseball in the USA. In the past few years, basketball has gained great popularity and is now Venezuela's number-two sport.

▶ TIPS ON DOING BUSINESS IN VENEZUELA

- Venezuela has as much in common with its Caribbean neighbors as it has with Latin America, and Venezuelans often display a Caribbean-style easygoing informality.

- In politics, as in business, Venezuelans tend to follow strong leaders. Leadership styles are often authoritarian, rather than inclusive.

- Venezuela is a highly status-conscious country. Power flows from the top down, and bosses expect compliance. Employees do not contradict their bosses, so foreign teams in Venezuela should be careful not to argue with each other in public, because Venezuelans will interpret this as demonstrating poor leadership.

- Venezuela's labor laws make it expensive to fire an employee or agent. Because of this, foreign firms often prefer to use commissioned agents rather than hired agents. (In most cases, a commissioned agent is not considered an employee.)

- Avoid dominating the conversation or putting pressure on your Venezuelan colleagues. Venezuelans like to be in control.

Cultural Note

Venezuela is a highly polarized country and has become even more so under the administration of President Hugo Chávez. The businesspeople you will deal with will almost all come from the middle or upper classes. If you deal with government officials, they may be from any background.

Venezuelan businesspeople can be divided into two types, with distinct differences in their styles of conducting business. Among the older generation, people will want to get to know you personally and will respond to you as an individual, rather than to your company or your proposals. The younger generations are often educated abroad and adopt foreign business practices. These executives may relate more to your firm, the proposal you are presenting, and so forth, than to you personally.

Many younger Venezuelans have been educated in the USA, and may own homes there. In fact, so many Venezuelans own property in Florida that the region around Miami has been nicknamed "Venezuela's twenty-first state."

⊙ COUNTRY BACKGROUND

Demographics

The population of Venezuela is approximately 25 million (2006 estimate). The ethnic makeup consists of mestizo (about 70 percent), Spanish, Italian, Portuguese, Arab, German and African. Only 2 percent of the population is full-blooded Amerindian.

History

The original inhabitants of Venezuela were several Amerindian tribes, including the Caracas, Arawaks, and Cumanagotos. After Columbus discovered the area in 1498, the Spanish began conquering the coastal regions and offshore islands. Explorer Alonso de Ojeda named the land Venezuela, meaning "little Venice," because many Indian homes around Lake Maracaibo and the coast were built on stilts—which reminded him of Venice. Spain controlled Venezuela for more than two centuries, save for a period from 1529 to 1546, when the Spanish crown paid a debt to a German banking house by offering Venezuela for exploitation. The Spanish empire in the Americas was shaken when Napoleon conquered Spain in 1810.

Independence movements grew among Venezuelans, and fighting broke out between rebels and royalists. Independence was finally secured when Simón Bolívar's forces (a Venezuelan) defeated the royalists at the Battle of Carabobo in 1821. The Republic of Greater Colombia originally contained Venezuela, Ecuador, and Colombia. In 1830 Venezuela seceded and became an independent nation.

Type of Government

For its first century, Venezuela was ruled by dictators. Since 1958, Venezuela has had continuous freely held democratic elections (peppered by several unsuccessful coup attempts). It is a federal multiparty republic, with a president who is both the head of government and the chief of state. There is a cabinet, or Council of Ministers, and a bicameral congress, composed of the Chamber of Deputies and the Senate. The judiciary is represented by the Supreme Court. Elections are held every five years. The administration of Hugo Chávez, who was elected president in 1999, rewrote the constitution and changed the way Venezuela is ruled. Whether or not the changes of Chávez's "Bolivarian revolution" will survive his administration remains to be seen.

For current government data, check with the Embassy of Venezuela at *www.embavenez-us.org*.

Language

Spanish is the country's official language. Venezuelans call their language *castellano*, not *español*. English and a variety of Amerindian dialects are spoken as well. There is also a native Venezuelan form of sign language, which has been taught in schools for the deaf since 1937.

Among older Venezuelans, there tends to be a great loyalty to one's regional dialect. Younger Venezuelans tend to accept the Caracas dialect as the most prestigious, whether they speak it or not. For data on the various languages of Venezuela, see Ethnologue at *www .ethnologue.com*.

The Venezuelan View

Venezuela has no official religion, but the vast majority of people are Roman Catholic (over 92 percent). Upper-class Venezuelans tend to be strongly Roman Catholic, and the Church is historically seen to have ties to the ruling class. However, the Church does not have great influence on the daily lives of most businesspeople. Evangelical Protestant groups have become more popular in the past few decades, especially among the poor.

The single most important institution in Venezuela is the family. Extended families are the norm, and relatives often go into business with each other. When deciding between competing offers, a Venezuelan is likely to select an offer coming from a relative—even a distant relative—instead of going with an unknown provider.

Younger Venezuelans still consider their families as a top priority, although their global awareness tends to be wider. It is more likely that the younger generation of Venezuelan businesspeople has been educated abroad. Post-1990 graduates came of age during hard times in Venezuela, and may lack the sense of entitlement and economic security that was present among their elders who prospered during the oil boom of the 1970s.

Venezuela is a male-dominated society. Sociologists who rank cultures along a masculinity index categorize Venezuela as one of the "most Masculine" in Latin America.

Another sociological finding puts Venezuela at the far end of the individuality index. This places the individual as the least-important person in a decision-making scenario. The best interests of one's family are considered first. (The USA ranks at the other end of this scale, with the individual decision-maker considering his or her self-interest above all.) A Venezuelan may make a decision by asking himself "Will this benefit or dishonor my family?"

In politics, business, and religion, Venezuelans tend to follow strong leaders. Leadership styles tend to be authoritarian rather than inclusive.

☑ Know Before You Go

Venezuelans tend to have casual attitudes toward the rules of the road. It is often stated that they regard traffic lights as "suggestions." Traffic accidents are a serious hazard to drivers and pedestrians alike. Because of the regularity of these accidents, companies with fleets of vehicles in Venezuela must factor in the cost of frequent damage to their vehicles.

Earthquakes are a constant hazard. Historically, the first Venezuelan Republic fell in part because a massive earthquake in March of 1812 damaged the seats of the Pro-Independence movement.

▶ CULTURAL ORIENTATION

Cognitive Styles: How Venezuelans Organize and Process Information

In Venezuela, outside information is accepted on most issues for purposes of discussion. However, Venezuelans do not change their attitudes easily. Their educational system has historically trained them to process information subjectively and associatively. Their personal involvement in a situation is more important than the rules or laws that might be used to solve the problem.

Negotiation Strategies: What Venezuelans Accept as Evidence

The truth is usually found in immediate subjective feelings. This may be influenced by their faith in the ideologies of humanitarianism, but not solely by the accumulation of objective facts.

Value Systems: The Basis for Behavior

Venezuela lost some of its humanitarian values when the oil market dropped and it had to increase taxes to maintain its economy. The following three sections identify the Value Systems in the predominant culture—their methods of dividing right from wrong, good from evil, and so forth.

Locus of Decision-Making

Individuals are responsible for their own decisions and any impact they may have upon their families or groups. The family, extended family, and friends are very important, and one must do nothing to shame them. Expertise is important in one's occupation, but less important than one's ability to get along with the group, so one usually has to make friends with the participants before meaningful negotiations can take place. The upper class dominates the economic structures of commerce and industry, but the middle class dominates politics.

Sources of Anxiety Reduction

Religion is not a strong force in their daily life, but Venezuelans are emotionally attached to the Church, and this gives them a sense of stability. The presence of the extended family also helps the individual to have a sense of security. Venezuelans seem to gain security by following charismatic leaders as well. Although they are always working on one or more projects, finishing them by a tight deadline does not seem to be a large priority. Time does not create anxiety.

Issues of Equality/Inequality

There are extreme contrasts between rich and poor, and Venezuelans feel that power holders are entitled to the privileges that come with the office. There is a small white elite, a large mestizo population, and a small black population. One notices some class and ethnic bias. Machismo is very strong. Women have some restrictions on their social and work behavior.

▶ BUSINESS PRACTICES

Punctuality, Appointments, and Local Time

- Unlike the inhabitants of many countries in Latin America, Venezuelans tend to be prompt. Foreigners are expected to be on time to business appointments. Social engagements also tend to start on time. It is better to be a few minutes early than a few minutes late in Venezuela. Allow yourself plenty of time to compensate for traffic, which is a serious problem in Caracas.

- As in most countries, Venezuelans write the date in this order: day, month, year; (e.g., December 3, 2010, is written 3.12.10)

Cultural Note

Business contacts should be initiated through local intermediaries. Get a Venezuelan representative to help you set up introductions before you travel. Many governments' consulates have a foreign commercial service officer who conducts research into industry segments and can provide you with company data. In certain cases they can arrange meetings at the correct management levels and within the appropriate social circles. Large legal and accounting firms also may have suitable contacts that can assist you as you enter new markets.

- Avoid scheduling appointments two or three days before or after a holiday. Venezuelans often take extended vacations.
- For further information on Venezuela's official holidays, visit *www.kissboworshakehands.com.*
- The country of Venezuela is four hours behind Greenwich Mean Time (G.M.T. – 4).

Negotiating

- In a business meeting, begin by getting to know everyone. Don't rush into a discussion of the deal. At the same time, do not try to be instant friends with your prospects.
- Under the leftist administration of President Hugo Chávez, there are other factors to business negotiations than whether a deal is beneficial for all parties. Issues revolving around privatization may impact your deal.
- Never change your team during negotiations.
- Letters, brochures, and other documents should be translated into Spanish and followed up with a phone call.
- If you receive a reply from a Venezuelan in your native language, you may begin using your language in correspondence. English is spoken by many Venezuelan businesspeople.
- It is best to send an individual rather than a team for the first contact with a Venezuelan prospect. Later, you should send other members of your team.
- Even among Venezuelans educated in North America, expect negotiations to proceed more slowly than in the USA.
- Do not mention bringing in an attorney until negotiations are complete.
- After the first business contact in Venezuela, it is appropriate for the senior executive of the foreign firm to write a letter of thanks to the senior executive of the Venezuelan company.
- The focus of the business deal should be long-term, not solely geared to immediate returns. Venezuelans have had bad experiences with foreign firms that make a quick profit, then leave the country. You do not want to be categorized as another short-term player.

- Topics to avoid discussing are the government, personal relationships, and a comparison of your country's policies to Venezuela's.
- It is rude to ask direct questions about a person's family. However, such information is useful, especially because nepotism is common, and several family members may work for the same company. Try to find this information out through a third party.
- Venezuelans appreciate visitors who have some knowledge of their country's history and cultural achievements.
- Present your business card immediately following an introduction. Treat business cards with respect. Have your card printed in Spanish on one side and your native language on the other. Be sure your job title is clearly identified; Venezuelans are very status conscious and will want to understand your position in your company.
- Venezuelans are generally comfortable with technological advances, and are open to conference calls, e-mails, Internet-based training, Web conferences, etc.

Business Entertaining

- It is good practice to follow up morning appointments with an invitation to lunch, where you can continue your business discussions.
- In a restaurant, it is common for Venezuelans to compete with you for the check, even if you issued the invitation. To avoid this, arrange beforehand with the waiters to have the bill given directly to you (or pay it away from the table). This is particularly important for women, as they may encounter some resistance from their male Venezuelan counterparts in settling the bill.
- Unlike lunch, dinner is for socializing, not business.
- Dinner generally begins at 8:30 P.M., and can last until midnight.
- Spouses are usually invited to dinner.
- Businesswomen should be aware that going out alone with Venezuelan businessmen may be misconstrued. It is better for businesswomen to come to Venezuela as part of a team.
- At the table, the senior executive from each firm should sit facing each other.
- The senior visiting businessperson may give a toast offering good wishes for the negotiations, adding a comment about the pleasure

of socializing with Venezuelans. This toast should be in Spanish. If the visitor does not understand Spanish, he or she should memorize it phonetically or be accompanied by an interpreter.

- If you are invited for a meal at a Venezuelan home, be aware that this is a sign of close friendship and is not to be taken lightly.

⊙ PROTOCOL

Greetings
- A firm handshake is the standard business greeting.
- While shaking hands, announce your full name; the Venezuelan will do the same.

Titles/Forms of Address
- For further information on the proper titles and forms of address for Spanish-speaking countries, please consult Appendix A.

Gestures
- Venezuelans greet friends with a brief embrace called an *abrazo*, a squeeze of the arm, and sometimes a kiss on the cheek.
- Venezuelans converse in very close proximity to one another. Try not to waver or move away during your conversation, as this will be interpreted as rejection.
- During a conversation, Venezuelans often touch each other's arms or jacket.

Gifts
- It is best to postpone giving business gifts until you have established a friendly relationship.
- The best time to present a business gift is during a long lunch. Try not to present a gift during business hours.
- For business, bring high-quality gifts that are useful—for example, a lighter with your company name, small electronics, carefully selected books, or an imported liquor (a twelve-year-old Scotch).
- Perfume and flowers (particularly orchids, the national flower) are good gifts for women, and are not generally considered too

personal. If, as a man, you feel the gift might be misconstrued, say it is a gift from your company.

- You may give gifts to the children of your colleagues; this will be greatly appreciated.
- In preparation for subsequent visits, ask colleagues if there is something from your home country that your Venezuelan counterparts would like you to bring back.
- Baseball is the national sport of Venezuela. If you are from Canada or the United States of America, sports attire from the professional baseball teams that have Venezuelans on their roster make good gifts.
- Foreign women should be wary about giving personal gifts to Venezuelan businessmen. This is best delegated to a male member of your team.
- When going to a Venezuelan home, bring a gift. Never arrive empty-handed.

Dress
- Venezuelan women are very fashionable. Women should pack their best business clothes and something more formal for evening wear.
- Expect Venezuelans to notice both your dress and your accessories. Details such as high-quality watches or jewelry increase your status among most Venezuelans. Poorly dressed businesspeople do not command as much respect as executives with well-made clothes.
- Men should dress conservatively, in dark business suits of tropical-weight wool.

Cultural Note

In addition to its position as Venezuela's capital and largest city, Caracas has become the city of gardens. To alleviate hunger among Venezuela's 24 million impoverished citizens, the government ordered citizens to grow food crops on every available plot of land in the city—and on rooftops and in containers as well. Many foreign observers call the effort well intentioned, but point out that such projects have failed to provide enough food when tried in Communist countries.

Appendix A

Titles and Forms of Address in Latin-American Countries

There are many naming conventions within *Kiss, Bow, or Shake Hands: Latin America*. For efficiency's sake, we have consolidated much of the information here. Some of this data may be repeated in certain chapters.

The following information is generally true for the Spanish-speaking countries of Latin America *except* for Argentina. The section "Titles/Forms of Address" in the chapter on Argentina gives information on the unique naming conventions of that country.

- Historically, many parents followed a Christian tradition, and gave their children compound names at their baptism. For example: Juan Antonio, or Maria Rosa. The first names would usually include a saint's name, or a name of a relative or godparent—or both.

- At a confirmation ceremony, a middle name was often added, which might be derived from the person's "Saint's Day" (e.g., October 18 is the Feast of St. Luke, so a child born on that day might receive the name Luke, or Lucia). Confirmation names are not often included in business or social interactions.

- First (and possibly, middle names) would then be followed by compound family names (or surnames): one from the father, which would be listed first, followed by one from the mother. The father's surname was commonly used when addressing someone—e.g., Señor José Antonio Martínez de García would be addressed as Señor Martínez, and Señorita Pilar María Nuñez de Cela would be addressed as Señorita Nuñez.

If the two people in the above example married, the woman would traditionally add her husband's surname and be known by that: Señora Pilar María Nuñez Cela de Martínez. Most people would refer to her as Señora de Martínez or, less formally, Señora Martínez.

- As women become increasingly independent, they may retain their maiden names, or use any combination thereof.

- As a general rule, use only one surname when speaking to a person, but use both surnames when writing.

- Additionally, it is important to address individuals by any titles they may have, followed by their surnames. For example, teachers may prefer the title *Profesor*, and engineers may go by *Ingeniero*.

- Don and Doña are additional titles of respect

- In Spain, the use of the familiar *(tú)* and formal *(Usted)* forms of address are different from their usage in Latin America. For example, Spaniards may speak to domestic employees in the formal (Usted) manner; they feel this confers dignity and shows respect for the person.

- Unlike the practice of Spanish-speaking countries, the order of names in Portuguese is first name, middle name, and, usually, two last names. The first surname is from the person's mother, and the second from the father. If an executive hands you a card with the name Joaquín Gilberto Silva Mantega, you would address him as Senhor Mantega.

  You may see the words *do, da,* or *de* between surnames. These mean "of" and are simply a connective. Senhor Joaquín Gilberto Silva de Mantega would generally still be addressed as Senhor Mantega.

Further data on naming conventions can be found on our Web site, *www.kissboworshakehands.com*, or in *Merriam Webster's Guide to International Business Communications*.

Why Learn a Foreign Language?

THROUGHOUT EUROPE, ASIA, and much of the world, business travelers are frequently multilingual. Their study of foreign languages begins in primary school, and often continues far into adulthood. Why do they study so hard to learn an unfamiliar tongue?

U.S. executives generally assume that foreigners learn English because it is the universal language of business. English has commonly predominated in business transactions for years, but that does not explain why German, Japanese, and Finnish executives expend substantial time and effort to learn Spanish, Mandarin, or Tamil.

The reason these business travelers study is to expand their trade in areas of the world such as Latin America, Asia, and the Indian subcontinent. And they understand that, in much of the world, business is built upon relationships. Speaking with prospects in their own language demonstrates a great deal of respect for that culture—it establishes a level of credibility for that executive, it builds trust, and it bridges the cultural gap.

Furthermore, many international executives are exceedingly self-reliant. They do not like depending upon interpreters. They resent missing out on various aspects of conversations, and they want clients to look at *them*—not the interpreters. So, frequent flyers from France, Austria, and Korea dedicate years to learning languages. And their clients respond.

Learning a country's language—and its regional dialects, accents, and vocabulary—gives one a deeper understanding of its culture. For example, when several French businessmen who had spoken perfect "British English" for twenty years were given new assignments in the Midwestern region of the USA, they started taking customized courses in "American-style English." Why? Because their Midwestern bosses thought that their English was "too Euro." Their "American English" training included television shows that reflected current U.S. cultural styles—like *The Apprentice*. It also taught them how to communicate in sound bites, write in bullet format, and pepper their communications with sports analogies. Just like their U.S. bosses.

But what if you do not have a background in languages, and want to begin learning the most widely spoken language on earth—Mandarin? Numerous multinationals now realize they will require employees who are fluent in Mandarin, and they are initiating programs to build their own multilingual workforces.

Bettina Anagnostopoulos, Manager of Language Projects at Cartus *(www.cartus.com)*, has been involved in this process for years. She has designed many projects, including a "Seven Level Mandarin" program at a corporate university in California. The training is not just for "high potentials" who are being considered for assignments in China, but also for non-traveling virtual team members, business travelers, and others who may be offered Asian assignments in the future. The program includes various courses, from "Beginner Chinese for Heritage Learners" (these are employees with Chinese parents, or those who grew up in China), to "Advanced Business Chinese," which includes accent modification for Chinese-Americans who need to adjust their pronunciation and inflections in order to communicate effectively with native Chinese. One interesting aspect of the "sustained training" that Cartus recommends is that it must be stimulating enough to motivate learners beyond their second or third year. The program integrates "Cultural Mentors" (or coaches) with language teachers, electronic training, videos, music, podcasts, and other personalized learning methods.

Of course, the best option for absorbing a language is still a formal educational program, starting at a young age. The USA is slowly catching on to the importance of teaching Chinese in public schools, and hopefully will soon implement programs like Seattle, Washington's twelve-year curriculum in Mandarin.

Besides formal educational programs and corporate training resources, you can find scores of language and translation options on the Web. A search on "foreign phrases" or "foreign language learning" will generate any number of products. As a start, try the British Broadcasting Corporation's Web site for languages at *www.bbc.co.uk/ languages*. Other links for foreign language programs and translation systems are available at *www.kissboworshakehands.com*.

Considering the kinetics of world demographics, English may not be the sole language of business in the decades to come. Be ahead of the curve, and *buon viaggio*!

"Una persona que habla dos lenguas vale dos personas."
A person who speaks two languages is worth two people.
—SPANISH PROVERB

APPENDIX C

Contacts and Resources

BECAUSE OF THE DYNAMIC NATURE of travel warnings, customs requirements, and so on, this section directs you to several large Web sites that provide broad-based, helpful data for international travelers. While every country has its own respective requirements, the U.S. Web sites included here are a reasonable start for international business contacts, travel advisories, medical information, passports, etc.

Government Sites

Make it a practice to contact your country's embassy when you travel, as it can prove helpful in emergency situations. Many embassies now allow registration of your information online.

Embassies can arrange appointments with local business and government officials; provide counsel on local trade regulations, laws, and customs; and identify importers, buyers, agents, etc. They may also provide economic, political, technological, and labor data. There are many lists of embassies on the Web, such as *http://usembassy.state.gov*. Other helpful government sites include:

www.state.gov/travel
This site provides:
- Travel warnings
- Consular information sheets
- Public announcements
- Passports and visas for U.S. citizens
- Country background notes

- Foreign consular offices in the United States
- Key officers at U.S. foreign service posts

www.customs.ustreas.gov
Produces a database that can be queried by topic, (e.g., travel requirements, importing procedures, etc.), or an individual's status (e.g., importer, traveler, carrier, etc.)

www.cia.gov
The U.S. Central Intelligence Agency produces several documents of note for global travelers. These include:
- The World Factbook (at *www.cia.gov/cia/publications/factbook*)
- An online directory called "The Chiefs of State and Cabinet Members of Foreign Governments," available at *www.cia.gov/cia/publications/chiefs/index.html*. This informational directory is updated weekly and includes many governments of the world, including some with which the United States of America has no diplomatic exchanges, and which are not officially recognized.

Corruption and Bribery
www.transparency.org
Transparency International, a worldwide nongovernmental organization, reports on corruption and bribery around the world. They issue an annual "Corruption Perceptions Index," which relates to perceptions of the degree of corruption as seen by businesspeople, academics, and risk analysts. In the "2005 Corruption Perceptions Index," the five least corrupt countries out of 158 were Iceland (number 1), Finland, New Zealand, Denmark, and Singapore. The five most highly corrupt were Haiti, Myanmar, Turkmenistan, Bangladesh, and Chad (number 158).

Medical Information
www.cdc.gov/travel
The Centers for Disease Control provides an abundance of medical resources for international travelers. It includes everything

from health information and vaccinations required for specific destinations, to advice on traveling with children and pets.

Of course, you will want to be thoroughly prepared for your trip, so schedule physical and dental examinations well before leaving. Remember that some vaccinations must be given over a period of time. Also take current medical documentation with you, and list any chronic conditions and current prescription drugs (including dosages). In order to avoid problems at customs, carry all medications in their original containers. Also, take an extra set of glasses, contacts, or prescriptions. In your bags, include the name, address, and phone number of someone to be contacted in case of an emergency.

Prepare a basic medical travel kit, which might include aspirin, a topical antibiotic, bandages, a disinfectant, 0.5 percent hydrocortisone cream (for bites or sunburn), sunblock, a thermometer, and diarrhea medication. Pack the kit in your carry-on luggage (if you are permitted a carry-on bag!).

Also confirm that you have sufficient travel medical insurance. There are two main types of travel insurance: 1) policies that make direct payments for medical care and provide assistance, and 2) policies that reimburse you for emergency expenses. (With the latter option, you might have to pay the doctor or hospital immediately—in local currency—and file a claim once you return home.)

While we do not endorse any specific organizations, the Bureau of Consular Affairs maintains an extensive list of Travel Insurance Companies, as well as Air Ambulance, Med-Evac companies, and Executive Medical Services. A list of these firms is available at *http://travel.state.gov/travel/tips/health/health_1185.html*

Appendix D

Seeing Red: International Colors and Symbols

WHY DOES RUSSIAN PRESIDENT Vladimir Putin rarely wear a red tie? Certain colors and symbols can have a tremendous impact in different cultures. Colors can be so powerful that they can influence voters and sway elections. Professor Jorge Contreras from the Universidad de Monterrey in Mexico described a situation where this has occurred:

> *"The Mexican flag has three vertical bands of color: green, white and red. At election time, each political party adopts a particular flag, which is prominently displayed at voting booths. One of the most important parties in Mexico, the Partido Revolucionario Institucional (PRI), generates controversy during every election because the colors they use on their campaign flags are green, white and red. This confuses people in rural sections of Mexico, where illiteracy can be a problem. As the people cannot read, or are not well educated, the colors of the PRI flag make them think they are voting for the Flag of Mexico."*

While politicians may be delighted to influence an election by virtue of their flag, they may blanch at the adverse reactions resulting from the misuse of a flag, or its colors.

When Not to Display the Flag

McDonald's made a serious mistake when they developed a disposable placemat illustrated with flags from different countries. It disturbed some patrons to deface the flag-decorated placemats with ketchup, fries, etc., and then throw them in the trash. After many complained to management, McDonald's pulled the placemats.

A more significant error is repeatedly committed during World Cup competitions. Ill-informed promoters create and sell World Cup soccer balls, decorated with the flag of each country that qualifies for the finals. Unfortunately, every time Saudi Arabia makes the Cup finals, some promoter puts their flag on a soccer ball, offending not only the Saudis, but Muslims in general. The name of Allah is on the flag of Saudi Arabia and must be treated reverently. Allah's name may never be associated with any commercial purpose . . . and it is particularly taboo to touch Allah's name with the foot! (The foot is considered unclean in many parts of the world, notably the Middle East.)

How People React to Colors

Although some scientists believe that the chemical reactions from the color-sensitive cones of the eyes to the pituitary gland generate uniform emotional responses in all people, cultural anthropologists disagree. In his book *Blunders in International Business*, David Ricks states that green may make Swedes feel healthy (or think of cosmetics), but people who live around the equator may associate green with disease. Clearly, people are not all alike, and their interpretations or reactions to colors and symbols vary greatly, depending upon their cultural background and physical location.

Just consider how one color, red, can be perceived around the world:

- In the United Kingdom and France, red is considered the most masculine of the colors, not blue.
- In parts of Africa, dark red is a color of mourning, or can be blasphemous.
- When someone dies, Buddhists write his or her name in red.
- In China, Japan, and much of Asia, red is an auspicious, lucky color.

- A red circle (in a logo or a design element) can remind people who were occupied by Japan during WWII of the Japanese flag. Not a good idea in the Philippines.
- The familiar red logo of Coca-Cola is almost synonymous with the USA, but sometimes generates feelings of Anti-Americanism. One firm "Mecca-Cola" has imitated the highly identifiable red can with white cursive lettering to promote a political agenda opposing U.S. global hegemony.
- Finally, in Russia, Romania, Moldova, and many countries of the former Soviet Union, red is still associated with blood and communism. According to Professor Andrei Muntean of Drexel University, you will not generally see a leader like President Vladimir Putin of Russia wearing a red tie. While Moscow is becoming a new center for haute couture, and he is quite aware that red is the "power tie" of choice in the West, he traditionally opted for more subdued colors: serious dark blue, brown, or even black neckwear.

Whether your event includes an ad campaign, a new logo, a floral arrangement, or just your day's attire, your colors definitely convey messages (intentional or otherwise) to those around you. Each shade is perceived differently in the countries you target, so be sensitive in your selection of color and symbols, or the target may be you!

Appendix E

Holidays

Every country in the world celebrates holidays, and little or no work is conducted during these celebrations. However, holidays are always subject to change. Governments frequently add, delete, or move certain official holidays. Furthermore, the dates for many holidays do not fall on the same day in the Western (Gregorian) calendar each year. This may be because they are dated using a calendar that does not correspond to the Western calendar (for example, the Arabic Hijra calendar is lunar, and is only 354 days long).

Some cultures use lunisolar calendars (for instance, the Hebrew and Chinese calendars—although these two are not similar in other aspects), and some have both the aspects of solar and lunisolar calendars (for example, the Hindu calendar).

Actually, there are over twenty calendars in use around the world! Indonesia is a good example of one country that uses multiple calendars. They include the Gregorian calendar, one which is similar to the Islamic calendar, a calendar used primarily in Java, and several others. In Java, when the fifth day of a month coincides on all the calendars various celebrations take place (businesses are opened, babies are named, etc.). This is because five is an auspicious number—there are five sacred mountains, five elements, and so forth.

Some holidays are purposefully consecutive, like "Golden Week" in Japan. It allows for Japanese workers to enjoy extended vacations and observe some important holidays together.

The work week may be different in various cultures as well. For example, in the Muslim world, the Sabbath is celebrated on Friday. Some Islamic nations have their "weekend" on Thursday and Friday, and their work week runs Saturday through Wednesday.

Whatever the calendar or work week in use, the only way to be sure your business trip is not interrupted by official or local holidays is to contact reliable, up-to-date sources before your trip. Consult with the country's embassy, call your associates at your destination, or reference our World Holiday Guide at: *www.kissboworshakehands.com.*

One additional note: You may see the traditional terms B.C. (before Christ) and A.D. (anno Domini, "the year of the Lord") being used interchangeably or replaced with the terms B.C.E. (before the Common Era) and C.E. (Common Era). The new notation "Common" refers to the most common calendar—the Gregorian, or Western Calendar.

Equivalents

Unit	Metric Equivalent	U.S. Equivalent
acre	0.404 685 64 hectares	43,560 feet^2
acre	4,046,856 4 meters^2	4,840 yards^2
acre	0.004 046 856 4 kilometers^2	0.001 562 5 miles^2, statute
acre	100 meters^2	119.599 yards^2
barrel (petroleum, U.S.)	158.987 29 liters	42 gallons
(proof spirits, U.S.)	151.416 47 liters	40 gallons
(beer, U.S.)	117.347 77 liters	31 gallons
bushel	35.239 07 liters	4 pecks
cable	219.456 meters	120 fathoms
chain (surveyor's)	20.116 8 meters	66 feet
cord (wood)	3.624 556 meters^3	128 feet^3
cup	0.236 588 2 liters	8 ounces, liquid (U.S.)
degrees, Celsius	(water boils at 100°C, freezes at 0°C)	multiply by 1.8 and add 32 to obtain °F
degrees, Fahrenheit	subtract 32 and divide by 1.8 to obtain C°	(water boils at 212°F, freezes at 32°F)
dram, avoirdupois	1.771 845 2 grams	0.0625 5 ounces, avoirdupois
dram, troy	3.887 934 6 grams	0.125 ounces, troy
dram, liquid (U.S.)	3.696 69 milliliters	0.125 ounces, liquid
fathom	1.828 8 meters	6 feet
foot	30.48 centimeters	12 inches
foot	0.304 8 meters	0.333 333 3 yards
foot	0.000 304 8 kilometers	0.000 189 39 miles, statute
foot^2	929.030 4 centimeters^2	144 inches^2

Unit	Metric Equivalent	U.S. Equivalent
foot	20.092 903 04 meters^2	0.111 111 1 yards^2
foot^3	28.316 846 592 liters	7.480 519 gallons
foot^3	0.028 316 847 meters^3	1,728 inches^3
furlong	201.168 meters	220 yards
gallon, liquid (U.S.)	3.785 411 784 liters	4 quarts, liquid
gill (U.S.)	118.294 118 milliliters	4 ounces, liquid
grain	64.798 91 milligrams	0.002 285 71 ounces, avdp.
gram	1,000 milligrams	0.035 273 96 ounces, avdp.
hand (height of horse)	10.16 centimeters	4 inches
hectare	10,000 meters^2	2.471 053 8 acres
hundredweight, long	50.802 345 kilograms	112 pounds, avoirdupois
hundredweight, short	45.359 237 kilograms	100 pounds, avoirdupois
inch	2.54 centimeters	0.083 333 33 feet
inch^2	6.451 6 centimeters^2	0.006 944 44 feet^2
inch^3	16.387 064 milliliters	0.000 578 7 feet^3
inch^3	16.387 064 milliliters	0.029 761 6 pints, dry
inch^3	16.387.064 milliliters	0.034 632 0 pints, liquid
kilogram	0.001 tons, metric	2.204 626 pounds, avoirdupois
kilometer	1,000 meters	0.621 371 19 miles, statue
kilometer^2	100 hectares	247.105 38 acres
kilometer^2	1,000,000 meters^2	0.386 102 16 miles^2, statue
knot (1 nautical mi/hr)	1.852 kilometers/hour	1.151 statue miles/hour
league, nautical	5.559 552 kilometers	3 miles, nautical
league, statute	4.828 032 kilometers	3 miles, statute
link (surveyor's)	20.116 8 centimeters	7.92 inches
liter	0.001 meters^3	61.023 74 inches^3
liter	0.1 dekaliter	0.908 083 quarts, dry
liter	1,000 milliliters	1.056 688 quarts, liquid

Unit	Metric Equivalent	U.S. Equivalent
meter	100 centimeters	1.093 613 yards
meter^2	10,000 centimeters^2	1.195 990 yards^2
meter^3	1,000 liters	1.307 951 yards^3
micron	0.000 001 meter	0.000 039 4 inches
mil	0.025 4 millimeters	0.001 inch
mile, nautical	1.852 kilometers	1.150 779 4 miles, statute
mile^2, nautical	3.429 904 kilometers^2	1.325 miles^2, statute
mile, statute	1.609 344 kilometers	5,280 feet or 8 furlongs
mile^2, statute	258.998 811 hectares	640 acres or 1 section
mile^2, statute	2.589 988 11 kilometers^2	0.755 miles^2, nautical
minim (U.S.)	0.061 611 52 milliliters	0.002 083 33 ounces, liquid
ounce, avoirdupois	28.349 523 125 grams	437.5 grains
ounce, liquid (U.S.)	29.573 53 milliliters	0.062 5 pints, liquid
ounce, troy	31.103 476 8 grams	480 grains
pace	76.2 centimeters	30 inches
peck	8.809 767 5 liters	8 quarts, dry
pennyweight	1.555 173 84 grams	24 grains
pint, dry (U.S.)	0.550 610 47 liters	0.5 quarts, dry
pint, liquid (U.S.)	0.473 176 473	0.5 quarts, liquid
point (typographical)	0.351 459 8 milliliters	0.013 837 inches
pound, avoirdupois	453.592 37 grams	16 ounces, avoirdupois
pound, troy	373.241 721 6 grams	12 ounces, troy
quart, dry (U.S.)	1.101 221 liters	2 pints, dry
quart, liquid (U.S.)	0.946 352 946 liters	2 pints, liquid
quintal	100 kilograms	220.462 26 pounds, avdp.
rod	5.029 2 meters	505 yards
scruple	1.295 978 2 grams	20 grains
section (U.S.)	2.589 988 1 kilometers^2	1 mile^2, statute or 640 acres

Unit	Metric Equivalent	U.S. Equivalent
span	22.86 centimeters	9 inches
stere	1 meter^3	1.307 95 yards^3
tablespoon	14.786 76 milliliters	3 teaspoons
teaspoon	4.928 922 milliliters	0.333 333 tablespoons
ton, long or deadweight	1,016.046.909 kilograms	2,240 pounds, avoirdupois
ton, metric	1,000 kilograms	2,204.623 pounds, avoirdupois
ton, register	2.831 684 7 meters^3	100 feet^3
ton, short	907.184 74 kilograms	2,000 pounds, avoirdupois
township (U.S.)	93.239 572 kilometers^2	36 miles^2, statute
yard	0.914 4 meters	3 feet
yard^2	0.836 127 36 meters^2	9 feet^2
yard^3	0.764 554 86 meters^3	27 feet^3
yard^3	764.554 857 984 liters	201.974 gallons

APPENDIX G

International Electrical Adaptors

This data is excerpted from a publication of the U.S. Department of Commerce.

The electricity used in much of the world (220–250 volts) is a different voltage from that used in North America (110–125 volts). Electrical appliances designed for North America may need converters to "step down" this higher voltage to the level required to operate. Some appliances cannot be converted for use elsewhere because they require sixty cycles per second (again, found primarily in North America), or they may have other requirements. Electrical wall sockets found around the world are also likely to differ in shape from the sockets used in North America. Electrical adaptor plugs are available to slip over the plugs of North American appliances for use in such sockets.

The following table and illustrations will inform you about the types of plugs you may encounter in various Latin American and Caribbean countries.

Type of Plug by Country

Country Plug	Type	Country Plug	Type
Argentina	C, I	Guatemala	A, B, G, H, I
Bahamas	A, B	Guyana	A, H
Barbados	A, B, F, H	Haiti	A, B, H
Belize	A, B, H	Honduras	A
Bolivia	A, C	Jamaica	A, B, C, D
Brazil	A, B, C	Mexico	A, B
Cayman Islands	A, B	Nicaragua	A
Chile	C, F, L	Panama	A, B, I
Colombia	A, B	Paraguay	C
Costa Rica	A, B	Peru	A, C
Dominican Republic	A	Suriname	C, F
Ecuador	A, B, C, D	Trinidad and Tobago	A, B
El Salvador	A, B, C, D, E, F, G, I, J, L	Uruguay	C, F, I, L
Grenada	G	Venezuela	A, B, H

Plugs in Commercial Use

Type A Flat blade attachment plug	**Type B** Flat blades with round grounding pin
Type C Round pin attachment plug	**Type D** Round pins with ground
Type E Round pin plug and receptacle with male grounding pin	**Type F** "Schuko" plug and receptacle with side grounding contacts
Type G Rectangular blade plug	**Type H** Oblique flat blades with ground
Type I Oblique flat blade with ground	**Type J** Round pins with ground
Type K Round pins with ground	**Type L** Round pins with ground

Index

abstractive thinking, xiii–xiv
altitude sickness, 31, 55, 70, 93, 139, 185
antiglobalization sentiment, 5, 147
anxiety reduction, xvi; *See also* value
  systems
appointments. *See* time
Argentina, 1–13
associative thinking, xiii–xiv
attire. *See* dress
attitudes: of Argentineans, 5; of Belizeans,
  18–19; of Bolivians, 30; of Brazilians,
  43–44; of Chileans, 55; of Colombians,
  69; of Costa Ricans, 81–82; of Ecuadorians, 93; of Guatemalans, 115; of
  Hondurans, 127; of Mexicans, 138–139;
  of Nicaraguans, 151; of Panamanians,
  163; of Paraguayans, 174; of Peruvians,
  184; of Salvadorians, 104–105; of Uruguayans, 197; of Venezuelans, 207–208

Belize, 14–25
Bolivia, 26–38
Brazil, 39–50
business entertaining: Argentina, 9–10;
  Belize, 23; Bolivia, 34–35; Brazil, 47–48;
  Chile, 60–61; Colombia, 73–74; Costa
  Rica, 86; Ecuador, 97; El Salvador,
  108–109; Guatemala, 119; Honduras,
  131; Mexico, 143; Nicaragua, 155–156;
  Panama, 167; Paraguay, 177–178; Peru,
  189; Uruguay, 201; Venezuela, 212–213
business hours. *See* time
business negotiations: Argentina, 8–9;
  Belize, 22–23; Bolivia, 33–34; Brazil,
  46–47; Chile, 58–60; Colombia, 73;
  Costa Rica, 85–86; Ecuador, 96–97; El
  Salvador, 107–108; Guatemala, 118–119;
  Honduras, 129–131; Mexico, 141–142;
  Nicaragua, 155; Panama, 166–167;
  Paraguay, 176–177; Peru, 188–189;
  Uruguay, 200–201; Venezuela, 211–212
business practices: Argentina, 8–10;
  Belize, 21–23; Bolivia, 32–35; Brazil,
  46–48; Chile, 58–60; Colombia, 72–74;
  Costa Rica, 84–86; Ecuador, 95–97; El
  Salvador, 107–109; Guatemala, 117–119;

Honduras, 129–131; Mexico, 141–143;
  Nicaragua, 154–156; Panama, 165–167;
  Paraguay, 176–178; Peru, 187–189;
  Uruguay, 200–201; Venezuela, 210–213

Centers for Disease Control (CDC),
  221–222
Central Intelligence Agency (CIA), 221
Chile, 51–63
closed-minded thinking, xii–xiii
clothing. *See* dress
cognitive styles, xii–xiv; Argentina, 6;
  Belize, 20; Bolivia, 31; Brazil, 44;
  Chile, 56; Colombia, 70; Costa Rica,
  82–83; Ecuador, 94; El Salvador, 105;
  Guatemala, 116; Honduras, 128;
  Mexico, 139; Nicaragua, 152; Panama,
  164; Paraguay, 175; Peru, 186; Uruguay,
  198; Venezuela, 209
collectivism, xv–xvi
Colombia, 64–76
colors, 223–225
corruption, 6, 56, 221
Costa Rica, 77–88
crime: Argentina, 6; Belize, 20; Brazil,
  44; Chile, 56; Colombia, 65, 69–70; El
  Salvador, 105; Guatemala, 116; Mexico,
  139; Nicaragua, 152; Panama, 163–164;
  Peru, 185
cultural orientation: Argentina, 6–7;
  Belize, 20–21; Bolivia, 31–32; Brazil,
  44–45; Chile, 56–57; Colombia, 70–72;
  Costa Rica, 82–84; Ecuador, 94–95; El
  Salvador, 105–107; Guatemala, 116–117;
  Honduras, 128–129; Mexico, 139–141;
  Nicaragua, 152–154; overview of,
  xi–xvii; Panama, 164–165; Paraguay,
  175–176; Peru, 186–187; Uruguay,
  198–199; Venezuela, 209–210

decision-making, xv–xvi; Argentina, 7;
  Belize, 21; Bolivia, 32; Brazil, 45; Chile,
  57, 58; Colombia, 71; Costa Rica, 83;
  Ecuador, 94–95; El Salvador, 106;
  Guatemala, 112, 116–117; Honduras, 124,
  128; Mexico, 140; Nicaragua, 148, 153;

About the Authors

TERRI MORRISON and WAYNE A. CONAWAY have coauthored five books on intercultural communications, hundreds of articles, and several databases—all of which are available at *www.kissboworshake hands.com*. Terri Morrison also offers keynote seminars on intercultural communications, which range from one to three hours. These highly informative, entertaining, and interactive presentations can be customized for specific industries, countries, and regions of the world. A speaker video, biography, and references are available at *www.TerriMorrison.com*.

Their electronic product *Kiss, Bow, or Shake Hands: Expanded Edition* (KBSH:XE) contains up-to-date business and cultural data on over 100 countries. Numerous private and public institutions have found KBSH:XE to be a valuable tool for facilitating globalization. Subscriptions are available for corporate, educational, governmental, and personal usage, and contain information on everything from Business Practices (appointments, negotiating, entertaining, etc.) to Intellectual Property Rights and Culturally-Correct Gifts. A demo of KBSH:XE is available at their Web site.

The electronic *World Holiday and Time Zone Guide* contains a useful format of cross-referencing holidays both by the country and by the day of the year. This database is a convenient feature for heavy travelers, meeting planners, and researchers who need current holiday information on 101 countries.

The study of intercultural communication represents a lifelong interest for the authors of *Kiss, Bow, or Shake Hands*. By way of continuing that research, the authors invite your comments. Whether your own experience confirms or diverges from the data in this book, they welcome your perspective. Please contact them at:

TerriMorrison@getcustoms.com
Phone: 610-725-1040

Or via these Web sites:

www.getcustoms.com
www.TerriMorrison.com
www.kissboworshakehands.com

Virtue is bold, and goodness never fearful.
—William Shakespeare